From Rose Rosetree's Enlightenment Students

Rose's vision, creativity and teaching are unmatched, and I am grateful every day for her work as an Enlightenment Teacher.

My understanding, awareness, and skills have developed considerably through sessions and classes with Rose. I have more confidence in, appreciation for, and enjoyment of, my human life.

Paula from Herndon, Virginia

....

I've been living in Spiritual Enlightenment (as validated by Rose) for about five years now. Without having an Enlightenment Teacher, I wouldn't have known.

I knew something was different — I felt different for one — but it wasn't until Enlightenment was validated in a session that I had words to explain what had happened.

Living in Enlightenment doesn't mean life is easy, but making choices that work for me is easier.

What I mean is, things that don't work for me anymore will become more obvious until I make a choice to let them go, change how I approach them, or get the help that I need in the moment.

Perhaps I've even become more resourceful. It seems like new resourcefulness grows in the background, now that I'm in Age of Awakening Enlightenment.

Gabrielle from Bowie, Maryland

....

I remember what my life was like before Rose validated Age of Awakening Enlightenment for me. There are a lot of differences between the way I lived before and how I live now.

One of the biggest differences is that, before Enlightenment, I would rely on other people's opinions of me and my work. Now my sense of self is way stronger, so I pay attention to the opinions of others but that no longer defines me.

In many ways I have grown immensely since moving into Enlightenment, and my life has improved tremendously. Thanks, God.

Anthony from Philadelphia, Pennsylvania

....

Living in Age of Awakening Enlightenment is really just a very comfortable, human way of being. Having Rose as my Enlightenment Teacher was radically different from other offerings from spiritual teachers.

She taught me her Program for Spiritual Enlightenment; in the process of following that I became a more active participant in my own life and, also, it became much easier for me to develop new social skills. In turn, this empowers me to do better at solving everyday problems.

None of this has involved straining to deny my own self, or attempting to become like someone else. That, to me, is the biggest difference in what to expect from Energy Spirituality vs. mainstream: That Rose teaches you how to be more fully yourself, and how to enjoy life so much more in the process. What she teaches is elegant in its simplicity.

Georgette from Jackson, Mississippi

....

It is a dream come true for me to have an Enlightenment Teacher! I'm so used to it by now, and it's so undramatic, that maybe I take it for granted most of the time. Having a teacher is at least as helpful *after* moving into Enlightenment, compared with before.

There's a lot to say, but one thing that stands out to me is the fact that Rose has developed a system for energetic literacy — and has taught it to me!

The very first time Rose Rosetree read my aura, I knew this was what I was looking for.

It was so truthful! I had explored aura readings with other people before, but they were, comparatively, a whole bunch of fluff. A lot of it was just flattery, or sugar-coated Spiritual Addiction talk (even if some of the healers were lovely people, wanting to help).

Energetic literacy is quite plainly the very practical way to see truth in life. How could any spiritual teacher living today ignore this?

Janice from Washington, D.C.

Rose, I am someone for whom you facilitated Enlightenment Validation. Since I'm now living in Age of Awakening Enlightenment, I want to speak to the idea that you spread love to others when you are in Enlightenment by avoiding, or not even recognizing, conflict.

Pre-Enlightenment, I did just that. I avoided conflict and worked at seeing the Christ in people. I let people treat me poorly, and turned the other cheek.

That's so over now.

How else am I personally growing in Enlightenment? Among other things, when conflict comes up I can tell. Instead of trying to forgive, I'll feel angry (or whatever else my spontaneous reaction happens to be). And I am even developing excellent new skills for using my power in situations of conflict.

Renee from Iowa City, Iowa

Through Rose's Enlightenment Teaching I learned to regulate my Technique Time — 20 daily minutes, tops.

No list of b.s. to check off, no vague notions about whatever. Only the truth delivered by Rose, one serving at a time, in bite-sized pieces.

And even though Enlightenment wasn't my goal (never thought I would "qualify," so never asked), it happened! To me!

Clarity of mind is hands down the best part of living in Age of Awakening Enlightenment. How I experience my life as Who I Am, growing from a place that propels me forward in all ways, especially being human.

Liane, from a very small town in Wyoming

I first heard the term "spiritual teachers" in the 80's when I ran in a New Age circle. Before that time we only had pastors and priests.

In these New Age groups, we studied and respected any and all psychics, like Edgar Cayce and Ramtha. We took their advice about how to live our lives, including how to practice our spirituality.

Interestingly, there was no talk or expectation about us mere mortals achieving Enlightenment. Instead we focused on becoming, for instance, more tolerant and loving… more like Christian saints.

Rose Rosetree has been the best spiritual teacher I've ever had, and the first one who actually helped me to see real improvements in my life.

As my Enlightenment Teacher (a relationship that I never expected to have), she has continued to assist with my spiritual and emotional growth. I'm so grateful! In many ways I am growing, and growing more quickly, in Enlightenment.

Allison from Minneapolis, Minnesota

The biggest surprise for me about living in Spiritual Enlightenment is that I approach my life from a more innocent, joyful perspective.

I get to laugh and joke, and enjoy my human experiences with no need for boring spiritual practices or living as if in a cave. No hair shirts or being hard on myself required!

Actually, I find it more important than ever to be good to myself and pay attention to what interests me, caring about what is happening at a human level. That's where the action is when you live in Age of Awakening Enlightenment.

Making good choices and following through on them leads to more growth, both emotionally and spiritually. I never expected to reach Enlightenment, let alone have that become the jumping off point for accelerated growth as a human being.

That growing is not always easy, and many times uncomfortable, but I keep at it because I want to get the most I can out of my life.

Violet from Minneapolis, Minnesota
....

Although I'm not in Enlightenment yet, I'm progressing toward it and enjoying a degree of fulfillment beyond what I used to think would ever be possible.

Rose Rosetree has been my spiritual teacher for over six years now, and she has helped me (with the aid of a Divine Being) in many areas of my life where I wished to grow. I hope one day I will live to my full potential.

Growing up, I learned to have pretty good manners and developed basic social skills; however, I never learned how to start a conversation, nor how to do small talk; nor did I understand that a conversation involves give-and-take, and it can take some work to keep a good conversation going.

Following Rose's Program for Spiritual Enlightenment has helped me to fill in other gaps in social skills too, skills that I didn't learn while growing up with my family.

In general, Enlightenment Teaching sessions also seem to have creativity built into them, and that is something I thoroughly enjoy about having Rose as my spiritual teacher. Creativity is becoming much more effortless in everyday life. No more squinting for me!

Edward from London, England
....

ENLIGHTENMENT TEACHING for the Age of Awakening, BOOK 1

Seeking Enlightenment in the Age of Awakening

Your Complete Program for Spiritual Awakening and More, in just 20 Minutes a Day

Rose Rosetree

Women's Intuition Worldwide
Sterling, Virginia

Seeking Enlightenment in the Age of Awakening

YOUR COMPLETE PROGRAM FOR SPIRITUAL AWAKENING AND MORE, IN JUST 20 MINUTES A DAY

Copyright© 2022 by Rose Rosetree

IMPORTANT: The information in this book has been researched over many years. However, the author and publisher assume no liability whatsoever for damages of any kind that occur directly or indirectly from the use of statements in this book. As the reader, you alone are responsible for how you use the information here.

This book is not intended as a substitute for the recommendations of mental health professionals or physicians. Rather, it is intended to offer information to help the reader to cooperate with mental health professionals and physicians as needed for that reader's personal growth. This book will teach you skills for self-healing only. To become a professional at Energy Spirituality℠, more training is needed. The Energy Spirituality℠ Mentoring Program aims to meet the growing demand for practitioners in this emerging field. For specifics, contact the publisher.

All rights reserved. No part of this book may be reproduced or transmitted in any form or by any means, electronic or mechanical, including photocopying, scanning, recording, or by an information storage and retrieval system, without written permission from the publisher. The exception is if a reviewer quotes brief passages in a review to be published in a newspaper, blog, or magazine.

First names used alone in this book are fictitious.

Energy Spirituality℠, Aura Reading Through All Your Senses®, Consciousness Positioning Consults®, Empath Empowerment®, Soul Thrill® Aura Research, Spiritually Sparkling® Energy Healing Skills, and Vibrational Re-Positioning® are regist237ered or unregistered trademarks of Rose Rosetree. All rights reserved.

ISBNs: 978-1-935214-53-3 (paperback KDP) | 978-1-935214-51-9 (paperback ingram)
978-1-935214-52-6 (ebook)
LCCN: 2022913635

Please direct all correspondence and inquiries to

Women's Intuition Worldwide, LLC
116 Hillsdale Drive, Sterling, VA 20164-1201
rose@rose-rosetree.com
703-450-9514

Visit our website: www.rose-rosetree.com

Also visit the Energy Spirituality℠ Blog, *Deeper Perception Made Practical*
Going to press with this first edition, Rose's monitored blog had over 104,000 comments.
Join our lively conversations with people like you, thought leaders.
www.rose-rosetree.com/blog

Dedication

*Calling this path to Enlightenment "some hills and valleys"?
That doesn't do you justice.
Yes, you,
the climber with a lion's heart, an angel's crown,
and sometimes awkward feet.*

*Inwardly more-than-ready but outwardly unprepared,
that's how you set out on this path;
maybe giving no thought to all the hills and valleys you'd face.
No mere scenery for you — these would require your active climb,
your relentless climb.*

*Equally unknowable,
how could anyone foretell all the mysterious grace?
Because sometimes that path of yours will suddenly open up
more-more-more,
Like revealing a valley of wildflowers,
blooming and shining and rare,
Until you find yourself breathing a delectable sweetness,
Never-forgettable to your eternal soul.*

*Sometimes you'll be given the tiniest moments,
and they will fill you up,
since any moment with strong God presence can change you forever
due to being so very familiar
more familiar than all you've encountered
since this lifetime began.*

*Take heart, Smart Spiritual Seeker.
When you look back, you will finally be able to see it:
how every single step you've taken, joyful or not,
has left footprints of gold.*

—Rose Rosetree, Sterling, Virginia, October 19, 2020

Contents

Dedication
Your Quick Preview i
Acknowledgments vi

PART I.
Homesick for Heaven — 1

CHAPTER 1.	Seeking Enlightenment, Could You Be Homesick for Heaven?	.5
CHAPTER 2.	Church-Wenters in the Age of Awakening	10
CHAPTER 3.	Your New Superpower, Enlightenment-Helpful	19
CHAPTER 4.	What WAS the Shift into the Age of Awakening?	35
CHAPTER 5.	Why Spiritual Awakening Is NOT Enlightenment	53
CHAPTER 6.	Content or Process? Don't Be Fooled	69
CHAPTER 7.	Energy Talk, a Seductive Substitute for Enlightenment	79
CHAPTER 8.	Can You Recognize Energy Talk?	88
CHAPTER 9.	Like Puberty, Except about Energy	94

PART II.
What the Enlightenment Establishment... Overlooked — 105

CHAPTER 10.	Humanity's Superhero Story	108
CHAPTER 11.	Defy the Allure of the Astral	115
CHAPTER 12.	Super-Comfy LOW Astral Vibrational Frequencies	128
CHAPTER 13.	Snapshots of Consciousness: Innovation for Smart Spiritual Seekers	135

CHAPTER 14.	Snapshots for SOPHISTICATED Spiritual Seekers. 142	
CHAPTER 15.	Learn More about a LOW Astral Vibrational Frequency 151	
CHAPTER 16.	Overcome Spiritual Illusions. 157	
CHAPTER 17.	Pleasantly Intoxicating MEDIUM Astral Vibrational Frequencies 167	
CHAPTER 18.	Learn More about a MEDIUM Astral Vibrational Frequency 178	
CHAPTER 19.	The False Grandeur of HIGH Vibrational Frequencies. 188	
CHAPTER 20.	Learn More about a HIGH Astral Vibrational Frequency 196	
CHAPTER 21.	Attention Spiritual Seekers: Astral Is NOT Divine. 207	
CHAPTER 22.	Uniquely Yours, the DIVINE Vibrational Frequency 221	
CHAPTER 23.	Learn More about the DIVINE Vibrational Frequency 229	

PART III.
Your Personal Program for
Spiritual Enlightenment — 237

CHAPTER 24.	Today's New Smarts for Seeking Enlightenment 243	
CHAPTER 25.	Technique Time: Why It Matters So Much. 254	
CHAPTER 26.	10 EXCELLENT Choices for Your Technique Time 263	
CHAPTER 27.	10 TERRIBLE Choices for Technique Time. 274	
CHAPTER 28.	Consciousness Lifestyles, the Test of Enlightenment 286	

CHAPTER 29. How this Program for Enlightenment
            Helps You 308
CHAPTER 30. Where You're Headed 323
CHAPTER 31. Summing up Your Program for
            Spiritual Enlightenment 336

Afterword — 339

Index — *Online at www.rose-rosetree.com/books-2*

Your Quick Preview

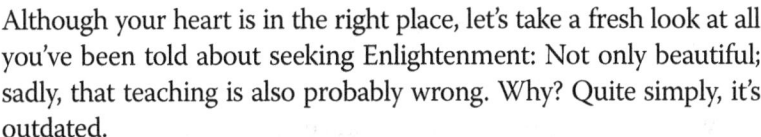

Although your heart is in the right place, let's take a fresh look at all you've been told about seeking Enlightenment: Not only beautiful; sadly, that teaching is also probably wrong. Why? Quite simply, it's outdated.

No insult intended to your meditation teacher, yoga teacher, non-duality teacher, guru, or anyone else who has been advising you.... But most likely they're members of today's **Enlightenment Establishment**. So far as these spiritual teachers are concerned, nothing has changed in thousands of years. According to them, spiritual seekers must continue to follow the age-old requirements:

1. Purify themselves.
2. Perform spiritual practices as much as possible.
3. Obey the authority figure in charge. Although it's no longer universally fashionable to call them gurus or priests, you shall know them by their high status.

Why Would that Enlightenment Establishment Ever Change?

Given their affluence and influence, it's unlikely these spiritual teachers would think, "Gee, maybe there's something I've missed." But hello! In 2012, the **Age of Awakening** began; as a result, the rules changed for seeking Enlightenment. (You'll be learning about them here, of course, culminating in Part III of this book, which will summarize the system that you're learning here.)

Also, to help you understand what has changed, do you know which essential skill became newly available to spiritual teachers, available ever since the Shift into the Age of Awakening?

Energetic Literacy, that's what. Energetic literacy means mastering precise skills for telling what's happening with any spiritual seeker's flow of consciousness.

Living now, we spiritual teachers can develop excellent skills of energetic literacy. Actually this essential skill protects teachers and students alike, allowing us to avoid mistakes that could prove spiritually costly.

Only why would today's all-knowing spiritual authorities bother developing today's emerging skills of energetic literacy? Why acknowledge that any important changes are needed at all?

Was the Shift predicted in the Bible, the Upanishads, the Analects of Confucius, etc.? Even America's high priestess of personal growth and spiritual knowingness, the great Oprah Winfrey herself, hasn't accurately proclaimed what matters spiritually about living in the Age of Awakening. Nor has she interviewed an expert with full energetic literacy, let alone learned those skills for herself.

So how could there be anything new to learn... according to today's Enlightenment Establishment?

Yet Important Changes HAVE Occurred

As you keep reading, you'll discover important information, not previously published elsewhere, about what's *essential* for seeking Enlightenment in the Age of Awakening. Among these essentials, you'll learn how today's skills for energetic literacy can keep the process of seeking Enlightenment on track — and honest.

Thus, you're starting a book that aims to bring a clarity which the Enlightenment Establishment won't be giving you. Not yet, anyway.

Of course, the Age of Awakening should matter to every spiritual seeker. Ever since the Shift, on December 21, 2012, it has become far easier and far faster than ever before... to reach Spiritual Enlightenment.

But why, exactly? In subtle ways, human consciousness — *your* consciousness — functions differently now. That matters.

You see, moving toward Enlightenment involves your personal consciousness.

> For thousands of years before The Age of Awakening, Enlightenment was called a *state of consciousness*. However, today's up-to-date experts now call Enlightenment a *consciousness lifestyle*. *(More on that to come.)*

Old teachings no longer work to develop an Enlightenment consciousness lifestyle. Soon you'll be discovering how much that matters. Sadly, traditional teachers don't know what consciousness lifestyle even means, let alone know how to help you with yours.

Old-fashioned approaches also ignore what has changed about how your consciousness works in everyday life. Yet for any effective Enlightenment teaching today? We must take into account all this and more.

Enter this unique resource for successfully seeking Enlightenment in the Age of Awakening. I can help you with that. By now I've helped other spiritual seekers to reach Enlightenment, using the same approach now available for the first time in this how-to book.

Keep reading and I'll guide you through an up-to-date **Program for Spiritual Enlightenment,** a set of flexible, customizable instructions, all expressly designed to work in the Age of Awakening.

Achieving Enlightenment Could Be Easier than You Thought

This program is easy. It won't take you more than 20 minutes a day. Probably you'll spend less time on your spiritual evolution, compared with what you're doing now. And guess what? You'll be working *smarter*. Thus, you'll evolve at top speed, both spiritually *and* emotionally.

As a side benefit, progressing toward Enlightenment can bring you results for solving everyday problems, plus a stronger sense of self; very likely helping you to enjoy your life considerably more.

Key to seeking Enlightenment now is learning about something else that's new, widely available only since the Shift into this Age of Awakening: Come learn about your new **Consciousness Positioning Superpower.**

Even if you don't yet know what that means, surprise! You're already using it. However, until you learn how to use it on purpose, you're almost guaranteed to misuse it. Of course, this book will reveal plenty about this superpower, and how to use it productively.

Another highlight of what you'll be learning? Join me for a fascinating survey of life's **Three Vibrational Frequencies: Human, Astral, and Divine.**

Each of these has a purpose for helping you to evolve spiritually, a purpose connected with how you use your consciousness.

Otherwise? Until you know the truth about your new superpower, you're probably spending most of your waking hours with consciousness aimed unproductively at one of these three vibrational frequencies.

This counts as a **Spiritual Side Trip**, like aiming for North but often twirling around without meaning to, somehow headed South for a while.

Avoidable, though! Since this book offers you….

The World's FIRST Program for Seeking Enlightenment in the Age of Awakening!

Maybe you're wondering, why has this particular Enlightenment Teacher discovered a way to make use of today's consciousness-related potentials? (And also help you to avoid today's sadly common problems with unintended side trips.)

It's as though my life experience was designed to make certain discoveries possible. Long story short, my background includes leadership at researching consciousness through parts of your aura called **Chakra Databanks**.

Besides that, I'm a spiritual teacher who's been active for 50 years, first working for Maharishi Mahesh Yogi as a teacher of Transcendental Meditation, later founding the field of Energy Spirituality™ in 1986.

This combo provided exactly the skills that made it possible for me to research what changed about consciousness after the Shift. Shortly afterward, I moved into Enlightenment.

During the years that followed, I began to develop the systematic training you'll find here. Both effortless and easy — and now it's yours for the reading.

What Else Is Important to Know Right Away?

Simply this:

- Although *spiritual awakening* is lovely, it won't bring you anywhere close to Enlightenment
- Step by step, this how-to manual will explain *exactly what to do* — and why — in order to pursue the real deal, Spiritual Enlightenment.
- Have you been feeling *homesick for Heaven*? Gain knowledge that can help you to solve the ache of separation from God.
- In the process you just might begin to *embrace your humanity* more fully than ever before.

In this Age of Awakening, millions of people can move into Spiritual Enlightenment.

Wouldn't you prefer to be one of them?

Acknowledgments

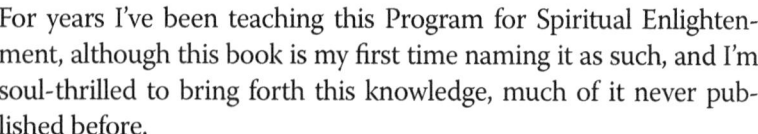

For years I've been teaching this Program for Spiritual Enlightenment, although this book is my first time naming it as such, and I'm soul-thrilled to bring forth this knowledge, much of it never published before.

If you have been my teacher, you know who you are. And I thank you.

If you have been my student, my client, or you've simply received Enlightenment Validation from me, you know who you are. And I thank you.

Mitch Weber, my husband; Matthew Emmanuel Weber, my son; I have a hunch that we know each other pretty well by now, so that (if you think about it) both of you know how much you have given me. I'll continue to pay that forward when bringing this bold, latest book into the world.

Editor Dana Wheeler, how I thank you!

Readers, I welcome you and acknowledge the greatness in you. May this book help you to bring even more greatness and truth into this world.

Divine Beings (like God, Jesus, and Kwan Yin) who have helped me to cocreate this book — as well as all of Energy Spirituality™ — thank you from the bottom of my heart, as well as every other direction. It is my honor to serve as an Enlightenment Teacher and the founder of Energy Spirituality™.

All my students quoted here have given permission. First names used alone are changed for confidentially; otherwise, full names are used for students who agreed to that, as well as being quoted.

Also, Some Realistic Acknowledgments

Recommendations in this book are meant for people with psychologically normal mental functioning; for example, excluding those on the autism spectrum.

What if you are on the spectrum? In terms of your spiritual growth, like every other human alive, during this lifetime you're pursuing important adventures for learning and service. The particular program in this book is not designed for you; other books and programs have been developed to help you more, developed by professionals whose expertise is different from mine.

Human life is not one-size-fits-all. For an evolving soul, Spiritual Enlightenment is definitely not the only game in town. Many groups of people are evolving in different ways, contributing uniquely and also learning different lessons, even while all of us live here at "Earth School."

Regarding psychiatric medication, such as medication prescribed for anxiety, appropriate medication can help your brain chemistry to function more normally. That's a good thing.

If you're taking this kind of medication, don't worry that this will disallow your spiritual evolution. Please know, I've helped folks on medication to move into Enlightenment. As you follow our Program for Spiritual Enlightenment, keep taking your meds.

PART I

Homesick for Heaven

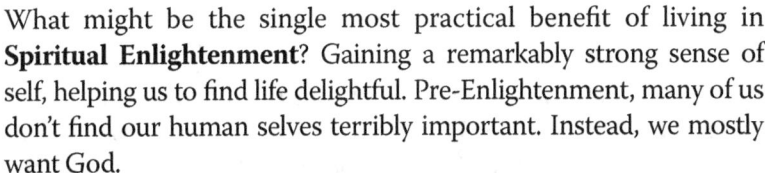

What might be the single most practical benefit of living in **Spiritual Enlightenment**? Gaining a remarkably strong sense of self, helping us to find life delightful. Pre-Enlightenment, many of us don't find our human selves terribly important. Instead, we mostly want God.

How we yearn to live with a closeness to God, and we sense (correctly) that this closeness will improve once we attain Enlightenment.

In reality, though, we can have both: Imagine yourself developing more *wholeness* as a person which, in turn, prepares you to hold more *experience* of God. Also called *"closeness."*

Spiritual Enlightenment has never been easier to achieve than right now, and for one simple reason.

Know it or not, all of us are living in the **Age of Awakening**. During this era, it is relatively easy to have experiences of spiritual awakening.

Even better, it's possible for millions of people — regular people, not only monks or nuns — to move into Spiritual Enlightenment.

Since we live in this new era, people like us have begun to do something near-miraculous; doing this super-subtle thing with our consciousness, doing it countless times every day, doing it automatically. You see, something new-and-spiritually-important has clicked into place for the entire planet.

This click occurred on one specific date, when the Age of Awakening began, on December 21, 2012. We humans were given a spiritual gift, a superpower. That's the single most important reason why, from a spiritual perspective, now is a new era compared with all that went before.

What exactly is new for each of us? Living in the Age of Awakening, you and I both possess a Consciousness Positioning Superpower. Definitely something new for the human race!

Using this properly will become a big part of our **Program for Spiritual Enlightenment**, a systematic way for you to progress at using more of your potential in life.

But in order for me to guide you effectively, we'll also need to take a clear-eyed look at where we are living. Not just *when* we are living, Smart Spiritual Seeker, but *where*.

You see, this is a world where millions of human beings are feeling terribly homesick for Heaven; sometimes, without meaning to, they're moving in a direction that's not quite their goal. Well, I aim to help you move full speed *ahead* — which won't be hard to do, not after you read the sort of info that's coming up, one chapter at a time.

Take heart. Humanity's new Consciousness Positioning Superpower can help you to attain a form of heaven on earth, Spiritual Enlightenment.

Quite soon you'll learn how this new superpower works, and then I'll coach you in how to make use of it. Along the way, I'll share my latest discoveries as an Enlightenment Teacher, discoveries based on extensive research, using refined skills of energetic literacy.

What Else Is Important to Know Right from the Start?

Thanks to this how-to book, you can expect to encounter many little **Aha!s** along the way. These subtle-and-fleeting insights into what's true for you... can add up to something big.

Fair warning though: While you're busily gathering up new bits of truth, a certain amount of illusion-removal will likely take place. But you can handle that, right?

Smart Spiritual Seeker, how can you gain the most from this resource for spiritual evolution? Write down all your Aha!s.

Granted, this recommendation may seem neither glamorous nor cosmic, but do it anyway. For best results, use a simple pad of paper or create an electronic document; keep this handy whenever reading, so you can quickly note your Aha!s.

Further, might I suggest this? Avoid buying some pretty-pretty journal where you would use lovely calligraphy. Likewise, do not "document" your experience on social media or YouTube, self-consciously sharing the story of how you're seeking Enlightenment.

Please don't aim for publication. It's plenty to aim for Spiritual Enlightenment. Given my experience as an Enlightenment Teacher, consider yourself warned. Self-consciousness like this can become its own sort of game, detracting from the innocence of your personal growth and spiritual awakening.

Hooray, Seekers of Spiritual Truth!

What else can you do to gain the most from this Program for Spiritual Enlightenment: something highly personal; something fun.

> **Look or listen or feel for truth, however it resonates personally for you. For the purpose of spiritual evolution, your easy recognition of what seems true to you... can help a lot.**

In case you're wondering, recognizing your truth can be easy. Starting now, give yourself permission to care about what's true for you. Recognizing this can be spontaneous and natural; never requiring that you scrunch up your forehead or squint.

Instead, something that strikes you as true will gently announce itself inwardly... brightening you up, helping you to make little connections, resulting in words or images that you can write down as some of your Aha!s.

Whatever seems meaningful to you... matters. This is *your* spiritual evolution.

CHAPTER 1

Seeking Enlightenment, Could You Be Homesick for Heaven?

My home is in Heaven. I'm just traveling through this world.

—**Billy Graham, Prominent American Evangelist**

Longing for Heaven won't help you to make the most of this lifetime, the one you have now. Especially if you're interested in Spiritual Enlightenment, don't treat this precious human life like some pathetic kind of consolation prize.

—*Rose Rosetree*

Many of us Enlightenment seekers feel a longing related to this simple fact: You weren't always human, you know.

- I happen to believe in reincarnation. Maybe that makes sense to you too.
- Alternatively, you may have been taught, "One and done." Because many of us have been promised that after this (only) lifetime, THE DECISION is made. Either you'll go straight to Heaven or else you'll burn forever in Hell.
- Whatever your current beliefs might be, doesn't this also seem likely to you? *Before this lifetime you were one with God.*

That said, how about now? Lately have you been experiencing anything remotely like "one with God"? No wonder so many of us have felt a deep kind of longing.

This Longing Is What I Mean by "Homesick for Heaven"

Clearly, you and I aren't living in Heaven, not unless we're doing a lot of lying to ourselves. I'd say, you and I are attending a school, **Earth School**.

Consider this planet to be a hotshot academy for spiritual evolution — a remarkably tough one, as you may have noticed. Human life here, on the whole, is no Disneyland, let alone Heaven.

Nonetheless, our world is a superb place for showing the best that we're made of. While enrolled at Earth School, character counts. Depending on what you say and do, every day you can progress spiritually. Maybe progress spiritually a lot!

But even if you do your reasonable best every single day, uh-oh. Sometimes you may feel a terrible homesickness for Heaven. For instance, you'll start asking, "Is that all there is?"

When did that asking begin for you? Maybe when you were young, maybe more recently? More important, asking and yearning and even praying: None of this can stop a person from feeling homesick for Heaven.

Same with being a religious believer, with your faith bringing *answers* that console you... but not necessarily the *experience* in everyday life that satisfies you.

What CAN Help?

Help you a lot, actually: First of all, let's acknowledge how respect is due to you for doing the best you can under the circumstances; and you also deserve respect for the unique spiritual path that you're creating for yourself. Acknowledging this, I'll be calling you **Smart Spiritual Seeker.**

Second, speaking of unique, I'm offering you a **Program for Spiritual Enlightenment** to help you, as you are, right now.

That means YOU, not some bland generic person. You can personally benefit from certain new-and-important spiritual truths.

For instance, it can help if you understand what **Spiritual Enlightenment** means *now* — not 2,000 years ago — which is why our program will supply up-to-date understandings, complete with specific DOs and DON'Ts and WHYs.

Basically, I'm aiming to provide all the essentials you need for making significant progress toward *your* goal.

Also, this program can help you to reconsider some common examples of **Spiritual Misinformation;** most likely, you've encountered a ton of that. Many terrible-and-obsolete, though nice-sounding, myths are now ridiculously popular; ironically, following these will move a person backward rather than forward.

Our Program for Spiritual Enlightenment will include Six Sweet Golden Rules, all of which are essential for making spiritual progress now, during this Age of Awakening.

Finally, wouldn't it be a relief if all these understandings could come with no strings attached? I happen to think that's really important. So, before you read another page, please know this about me: I'm an experienced **Enlightenment Teacher.** Meaning, I've helped many people like you to move toward Enlightenment, even helping some to cross that threshold.

Seems to me, this next point also needs to come NOW, since it's closely related to the no-strings-attached idea.

This Teacher's Personal Agenda

What is my agenda in offering you this Program for Spiritual Enlightenment? I'd love to help you to overcome any homesickness for Heaven; yet I'm not going to make a fairly common mistake, which is to teach you in such a way that I set myself up as some holier-than-thou member of the Enlightenment Establishment, a superior guru or preacher with power over you. Meaning:

1. You can read this book without having to join my church. (I run no church.)
2. Likewise, you won't need to join my religion. (Aren't there enough great ones already?)

3. Moreover, this program won't require that you change your religion, although you may decide to adapt it a bit.

Another option is that you're into your own kind of "disorganized" religion. No problem about sticking with that, because **Disorganized Religion** (living according to your own personal set of beliefs) may be all that you need — even if what you're needing most is God.

With all respect to those who prefer to worship God through an organized religion, consider this: In order to gain Enlightenment now, following a religion is beautiful but optional.

Seems to me, there's only one reason why worshiping God through religion would be *required* of us humans: because God demands it. But why would an Almighty, All-Loving God need human worship?

Whether you consider yourself *spiritual but not religious* or you are *deeply religious,* or *anything in-between,* you can follow this Program for Spiritual Enlightenment. Actually, you can benefit even if you're an *atheist,* and you've never felt the slightest bit homesick for Heaven, yet you'd like to use more of your full potential in life.

Regardless of how you reacted to that last paragraph, your freedom to react IS the point that I'm aiming to make here: In general, this Program for Spiritual Enlightenment allows you to show up as *yourself* and choose for yourself how you'd like to relate to the Divine.

Frankly, the more curious you are about all this, the better — which is implied when I call you SMART Spiritual Seeker.

Does that mean I have the right to ask questions?

Definitely! And yes, I'll even be supplying some good student questions, bolding them like our first one here, which you just read. Immediately afterward I'll proceed to provide the best answer I can.

By all means, as we team up together, ask questions. For that matter, bring along your B.S. detector. When and if it feels safe to you, maybe you'll also wish to open up your heart — your same heart that may sometimes yearn for more in your life, spiritually more.

And why, exactly, might you sometimes feel that way? Consider the possibility that subconsciously you remember a time when there really *was* more.

For sure, around here, **Seeking Enlightenment** is a freewillish activity — neither a faith nor a path. And if you already follow a spiritual path, our program will likely improve how well you follow it.

Realistically Speaking

Look, I can't promise to help you feel as though you're back living in Heaven. After all, you've been a flesh-and-blood mortal for quite some time now.

However, I'd like to help you make this current life of yours more joyful, including plenty of personal success and also service to others; a life made juicier because you're living your full potential spiritually. (All of the above being a practical definition of what I believe it means to live in **Spiritual Enlightenment**.)

Whether you attain that spiritual goal, or else you're simply making good progress toward it every single day you're alive, how can you tell when your spiritual path is really working?

In a quiet moment you'll realize, "Hey, I've stopped feeling homesick for Heaven."

CHAPTER 2

Church-Wenters in the Age of Awakening

I prayed for twenty years but received no answer until I prayed with my legs.

Frederick Douglass, Abolitionist and Social Reformer

Organized religion can inspire you. But it won't help you evolve spiritually, not now in the Age of Awakening, not if you're intent on growing beyond your usual limitations.

Rose Rosetree

Like the leaders of today's *Enlightenment* Establishment, leaders of America's *Religious* Establishment are often quite stuck in terms of using their full potential in life.

Mysteriously, what has happened in these early years of the Age of Awakening? An awful lot of church*goers* have turned into church-*wenters*. But why?

By 2019, only 50% of Americans identified as *church members*, compared to 70% just 10 years before. Could that statistic suggest that half of today's population no longer trusts organized religion to help solve their problems?

Meanwhile, the percentage of people who describe themselves as *atheist, agnostic,* or *"nothing in particular,"* has surged to 26% of our population, up from 17% only 10 years before.

So that's more than 1 in 4 Americans who might still feel home-sick for Heaven, yet they no longer rely on religion.

Such a big change over one decade! For you, personally, has your involvement in religion changed much since the Shift in 2012?

Mysterious Changes

This Program for Spiritual Enlightenment aims to help you sort through the social changes around you and find a way to progress inwardly, a way that helps you to use more of your full potential in life. Mainly, that's the goal of this book.

In the background, though, we're going to be solving a mystery, the **Church-Wenters Mystery**. You see, this somewhat uncomfortable mystery turns out to be closely connected to our very inspiring goal of seeking Enlightenment. Parallel sequences of knowledge will be unfolding, chapter by chapter.

Why include this kind of detective work? For one thing, Enlightenment Teachers aim to solve spiritual mysteries, and right now you happen to be living through one.

Smart Spiritual Seeker, aren't you a born problem solver? Then it may seem familiar to you how, like a good mystery novel, this Program for Spiritual Enlightenment can move you forward bit by bit: Helping you to discern red herrings versus really good clues — and that happens to be where the Church-Wenters mystery can also become relevant.

From this chapter onward, what will I be sharing that's related to this mystery? Ideas that are unconventional; unconventional according to today's religious standards; unconventional, probably, until the deeper perception skills that I've been teaching for decades... go mainstream.

Glad to say, you don't have to wait for mainstream society to catch up with what you'll learn here; nor will you have to spend 100,000 hours of research, as I have, using skills of **Energetic Literacy**.

Incidentally, I use these words as a term of art. "Energetic literacy" allows us to delve into consciousness patterns deep within different people; research that delivers something altogether different from psychic readings, being more akin to how you're reading this chapter right now, by using **Word Literacy**.

As we proceed, occasionally I'll share some of these consciousness-related findings; they'll read like ideas about human life, nothing terribly fancy. But why include this, if you're not expecting it?

Overall, I'm aiming to give you nothing less than a practical, current guide to the *effective* pursuit of your spiritual evolution, helping you to attain a degree of clarity that's quite feasible, thanks to living in the Age of Awakening.

Smart Spiritual Seeker, our pursuit will include knowledge that may be new to you. Enlightenment-related, subtle yet very real, definitely this is not yet *common* knowledge. Honestly, do you often talk with your friends about…

Consciousness Lifestyles?

Sure, you've heard of Enlightenment. Well, that's a Consciousness Lifestyle. But how many of the people you know have even *seen the term* "Consciousness Lifestyle," let *alone understood its importance*?

For instance, did you know? Because we're living in the Age of Awakening, you and I and all human beings have a particular **Consciousness Lifestyle**, or pattern to how we think and feel, due to everyday habits with using our consciousness. (**Consciousness** means how we inwardly experience life during our waking hours.)

Here's an analogy about having different Consciousness Lifestyles; they're like wearing rose-colored glasses versus glasses colored charcoal gray. In that sense, the consciousness lifestyle of Enlightenment is like wearing glasses that give you excellent eyesight.

> But if consciousness lifestyles are so universal, and they matter, how come everybody doesn't talk about them? Like I should be seeing a ton about this on social media.
>
> Here's the main reason why folks aren't tweeting, etc., about consciousness lifestyles, at least not yet. You see, throughout

most of recorded history, nearly every human adult with normal mental functioning... has possessed the identical consciousness lifestyle as everyone else.

Now that we're in the Age of Awakening, *several different consciousness lifestyles have become available.* Over time that may change, but for now, each of us has one particular consciousness lifestyle at any given time. Everybody does.

And Guess Who's Responsible for Yours?

You are, of course. So I aim to teach you in such a way that you can develop a consciousness lifestyle that's far, far better than that of the famous pastors whose churches are emptying out. This Program for Spiritual Enlightenment can help you develop a consciousness lifestyle that safely accelerates your spiritual evolution.

As a preview, what are the best options for your consciousness lifestyle? Spiritual Enlightenment would be great, but I can't promise you that one. No honest Enlightenment Teacher could.

However, coming close to that is the consciousness lifestyle called **The New Strong**, which this book can help you attain.

Hold on — why can't you promise us Enlightenment?

Because God decides when you're ready for that, neither you nor your humble teacher. Based on helping real-life students, I can tell you unequivocally that living The New Strong will greatly accelerate your progress toward Enlightenment.

For instance, what did I do today... before starting work on this book? At my blog, I happened to publish the latest article about one of my students moving into Spiritual Enlightenment.

Before that happened, what was her consciousness lifestyle? Yes, it was The New Strong!

Besides these Two Consciousness Lifestyles, Do Other Options Exist?

Definitely. Later I'll go into detail about all seven of today's consciousness lifestyles. Meanwhile I'll share my *conclusion* with you upfront: Spiritual Enlightenment, The New Strong, and Human-Based Spirituality are the best ones available. Period.

Sadly, the other four consciousness lifestyles are more like being stuck inwardly, flying in one kind of holding pattern or another; basically, *hanging out* spiritually rather than *moving forward*.

Of course, you'll have a chance to draw your own conclusions. From my side I've got so much to share with you, informed by working since 1986 in the field of **Energy Spirituality**™, by now having facilitated some 37,000 hours of personal sessions with clients.

What IS Energy Spirituality? It helps people like you with personal development and spiritual awakening, using energy skills that work now... in the Age of Awakening.

Living now is complicated, despite the innumerable advantages we have over spiritual seekers from bygone days, who struggled with much harsher circumstances in order to survive.

Foremost among our advantages now: How, absent any fanfare, at the start of the Age of Awakening, each of us was given... that new Consciousness Positioning Superpower, which you've read a little about so far. Expect to learn much more about that, along with other updates about spiritual seeking now, information that's needed for success with our Program for Spiritual Enlightenment.

Meanwhile, in the background, you'll receive a series of clues that can help you solve the Church-Wenters Mystery. For now, suffice it to say that popular preachers are only some of the folks who've run into trouble, working so hard, as if they'd never been given their Consciousness Positioning Superpower. (Although they still have it anyway.)

Worshiping God as if they still lived pre-Age of Awakening? And clueless that they possess this awesome new superpower? All this pretty much guarantees that religious leaders will be *misusing* it.

Such a Spiritual Mystery,
How to Live Well with Your Superpower

For sure, I aim to teach you the ins and outs of using your superpower *productively*. Meanwhile, maybe you're wondering, is seeking Enlightenment compatible with your religion? It can be. Important to know if you're a churchgoer!

And what else might matter to you, related to religion, as you continue reading what follows? These days you might still go to church, for any number of reasons. Yet you may find it distressing how, sometimes, your fellow believers don't seem to be living that religion, almost as though they lack the inner experience of God.

> In which case, maybe you've tortured yourself. "Who am I to judge?"
> Might I suggest this alternative? You do have the right to notice whatever you happen to notice. Discernment isn't the same thing as judgment.

As much as anyone else reading this book, you can benefit a lot from solving a certain spiritual mystery, with clues that will be unfolding in the background.

To Be Clear

Smart Spiritual Seekers, when introducing you to the Church-Wenters Mystery, I don't aim to blame anyone. Nearly everybody alive has some trouble adjusting to life in the Age of Awakening. But think about this. Who would be the last people willing to change during this new-and-challenging era?

Surely, the biggest change-resisters are those who are dead certain that, "I know it all."

Ironically, that rock-hard certainty might not be compatible with having much up-close-and-personal experience of God, or Jesus; Buddha or other spiritual masters. Why not? Because religion without direct experience of the Divine can lead to adamant certainty.

> Dead certainty is for corpses. In truth, who among us knows it all?

When this era began worldwide, much was set in motion. Humankind received a great many *big* changes that were also *subtle*. These subtle-and-unprecedented changes, not yet officially acknowledged by cherished religious and spiritual traditions; these potentially magnificent changes are altering the inner experience of humanity.

Seems to me, to the extent that we cling to beliefs from the past, we'll be ill-prepared for new challenges in this Age of Awakening.

Let's complete this chapter with a teaching tale to illustrate how confusing it can be, being dead certain about what to believe, despite living in this new era.

What Would You Have Done?

Once upon a time, Brian lived in a nice little house. He had two floors to himself, plus a gorgeous view, given that his home was just a few blocks away from a river.

Unfortunately, one day that river began to flood. At first, Brian started seeing a few notifications on his phone. Soon he turned on cable news, and began to see urgent warnings. However, Brian was a man of faith; no way was he going to worry about folks who weren't saved (like him). "If only they'd believe," Brian thought, "They'd stop complaining about every little thing."

Looking out his window, Brian didn't see much but rain. However, a sudden noise made him take another look. A jeep screeched to a stop right in front of his house; shortly after, a man came out and began pounding on the door. Opening the door, Brian looked at him suspiciously.

The jeep man said, "You're in danger. This flood could be a matter of life or death. Get in my jeep. I can help you evacuate."

Brian looked down at "The Jeepster" and smiled sweetly. "You don't understand. I'm a man of faith. This flood is only a passing trial.

But after you go, how about this? I'll say an extra prayer for your soul. As for me, I'm in no danger. Jesus will take good care of me."

True to his word, Brian prayed. After opening his eyes, it looked to him like the water might be rising. To get a better view he went up to the second floor of his house.

Okay, this must be a test of his faith, Brian thought. After one hour — and quite a few prayers — he looked out the window and saw a motorboat moving toward him. It paused in front of his window.

Through a bullhorn, some guy from the boat started shouting, "You're in danger. Let us help you evacuate. Otherwise, you could drown in this flood. Get moving."

Brian looked over at "The Boatster" and smiled extra-sweetly. Raising his voice, Brian yelled, "You don't understand. I'm a man of faith. This flood is just a passing trial. But after you go, I'll say an extra prayer for you. As for me, I put my faith in Jesus."

Before Brian started praying this time, he admitted to himself that the situation around him was unusual. Could the Rapture be starting? All that rising water made him think of Noah's ark. Maybe he'd better go onto his roof, which Brian had remodeled into a nice party area where he'd entertained friends from church.

A few seconds after closing his eyes in prayer, Brian heard an interruption. Annoyed, he looked up to see the source of that terrible din. Amazingly there was a helicopter, hovering right above Brian's house. Somebody threw down a ladder. And then Brian heard another bullhorn. What a nuisance!

"Grab the rope ladder. We can rescue you, but we don't have much time."

Brian wasn't the least bit tempted by "Noisy Helicopter Man." Brian looked up at him and tried to send a message of sweet serenity through his eyes.

"You don't understand," he hollered into the noise. "I'm a man of faith. This flood is just a passing trial. But I know you mean well. After you go, I'll say a prayer for you. As for me, I'm so close to Jesus that it can help a lot, having me put in a good word for you."

Soon the flood rose even more. Before he quite knew what was happening, Brian found himself standing before Jesus. Of course, that was wonderful, except that Brian felt physically weird. Somehow it seemed as though he was hovering above his own physical body, and it sort-of felt to him as if that body had drowned.

Not being a fool, Brian quickly figured out what was going on. He said this:

"Jesus, how I've longed to stand before you at last! Only I never expected to meet you before my time. I hate to say this, but shame on you. Weren't you supposed to rescue me? Right to the end, I believed in you."

Jesus answered, speaking in a voice that sounded like a beautiful chime. Brian could hear the love in it.

Only what was Jesus saying? "Look, Brian, I sent you a jeep, a boat, and a helicopter. Every single time, you made your own choice about what to do."

Never once had Brian thought of that.

CHAPTER 3

Your New Superpower, Enlightenment-Helpful

We suffer primarily not from our vices or our weaknesses, but from our illusions. We are haunted, not by reality, but by those images we have put in place of reality.

Daniel J. Boorstin, Political Historian

To avoid suffering, don't keep asking, "Did I really receive this amazing consciousness superpower?"
The important question goes, "How can I use it?"

Rose Rosetree

Ever since the dawn of the Age of Awakening, you've had an awesome new superpower. Use it wisely and you'll make rapid progress toward Spiritual Enlightenment.

Misuse it, though? Like Brian waving away "Noisy Helicopter Man," you might find yourself terribly confused. No wonder it's vital for every Enlightenment seeker to learn the truth about humanity's new **Consciousness Positioning Superpower.**

- Although it's abstract.
- And maybe nobody ever told you about it before.
- Yet, if you really aim to use your full potential in life, knowledge in this chapter will prove indispensable for moving toward Enlightenment.

Obviously, given the name of this chapter, soon I will define this Consciousness Positioning Superpower. But like anything that's authentically new, sometimes it takes some preparation to comprehend it.

Please be patient as I prepare you, Smart Spiritual Seeker. Because this new superpower is a big deal, it's worth taking a little time to understand it. By the end of this chapter, you'll have the essentials.

What to do if this chapter ever seems heavy going? Skip forward to our next chapter. Later, though, come back and absorb more of the foundational knowledge here. Sooner or later, you'll likely find it abstract yet tasty. Maybe akin to sampling some chocolate cake with an amazing aftertaste?

Now, Yum, Let's Talk Consciousness

Sure, we can dare to talk consciousness. Already, Smart Spiritual Seeker, you may know quite a bit about consciousness; equally likely, though, your current knowledge *doesn't* include what follows, even though every bit of this is essential for seeking Enlightenment now. So let's get started.

> **As you already know, consciousness means being AWARE — just as you are right now.**

This consciousness of yours is an extraordinary spiritual gift. Usually it works for you just fine. For instance, every day, a certain amazing thing happens to you, and happens effortlessly.

At a certain point after arising, you realize something like, "Hello, World! I'm here, noticing things. Golly, I can keep on doing that all my waking hours. Hey, I'm going to have me ANOTHER DAY."

Probably you already know quite a lot about consciousness, at least if you've sampled the work of spiritual teachers. Commonly they teach techniques that involve consciousness.

Most famously, there's **Meditation**. As traditionally used by Enlightenment seekers, meditation means the practice of using a particular technique, one with a very specific way to direct your consciousness.

In addition, Eastern forms of meditation are often bundled in with many lifestyle ideals. The full package of duties is beautifully gift wrapped with promises, Enlightenment-related promises, grand promises that may never be attainable — realistically, speaking.

Even worse, how well does any method of meditation work, now that we're living in the Age of Awakening? Maybe not as well as back in the Age of Faith. (See Chapters 26 and 27 on "Technique Time.")

Meanwhile, here's a quick update about meditation practices: No longer are they necessary...
For this you can thank your new Consciousness Positioning Superpower.

Whether or not you've been meditating, that new superpower of yours has been influencing you, switching off-and-on throughout your waking hours.

Most likely, this superpower has caused countless subtle experiences that you've been having ever since the Shift.

How could that be? I haven't noticed a thing.

That superpower is subtle, impacting how your consciousness works, impacting you subconsciously and energetically. Keep reading and you'll learn much more about this.

Clarity will unfold one page at a time. In advance, might I suggest? Don't skim over the rest of this chapter. If anything, slow down a little, because this is going to be the story of *your* consciousness, highly relevant to helping you as a Smart Spiritual Seeker.

The Story of Human Consciousness NOW, After the Shift

Do you already know this next concept? It concerns how your consciousness operates now, whether you've noticed this happening or not.

> Smart Spiritual Seeker, you're capable of experiencing three very different varieties of energy.
>
> But never more than one at any given time — at least, not unless you've got three different heads.

Seriously, at any given time, you'll experience only one of this world's three types of non-physical energy.

> *Look, do you really think it's a big deal, telling us about energy? Being energy sensitive, I already know more than most people. Isn't all this a little basic?*
>
> *Not basic at all, so please keep reading.*

In my experience, few people who talk about energy know much about what has changed with this Age of Awakening. In this chapter let's continue to explore little-known essentials for gaining Spiritual Enlightenment.

Energy Isn't Just Energy. Not in the Age of Awakening

Since we're living in this new era, seeing energy — or feeling it or sensing it — this is no longer an end in itself, but more like a good start. Today's spiritual seekers need to become familiar with *three different kinds of nonphysical energy*: Each one has an important purpose for your spiritual evolution.

To up your discernment, let's start calling each major kind of energy… by its rightful name. Never again make the newbie mistake of just calling it "energy." Rather, let's talk in terms of one or another **Vibrational Frequency.**

Why use that term of art? Different kinds of energy possess very different characteristics. In turn, these differences impact your spiritual evolution, which is the practical reason why, in this chapter, you'll start learning more about all three *very distinctive* vibrational frequencies.

To begin, did you know? Whenever you're aware of energy, you're having an experience at one particular kind of vibrational frequency. But which kind? That matters.

Shocking but true: Countless times each day you're noticing life at one or another of the three major vibrational frequencies. AND that spontaneous experience isn't necessarily helpful, not if you're seeking Enlightenment.

In short, you've got some *good news* and also some *room-for-growth news*.

- First, your *good news*: Referring to "energy" indicates talent for recognizing energy in general. Excellent!
- But does recognizing energy mean the same thing as knowing *how to use* experiences at each vibrational frequency? This matters for progressing toward Enlightenment.
- How about protecting yourself as a spiritual seeker? In this Age of Awakening, naïvely playing around with energy can lead to trouble. Yes, consider this your *room-for-growth news*.

Look, I aim to help you to avoid any trouble. Sadly, countless spiritual seekers today are getting sidetracked, wrongly assuming that all kinds of energy are created equal.

Also, guess what else? This very same *room-for-growth* topic might be essential for solving the Church-Wenters Mystery, that being the mystery we're exploring in the background. Now, Smart Spiritual Seeker, let's learn more about vibrational frequencies.

Goodbye, Energy. Hello, Vibrational Frequencies

Yes, I'm thrilled to start introducing you to Earth's three vibrational frequencies. Are you used to the vibing-out process of noticing energy? Today that's so common, but did you ever wonder: Whenever you vibe somebody out, which kind of energy are you noticing? Given your new Consciousness Positioning Superpower, "energy" could mean any of the three major kinds of vibrational frequency.

Due to your new freedom related to consciousness, most often these energy experiences are quite different from what was available before the Age of Awakening. You see, thanks to your new superpower, now you're really clever at experiencing life at different vibrational frequencies — and please remember, that's *frequencies* (plural), not simply one default kind of energy.

What's the catch? When your new superpower was installed, did it come with an owner's manual? No. Actually you weren't given any reliable knowledge at all for using this superpower.

Sad to say, thus far into the Age of Awakening, most people who are into energy are hindering their spiritual evolution, not helping it.

Based on research I've done with energetic literacy, approximately 85% of Americans are drastically underusing the power of their consciousness. Rather than evolving spiritually or progressing emotionally, they're developing problems with paying attention to human reality, falling into — there's that term again — *consciousness lifestyles* — that aren't Enlightenment at all.

Even worse, millions of folks have fallen into consciousness lifestyles that completely disallow spiritual evolution. Ironic, when that is happening to good people, working hard on themselves every day, believing that they are doing just great, and why? Because they feel or see energies.

Building Blocks of Understanding

Smart Spiritual Seeker, in this chapter (and later ones as well) I'm going to give you building blocks of understanding; these can help you to develop a new discernment about different vibrational frequencies.

Although you'll be learning new *concepts*, guess what won't be new?

Already you're used to the *process* of sorting through abstract ideas; for instance, back in the day you did exactly this kind of sorting when you learned how to tell apart letters like A, B, and C.

Ever play with alphabet blocks? Then you can remember how, as a kid, it was a big deal when you learned that A, B, and C are all *letters of the alphabet*. Maybe you had a set of colorful blocks, and each block was decorated with one of these letters.

At first, it was a super-easy kind of fun playing with your blocks... easy because the differences between letters didn't matter; whether those blocks were labeled A, B, or C, all of them were exciting new toys. Later though, you learned more. What a breakthrough it was when you discovered how to tell alphabet blocks apart, proudly realizing that:

- Some blocks had the letter A — which meant a certain kind of sound.
- And other blocks had a letter B — which meant a different kind of sound.
- While still other blocks, had a letter C — meaning an altogether different kind of sound.

Definitely a big deal! Besides being fun in itself, learning about specific letters was essential for moving toward the important grownup goal called, "Look at me. I can read."

These days, as an adult, it might be rare for you to feel a childlike thrill of discovery. Quite possibly though, that might start happening as you continue to read this chapter. You see, we're beginning to explore three building blocks of understanding, *and each one* will inform you about a different kind of energy.

Basically, you're learning how to distinguish three altogether different things, akin to when you first realized: Similar looking blocks could signify completely different letters.

I'm here to help you put words to your subtly different experiences of consciousness, and why? Because each building block of understanding, each letter, matters for *hastening your spiritual evolution*. So let our introductions continue!

Some Energy Exists at HUMAN Vibrational Frequencies

Of course, being human, you're a natural at noticing this kind of energy. Except wait a minute. Even this may not be as duh! as it seems.

- Every physical object on earth has *physicality*, with characteristics like shape and size and color. Physicality is something you're used to, just like handling ABC blocks.
- In addition, every physical object on Earth also has an underlying quality of *energy*.
- That underlying *energy*, distinctive to all people and things on Planet Earth, is something we tend to take for granted; being as familiar to us as the vowels in words.
- By contrast, *physicality* could also be compared to the oomphy consonants in words, and aren't consonants more attention-grabbing than vowels? (Entire systems of shorthand involve dropping the vowels in words.)

Back to the energy (and physicality) we earthlings are so familiar with, what quality does it have? Which quality have you come to take for granted, ever since you were a baby? It's **Human Vibrational Frequencies.**

These vibrational frequencies are low and slow, possessing a quality like the expression *down-to-Earth*. Within the abstract-seeming category of Human Vibrational Frequencies, there are actually many variations, such as LOW or MEDIUM or HIGH Human Vibrational Frequencies. However, human is the unmistakable common factor with all the energies that underlie every physical thing on this planet.

Simply put, Human Vibrational Frequencies include the solid-and-real quality common to everything you might notice in physical reality, be it feet or desks or staplers.

In addition, your thoughts and feelings don't have physicality. Nonetheless, they still exist at a Human Vibrational Frequency... provided that whatever you're noticing is surfacy enough.

For instance, in a surfacy way, can't you tell how you happen to feel right now, whether it's mostly happy or sad or scared or angry?

If I understand what you mean by "surfacy," everybody can do that. So why bother to state the obvious? Please, I'm interested in Enlightenment, not being boring like ordinary people.

Many spiritual seekers today sneer at Human Vibrational Frequencies. Yet these can become very important to you, even for the goal of seeking Enlightenment. It's a serious mistake to consider human experience to be boring or "unspiritual."

Let's start setting the record straight. While living with your new Consciousness Positioning Superpower, you are definitely capable of exploring life at two fancier — and entirely different — vibrational frequencies, neither of which is designed to inform you reliably about anything human-and-surfacy.

Granted, each of these two fancier vibrational frequencies still has a role to play in your spiritual evolution. Remember when I mentioned earlier that each of the three vibrational frequencies has a distinctive *purpose* for your spiritual evolution? Hardly a mainstream notion, not today!

Human Vibrational Frequencies have the spiritual purpose of serving as an essential default for your life experience. Whereas Astral and Divine Vibrational Frequencies can contribute differently to our Program for Spiritual Enlightenment.

More, much more, about this is to come in Part III. Meanwhile I wonder, what do you know so far concerning our second kind of vibrational frequency? Let's explore.

Some Energy Exists at ASTRAL Vibrational Frequencies

All **Astral Vibrational Frequencies** move faster than low-slow Human Vibrational Frequencies; also, astral means more subtle; technically you could even say that astral experiences are vibrationally *higher*, compared with anything human.

For sure, when consciousness is positioned at any Astral Vibrational Frequency, we experience only energies.

Not only do all astral experiences *lack physicality*; in addition, all astral experiences lack the familiar-though-subtle *energy* of Human Vibrational Frequencies, these being building blocks of all animate and inanimate life forms on Earth.

Also interesting to know, what else is tucked into Earth School? Every living *human, animal,* or *plant* contains a full set of astral equivalents, layer around layer around layer.

Trippy, huh? But we're unlikely to experience this directly unless under the influence of recreational drugs; so let me give you a little thought experiment to help the concept come alive.

Suppose that you're looking at your Aunt Penelope. Technically speaking, how do you make contact with her? You perceive one version of her at a time. Meanwhile multiple other versions of her exist at every vibrational frequency, whether human or astral or Divine.

Being human, you'll perceive only one version out of this huge assortment, depending on the vibrational frequency that your consciousness happens to be noticing right now.

Imagine further — since it's true — that tucked into your aunt's sweet face is a full set of astral versions; the number of Penelopes at Astral Vibrational Frequencies greatly outnumbering those at Human Vibrational Frequencies.

So, what's it like to experience at Astral Vibrational Frequencies?

Given our new Consciousness Positioning Superpower, astral often feels normalish, like a new-and-improved kind of normal, feeling energetically ordinary, except that somehow whatever you're noticing is a bit cooler than usual.

Here's an Everyday Example, about YOU

Everyday examples abound, since we humans are able to pay attention to any nearby fellow human, or other kind of animal, or plant. How about perceiving that physical body of yours, the one right here?

Smart Spiritual Seeker, you might start by noticing your toes. That's easy enough. Even as a baby you could do that, and not only by sticking those toes in your mouth. Being human, with normal mental functioning, you're designed to notice what exists at Human Vibrational Frequencies.

However, those physical toes of yours are only the start of noticing who you are, since you've also got an **Aura**. What does that mean? Your aura is a set of energy bodies around your physical body.

As you may know, auras are full of information. (For that reason, **Aura Reading** in the Age of Awakening means this: Using skills to download some of that info; in sharp contrast to the vague, outdated idea that reading auras means "seeing the colours.")

Technically, extra astral versions of you — or Aunt Penelope, her 17 cats, or her beloved red prayer plant — every living thing is more than its physical form.

Every human alive is packed-and-stacked with energy bodies that, together, make up our auras. Mostly our auras are made of energies at Astral Vibrational Frequencies.

Mostly made? Mostly???

Nice catch, Smart Spiritual Seeker. Within your aura, the subtlest part isn't astral at all. Instead, this exists at an altogether different vibrational frequency, neither human or astral, which brings us to...

Subtlest of All, the DIVINE Vibrational Frequency

Ah, simplicity! If you're seeking the highest kind of energy, there's only one option; it's very different from the nearly infinite varieties of Astral Vibrational Frequencies; or even the countless subtleties with our so-familiar Human Vibrational Frequencies.

You see, Smart Spiritual Seeker, there's only one **Divine Vibrational Frequency**. We could also call it *Perfection Everywhere Now*.

Hey, if you think this perfection might have something to do with the goal of our Program for Spiritual Enlightenment, you'd be absolutely correct.

Annoyingly and/or beautifully, this highest vibrational frequency is the most deeply hidden of all. Yet it's tucked into every single human being — yourself included.

A Divine version of me?

Absolutely, that's built right in. You exist at the Divine Vibrational Frequency, regardless of your religion (or lack thereof). Ultimately, your Divine nature is at the core of your magnificent human life, the person you are right now.

Take that as confirmation of what you've probably felt already: The Divine Vibrational Frequency lies within you.

In addition, long before attaining Enlightenment, it's possible for you to actively position your consciousness at the Divine Vibrational Frequency — this happening on occasion, such as sometimes while doing Technique Time. When you manage that, ah! Your thoughts and feelings are tinged with Perfection Everywhere Now.

Hey, did you catch the phrase I just used, *position your consciousness*? That matters.

HOW You Position Your Consciousness Matters

Smart Spiritual Seeker, in later chapters you'll learn much-much more about positioning consciousness. Meanwhile, let's explore essential concepts before racing forward to the more advanced ones. Ever hear the saying: "You have to walk before you can run"?

Excellent advice to this day, even though that saying was coined in the 15th century!

So, what does it mean to **Position Your Consciousness**? Look, I know you've already learned a lot in this chapter, but while we're at it, let's fit in some equally important essentials. What else do you know, vibrationally speaking, about how your consciousness works?

Long before receiving your new Consciousness Positioning Superpower, you've had a couple of consciousness abilities, granted; standard abilities that human beings have likely used for thousands of years, long before the Age of Awakening. (Used AND taken for granted.

Let's consider each one in turn — standard human abilities, not new but wonderful nonetheless. First of all, give yourself credit for....

Standard Human Ability #1. PAYING Attention

Being human, you have consciousness. This helps you to choose how you're **Paying Attention**. All your waking hours, you're paying attention to one thing after another; this process requires no special effort, provided that you have normal mental functioning.

Sweet, how your consciousness flows automatically, flowing like a gentle stream, a stream of consciousness flowing dependably... simply because you're human.

Throughout human history until the Shift, paying attention meant that your consciousness flowed *predictably* at Human Vibrational Frequencies. All your waking hours, you'd notice human-type things, easy-peasy.

Likewise, Standard Human Ability #2. DIRECTING Your Attention

Equally automatic and easy! Even tiny babies can do more than passively *pay attention* to whatever is before them. As we humans grow up, we get really good at a more active alternative; from time to time, we'll actively **Direct Our Attention**. This counts as a choice, albeit a tiny-and-effortless choice.

Countless times today, for instance, you might have found your mind "wandering." For instance, suppose that you attended a lunch meeting that (between you and me) wasn't totally fascinating. A series of boring presentations went on. And on. And on.

Hello! You might have given yourself a tiny vacay by directing your attention to something that seemed more charming.

- Maybe you looked out the window and spent a few seconds directing your attention toward a cute dog.
- Or you might have looked down at your lunch, directing your attention toward some mouth-watering cheese.

Next, a Mouth-Watering Truth about Consciousness

Call it spiritually delicious, if you like. Human lifetimes have always included certain built-in ways to *direct* our attention. For example, we can aim our eyes at something colorful, or listen for a pleasant sound; other times, we'll direct attention to our bodies with a bit of fidgeting; or maybe we'll start sniffing flowers in order to smell a lovely fragrance.

So human, doing any of this! Throughout most of human history, directing attention meant that your consciousness flowed wherever you aimed it AND, quite predictably, your consciousness would flow toward something at a Human Vibrational Frequency. Important point…

> **Throughout human history, all your waking hours, you'd notice people or things at a Human Vibrational Frequency.**
> *Before* **the Shift, you could choose WHERE to direct attention; however, you had little choice about WHICH vibrational frequency.**

So what's new, now that you're living *after* the Shift? Nothing's new about being able to *pay attention.* Nor is it unusual that sometimes you'll purposely *direct* your attention.

Beyond all that, something new has become available, effortlessly available every day of your life since Dec. 21, 2012. Living now, sometimes you'll start *positioning your consciousness* at an Astral or Divine Vibrational Frequency.

Goodbye, automatic consciousness positioning at Human Vibrational Frequencies.

Hello, NEW Human Ability: Positioning Your Consciousness

To be clear, *directing* your attention is not the same thing as *positioning* it. Remember what you've already learned in this chapter, about the three different vibrational frequencies? That's going to become very relevant. (Ooh, your consciousness plot is thickening.)

POSITIONING Consciousness Began after the Shift.

Finally I can answer our earlier question properly. What does it mean to **Position Your Consciousness**?

With the Shift into the Age of Awakening, every human alive gained a new Consciousness POSITIONING Superpower — that make-or-break ability which, earlier in this chapter, I promised to explain.

Now you're ready to put together some building blocks of understanding about energy, these understandings being vitally important for seeking Enlightenment in the Age of Awakening.

Before the Shift, human consciousness was nearly always locked into experience at Human Vibrational Frequencies.
Only very rarely would a person's consciousness shift up to a more refined Astral or Divine Vibrational Frequency. But now?

Spiritual seekers (and others) are spontaneously positioning consciousness away from Human, and doing this frequently.

Millions most often position their consciousness at an Astral Vibrational Frequency. AND, these sweet spiritual seekers have no idea of what they're doing.

Please, please, please keep reading the chapters that follow; you'll systematically learn how to use your new Consciousness Positioning Superpower to *enliven* your path to Enlightenment. Not *sabotage* it.

In case you're taking all this to heart, Smart Spiritual Seeker, here's a warning: Never give yourself the job of monitoring where you position your consciousness. Our Program for Spiritual Enlightenment includes nothing like that.

Spontaneity — not effort — will serve you far better; provided that you also use a bit of discernment in selecting activities during your day. (Keep reading. You'll see.)

Sadly, Few People Today Know What You Now Know

Well done, Smart Spiritual Seeker, how you've stuck with this chapter and developed vital concepts about three very different vibrational frequencies! Unfortunately, many seekers today assume that they know all that really matters about energy. Which is what?

- How, supposedly, energy is either GOOD or BAD.
- And the more time these folks spend noticing energy, the more spiritual they are.

Common "understandings" like these worse than untrue. They'll backfire for anybody seeking Enlightenment in the Age of Awakening.

Whereas the knowledge that you've just gained about your new Consciousness Positioning Superpower... can definitely help with your **Spiritual Evolution**, which means making authentic spiritual progress toward Enlightenment.

Apart from this new superpower, what else has changed with the Shift into the Age of Awakening? Is anything else different for those of us who are seeking Enlightenment?

Yes, actually. Your answer deserves a whole chapter. Coming right up.

CHAPTER 4.

What WAS the Shift into the Age of Awakening?

The ability to recognize opportunities and move in new — and sometimes unexpected — directions will benefit you no matter your interests or aspirations.

Drew Gilpin Faust, First Female President of Harvard University

Unless you're shopping in a store, "new" does not come with a label attached, nor with a price tag.

Rose Rosetree

Imagine that you're lucky enough to live in a pleasant neighborhood. The crime rate is low. Your neighbors are pleasant too, although these days nearly everybody is far too busy for friendship. Chats with your neighbors can race by so fast… if you pause to catch your breath… you might miss the entire conversation.

Imagine further that today is an ordinary Tuesday. In your neighborhood that means Trash Day. This particular morning you're wheeling your garbage can out to the curb. Unexpectedly you see Next Door Neighbor Kaitlyn; she's doing the same.

As usual, she's wearing stylish jeans and a busy t-shirt, picturing some celebrity you don't recognize; as always, her yellow-blonde hair is cheerfully bright; and when she turns toward you, her big, brown eyes look warm and friendly.

Both of you pause in your usual rushing (meaning, technically you do pause, although not for long). First you exchange a wave, then a "Hey." Following that, both of you take a sec to draw closer.

"Did you hear about Bill?" you ask.

"What?" Kaitlyn answers.

"He lost his job. The company went out of business."

For a moment Kaitlyn looks sad. Almost instantly, though, her face brightens. Kaitlyn gives one of her megawatt smiles, as she says with feeling: "You know what they say. *When one door closes, another door opens.* You've just got to believe."

Conversation handled, Kaitlyn turns away and heads for home.

Smart Spiritual Seeker, what's with that saying? How on earth is that door idea supposed to work, exactly?

"When One Door Closes, Another Door Opens"

Such a feel-good saying! However, when you think about it, this door business turns out to be quite relevant to what you'll learn in this particular chapter. You see, I'm aiming to help you understand more about the Shift into the Age of Awakening, so you'll be able to spot the consciousness implications of incidents like the hypothetical one just described here.

How has the Shift changed your everyday life?

Oh, Smart Spiritual Seeker, I've got big learning plans for us. Here's a preview of what we'll cover in this chapter.

1. Concerning, "When one door closes, another door opens," why is that so very Age of Faith?
2. Consider how the Age of Faith reached its culmination — and potential for absurdity — during the New Age Years.
3. What does it mean for you, having all that New Ageiness followed by humanity's *totally unprecedented* Shift into the Age of Awakening?
4. Which are the most popular ways that folks have responded to the thinning of the "Psychic Barrier" during the New Age Years?
5. How about post-Shift? Countless New Age fads are with us still, despite the complete absence now of the Psychic Barrier.

Of course, all this info is extremely relevant to your spiritual growth toward Enlightenment.

Why devote a whole chapter to this Age of Awakening business? Won't a quick summary be enough? I want Enlightenment and I want it quick!

No doubt, your time is scarce — like time for Neighbor Kaitlyn. But no, it wouldn't be wise to skip this chapter, figuring that someday you can google it all later, or wait until all the important spiritual info comes out as a movie.

Good luck with finding any of that: Smart Spiritual Seeker, this Program for Spiritual Enlightenment is leading edge, not like reruns of "Friends."

Besides, it's vital to delve more deeply into these topics. Not only will you learn more about consciousness possibilities in everyday life. Lacking these understandings, you'll be at a serious disadvantage for seeking Enlightenment now. As for the Church-Wenters Mystery that we're solving, in the background? Many clues are coming right up.

Altogether, the clarity available from this chapter alone... can start advancing you considerably toward fulfilling your spiritual goals.

Overview First, Smart You

Picture a Learning Planet, **Earth School.** Did you know? From an Enlightenment perspective, this amazing world is organized expressly to benefit courageous souls like you, seekers of spiritual evolution.

For thousands of years, human life at Earth School was set up in a certain way, seemingly how life *was in the beginning, is now, and ever shall be.* Only that "ever shall be" part didn't quite work out as most spiritual teachers have expected.

Still, Earth School's original setup with consciousness did endure for many thousands of years, lasting until the Shift on December 21, 2012. Let's call that bygone era **The Age of Faith**.

During the very end of that era, humanity went through a wildly exciting transition period, the **New Age Years**, lasting from 1980 until that Shift, about three decades.

Spiritual historians from the future may delight in unpacking that zany time, especially curious about why it took so long for most humans to know that the Shift even happened, let alone adjust to it.

Compared to those wise historians from the future, we lack hindsight. Besides, like Kaitlyn, we lack time. Quickly as possible, then, let's get to the practical parts. By now, the Age of Faith has ended for good. Every human on earth is living in The Age of Awakening — know it or not, like it or not.

Speaking of not knowing, that might include most of the people in your life, including the coolest influencers you know from YouTube, etc. Take your own survey:

> **How many people in your life know** what it means that the Shift happened? Humanity's previous consciousness era is totally over. Well, who cares about this new era? And who's got much clarity about what, exactly, changed?

Good luck with getting even one reasonable answer from all the people you know. However, Smart Spiritual Seeker, you're about to learn all the juicy parts, beginning with this very chapter.

During the Age of Faith, People Craved... Faith

Often they found it, too. In a way, this seems lovely.

But what if a lot of this faith covered up a limited ability to *experience* beyond Human Vibrational Frequencies, to *feel* beyond human, and even to *progress* much spiritually? True-true-true!

Human experience then, versus living now, is way different: Based on my research, the consciousness contrast is startling. By now we're all somewhat used to living in the Age of Awakening. Consequently, there's something you probably take for granted, Smart Spiritual Seeker. What would that be?

Our Consciousness Positioning Superpower, that's what. We've been taking this for granted, even before knowing much about what it is or how it works.

Smart Spiritual Seeker, since your goal is to evolve spiritually, all this matters. so you'll find more chapters in our Part I that give you just enough background to help you benefit from the goodies in Parts II and III.

All this learning builds toward a practical goal, for you to use your new Consciousness Positioning Superpower; and use it powerfully, using it like the motor in a motorboat. Don't you deserve to experience that power?

Today's Spiritual Progress Demands Direct Experience

Already you know how popular it is today, whatever the context, valuing direct experience.

For instance, some folks you know may prefer *experience presents* over *material gifts:* "Please don't give us your heirloom china. Help us pay for a honeymoon in Beijing."

Such an Age of Awakening preference! This Program for Spiritual Enlightenment requires well-chosen *experiences* at Human or Astral or Divine Vibrational Frequencies.

But which type of experience to have when?

Today's Consciousness Game Is New

Back in the Age of Faith, most people's consciousness was locked into Human Vibrational Frequencies. Therefore, their Age of Faith limitation involved *process*. In terms of *content*, folks could still talk a good game about the Great Spirit, Buddha, or Jesus.

> *Why was Earth School set up so that people in the Age of Faith had this big limitation?*
>
> *Wherever and however and whenever you happen to incarnate, the consciousness era on earth is non-negotiable; automatically that's going to set up your game of life this time around.*

Human life is always designed with certain limitations. By analogy, think of games like Candyland, Monopoly, or Catan. Would games like these be any fun unless they had a basic setup? Like that, back in the day....

One of the Biggest Rules for the Game of Human Used to be the "Psychic Barrier"

During the Age of Faith, the consciousness setup for human life on Earth included a **Psychic Barrier**, an abstract rule of the game, ineluctable like, "Just one sky. Only one Moon."

To get super-technical, the Psychic Barrier was a **Causational Process,** built into the operational design for human consciousness. This barrier worked like a circuit breaker, preventing nearly everybody from being able to position consciousness at any Divine or Astral Vibrational Frequency.

Quite the opposite of what we have now, given how each of us is now equipped with our Consciousness Positioning Superpower.

Back then, folks could talk about religion (*content*) but they couldn't experience it directly (*process*). Only through beliefs and happy imaginings could most people move past human limitations. Sigh! Under the circumstances, even that felt pretty great.

Consciousness limitations applied whether believers were taking Communion at church or praying their hearts out at their ashram. "God" meant *content*, not *process*.

The best most believers could do was to adore their cherished beliefs (while lacking much direct experience). Century after century, with very few exceptions, spiritual seekers were stuck with illusions. That was the best they could do.

No Wonder So Many Believers Depended on Faith

Smart Spiritual Seeker, not to diminish how much *you* have suffered from that sweet ache of *homesick for Heaven*, but consider this. Quite likely your ancestors felt far more homesick than folks living now.

Back then, human consciousness was locked into Human Vibrational Frequencies. Consequently, what happened to almost everybody during the Age of Faith? Whether desperately or dully, folks turned to shamanism, religion, you name it.

Authority figures mattered greatly, either well-credentialled authorities or, more infrequently, spiritual masters with rare consciousness talent who could actually teach their followers something about *process*, masters like Jesus and Buddha.

As human societies developed over millennia, *something* was always provided to ease that ache of homesickness. Maybe one didn't have much choice over which something. But at least you could have faith in *someone*. Which kind of someone would that have been?

Age of Faith Categories for Religious and/or Spiritual Help

Here's a short list of some of the likeliest helpers:
1. Your hardworking neighborhood witch doctor
2. The super-powerful tribal shaman
3. Your mighty medicine man or woman
4. Dedicated spiritualists and psychics
5. The local purveyor of wine or beer or psychedelic drugs
6. Sanctuary staff devoted to a particular God or Goddess, like the Delphic Oracle at a famous temple dedicated to Apollo; or worshipers of Amitabha Buddha at a Pure Land Buddhist temple.
7. Your priest. Or pastor. Or rabbi. Maybe your imam.

Overall, you get the idea. *Whenever* you lived during the Age of Faith, and *wherever* you lived, somebody was in charge, bringing desperately needed reassurance; somebody was considered "connected," and that somebody had to stay strong—even if secretly feeling crushed by the weight of human suffering.

So many beautiful people, giving their lives to help; yet they could only help so much. Even so, they might have helped others more than they knew, helping struggling humanity to get past the familiar trapped feeling of, "Is that all there is? Me so small. Life so big."

Now Let's Develop MORE Savvy about that Seeking

Aiming for Enlightenment, you need optimal savvy, right? Let's expand upon what you know thus far about the three different types of vibrational frequency.

An improved understanding will serve you well in later chapters. Rest assured all these juicy findings are based in a great deal of energetic literacy research. (What, you'd like me to share some of that with you? Then consider taking a series of online workshops called *The New Strong*. Go all the way through Level 103.)

Here my job is different, preparing you to succeed at our Program for Spiritual Enlightenment. So join me now in taking another look at our previous numbered list, all seven of those Age of Faith Categories for Religious and/or Spiritual Help. Technically speaking:

1. Categories 1–5, above, included beautiful "clergy" of different kinds, mostly accessing help from Astral Vibrational Frequencies. (Incidentally, to this day, aren't bartenders some of the most compassionate spiritual servants around?)

2. Whereas Categories 6-7 might have brought help from The Divine Vibrational Frequency. (Regarding *content*, at least. As a *process*, maybe that didn't happen terribly often.)

3. Important to note, during the Age of Faith, believers considered all seven of those occupational categories to be "spiritual." Even today many people mistakenly believe, "It's all the same thing," whether astral or Divine.

Granted, it was an achievement providing any of these otherworldly services. Picture the frustration of those devoted servants of God, struggling to do their best, practically smashing their heads against a wall, again and again, day in and day out.

What was that wall? It was a causational wall, the Psychic Barrier, and it represented no less an obstacle due to being invisible.

Gradually, Imperceptibly, that Psychic Barrier Thinneeed

As best I understand what happened, most of that thinning was a very slow process, stretching over tens of thousands of years.

Eventually, during the last 100 years of the Age of Faith, the pace of thinning accelerated exponentially. Even then, the Psychic Barrier held; consequently, human consciousness couldn't travel far, even if folks avidly followed their society's most venerated masters.

Human Vibrational Frequencies — that's where consciousness was stuck, sometimes with astral-type relief that seemed reassuringly holy.

Even for clergy who were fluent speakers of religious *content*, usually the *process* of using their consciousness meant just one thing: Consciousness positioning wouldn't generally budge, but stayed put at Human Vibrational Frequencies.

Like most spiritual teachers, even devout believers could seldom move far in consciousness. Many became expert quoters of the current theology; others developed a knack for **Mood-Making.**

Yes, Mood-Making

For instance, "Believe that you're in the presence of God. Make a good showing of faith in order to inspire the others."

Maybe, too, "Believe with all your heart. Until your faith is strong enough, you won't feel fulfilled." In which case, the one to blame wouldn't be Perfect God, nor Perfect Religious Leaders, but the sinful worshiper.

Sadly, Smart Spiritual Seeker, even the most brilliant, dedicated spiritual leaders couldn't do much about this general stuckness. With unpredictable-and-rare exceptions, nearly everyone's consciousness was locked into Human Vibrational Frequencies.

No Wonder Faith Mattered So Much

Look, Smart Spiritual Seeker: You've had your share of suffering, I have no doubt. But, with all due respect, there's suffering and then there's suffering. Famously, in 1651, "Leviathan" writer Thomas Hobbes characterized human life as being "solitary, poor, nasty, brutish and short." Even the *greatest* civilizations were pretty disgusting.

To see what I mean, hello! Study human history with an eye to seeing the quality of life for the vast majority of people, ordinary folks, not just the rich and aristocratic.

Or simply ask your oldest living relatives for stories about long ago. Get them in a good mood and then ask revealing questions like these:

- What were the family secrets?
- Which stories were too terrible for your own parents to tell you and the other kids?
- How horrendous were some of the things your family had to endure, with no choice, just to survive?

Even 100 years before the Shift, survival was tough. Granted, now that the Shift is over, physical survival isn't generally as harsh; still, it's hardly easy-breezy for you to live now, is it?

Physically, people used to be purer. The air they breathed was less polluted. Presumably they felt closer to nature. Didn't that make them more spiritual than people today?

Yes, those first three statements may be true, but let's take a closer look at the so-called "spiritual purity" of people long ago, more than 100 years deeper into the Age of Faith.

Sure, People Used to Be Keen Observers of Nature

Clearly, that's easy to romanticize; such as how humanity's physical environment was purer than what we've got now, considering air pollution and climate change. And hey, food was organic.

However, let's avoid feeling too nostalgic for humanity's "good old days." Consciousness-wise, what were the typical Age of Faith limitations to thought and feelings?

Look, it shocked me at first, doing research into consciousness; researching auras of people in daguerreotypes; learning about consciousness patterns of people who lived 100 years before the Shift. Although these folks looked recognizably human, their inner experience was anything but.

Much that makes your life worthwhile was rare or missing altogether. Inwardly, quality of life meant:

- Precious little use of imagination.
- Seldom noticing emotional nuances.
- Let alone having even much experience beyond Human Vibrational Frequencies.

Basically, how was inner experience for your Age of Faith ancestors? Their *process* of being alive reminds me of something car manufacturer Henry Ford famously told his customers back in 1909:

"Any customer can have a car painted any colour that he wants, so long as it is black."

Likewise, you could pay attention to anything... at any vibrational frequency that appealed to you... so long as it was at a Human Vibrational Frequency.

No wonder, religion brought consolation to those who searched for more meaning in life. Faith, obedience, and surrender provided *content*, if not *process*. Spiritually correct beliefs could help a person to feel spiritually safe. As for the more idealistic among us, faith brought hope of an "eternal reward."

All this Age of Faith dependency on religion came to a climax during the New Age Years. So let's delve further into those wildly enthusiastic decades, occurring right before the Shift into the Age of Awakening. During those New Age Years, some really wacky fads went mainstream.

Seven Popular Fads

Which fads peaked during the New Age Years? You might remember some of them. Take a deep breath. Then let's explore seven of the most popular New Age fads, from the perspective of consciousness.

How truly bizarre it was, living while the Psychic Barrier was thinning crazy-fast. This Enlightenment Teacher will summarize both *what* happened and also *why* I believe it happened.

Although that Psychic Barrier had gently been thinning throughout human history... What happened right before the Shift is almost impossible to believe, even if you lived through it.

Do you, personally, remember any of the New Age Years (from 1980 until the Shift)? Then maybe you recall how intense it was; although it's unlikely you knew a single soul who understood at the time what was collectively changing about human consciousness. I sure didn't.

In hindsight, we can appreciate how the range of human consciousness began to expand; in the background, the Psychic Barrier grew thinner daily; in the foreground, people began to discover something amazing!!!!!

Energy Sensitivity

Yes, countless people realized that they possessed **Energy Sensitivity**: Becoming able to notice energies in themselves and others. Did that happen to you, Smart Spiritual Seeker? If you hadn't already noticed energies before 1980, didn't you begin to notice them during the New Age Years?

Such mysterious energies, feeling spiritual or at least otherworldly; those energies seemed to promise a way to escape feeling so gosh-darned homesick for Heaven!

All this felt *amazing*, even if humanity hadn't quite developed the Consciousness Positioning Superpower which would soon become a defining characteristic for consciousness in the Age of Awakening. Nonetheless, personal consciousness was certainly moving toward much greater freedom. Emerging energy sensitivity wasn't a fad but a new capacity, a capacity that's here to stay.

By contrast, Smart Spiritual Seeker, here comes a list of seven fads from the New Age Years, fads related to *process*-related changes to consciousness, fads based on energy sensitivity, fads that became wildly popular. While reading, ask yourself, "Did I try any of them?" If you didn't try them personally, haven't you known folks who did?

New Age Fad #1. New Expectations for Religion

More people than ever *felt something special* while going to church, whether a traditional service or a "new thought" worship community. And if folks didn't feel a special something, very likely they proceeded to shop around.

By comparison, how common was "church-shopping" *before* the New Age Years? Not very.

Often, church was enjoyed primarily as a social experience. Although some worshipers believed that religion helped with their faith; others simply liked attending church in order to hear again-and-again how they were spiritually saved. (Or whatever other *content* was the equivalent of "saved," depending on the local variety of worship.)

By contrast, between 1980 and the Shift in 2012, many worshipers began to care most about how their religious leaders *made them feel*.

New Age Fad #2. Law of Attraction (LOA)

At a time when income inequality was growing in the U.S. (and elsewhere), did most people *notice* that, let alone *complain* about that? Hardly! Evidently economic facts weren't energy-sexy enough.

Instead, seekers swooned over an energy-sexy version of a *get rich quick* scheme, which explains why the preposterous Abraham-Hicks **Law of Attraction (LOA)** became a fad.

LOA theories appealed to those with energy sensitivity. Millions fell, and fell hard, for promises that they could develop a "spiritual" ability for manifesting money. Subconsciously, spiritual seekers might have been drawn to this particular fad for an understandable and deeply personal reason.

> Before this incarnation, as an angel living in a Heaven, each of us could manifest objects as quick as thought; for instance, imagining a dream home that would instantly become real — that is, exist in an astral energy form as something "real."

Only catch? Remembering this knack for manifestation wasn't a memory from any human lifetime but, rather, fond recollections of being an angel.

- Thoughts become things only while we're astral beings, living in an astral Heaven.
- While we're living humanly here on earth, the game of life is entirely different. Promises from an astral being, like Abraham, don't really work for humans.
- But back then? How could seekers, enthralled by their newfound energy sensitivity, be capable of clarity on that score?

New Age Fad #3. Channeled Teachings

Ooh, the special vibes! Another fad during the New Age Years involved exploring alternatives to organized religion, turning to channeled teachings that (supposedly) came from God, such as "A Course in Miracles."

As you may know, **Channeling** happens when a psychic like Lee Carroll allows an astral being like Kryon to take over his mouth and mind, using him like a ventriloquist's dummy.

In terms of vibrational frequencies, channeled teachings are often called "spiritual." Not true. Channeling comes from a discarnate astral being who uses a human channeler for a mouthpiece.

Thus, trance channeling is not Divine but astral; God does not take over humans and use them as puppets. (Among other reasons, why not? Because it's not terribly good for the spiritual evolution of the channeler.)

During the New Age Years, "spiritual" channeling went mainstream, which was hardly surprising, given widespread enthusiasm for "higher energies." How many believers guessed that *exponential thinning of the Psychic Barrier* was the underlying cause of this fad?

New Age Fad #4. "Everyone Is a Healer" — Supposedly

Why, exactly, did this absurd idea ever turn into a fad? You guessed it. Seekers of love and light were very susceptible, since they could suddenly *feel the energy.*

Common sense went out the window for many of us who became energy sensitive. Millions of kind-hearted people, who loved *feeling* that energy, conflated this process with skill at *healing* through energy; therefore, they flocked to New Age workshops on Reiki, Crystal Healing, Pranic Healing, etc. (Many caring energy enthusiasts still do, to this day.)

In their sweet enthusiasm, these aspiring healers believed teachers who told them that feeling energy was proof positive of their special gift. And did you ever notice this? Popular workshops often told students that the healing came from God, or else claimed the energy came from "**Spirit**," a popular synonym for the Divine — an inaccurate synonym, actually.

No wonder millions felt spiritually called to become energy healers. For example, during the New Age Years two different friends of mine — neither writers, nor healers, by any stretch — both self-published a how-to. Each author proudly entitled her book, "Everyone Is a Healer."

New Age Fad #5. Grand Promises of Mind-Body-Spirit

Smart Spiritual Seeker, are you old enough to remember when the grand promises of **Mind-Body-Spirit Healing (MBS)** began to revolutionize pop culture?

Whichever technique was employed, clients loved feeling what happened to their energies. Whether giving or receiving some form of energy "medicine," it felt so special. Surely that special feeling meant either God or healing or both.

But why, exactly? In my view, belief in MBS was mostly an expression of excitement over burgeoning energy sensitivity. Significantly, the "healing" came as a direct experience of energy awareness (*process*) rather than an intellectually rigorous system for learning how to facilitate healing (*content*).

Touching astral energy, moving it and/or seeing it? So spiritual — or so it seemed! And it didn't stop there. Millions of idealists believed that if you healed the body, automatically you'd heal the mind; if you fixed some energy problem physically, instantly you'd become more "spiritual," and so forth.

Even leading teachers and writers on MBS, including some who've been friends of mine, couldn't tell the difference between an idealistic fad versus a true causational connection between mind, body, and spirit.

New Age Fad #6. The Magic of "Being Positive."

During the New Age Years, millions of spiritual idealists also developed an allegiance to a higher way of living, positive thinking. Dr. Norman Vincent Peale is credited for launching *The Power of Positive Thinking*, first published in 1952; that is, 61 years before the Shift.

Incidentally, what kind of physician, exactly, was the good doctor? Peale happened to be a minister. Smart Spiritual Seeker, whichever credentials a "doctor" like Peale might have, does it make sense to you that emerging energy sensitivity would greatly enhance the appeal of his belief in "being positive"?

Mostly that appeal comes from feeling energy (at an Astral Vibrational Frequency). Of course, astral energy might seem way more uplifting than facing the familiar heaviness of life at Human Vibrational Frequencies; eating nothing but sugar might also seem like an improvement, for a while at least.

As you may know, the drive to positivity has only gained momentum since the New Age Years. Intensifying the energy emphasis, by now "Positive Vibes" aren't enough. "**Positive Vibes *ONLY***" has become crazy-popular.

Seems to me, positivity beliefs (*content*) haven't gained popularity on their own merits; the oomph comes from each seeker's growing ability to notice energy (*process*).

According to energetic literacy research, how do human beings today "become positive"? Usually they position their consciousness at an Astral Vibrational Frequency. In case you're wondering, that's nothing like living in Enlightenment.

New Age Fad #7. Megachurches

Megachurches? What a doozy of a concept! This fad led to the construction of ginormous houses of worship, churches that make money almost as fast as counterfeit operations, only perfectly legal.

Megachurches are run by religious celebrities called Televangelists; popular influencers via TV, then YouTube; many becoming household names in the New Age Years.

> By the Age of Awakening, countless megachurch members found certain preachers to be "godly." Honestly, couldn't everyone in the congregation feel the energy?

Energy-Energy-Energy

In this chapter, Smart Spiritual Seeker, we've summarized seven New Age fads related to energy sensitivity before the Shift. After the Psychic Barrier disappeared, energy sensitivity morphed into today's fully operational Consciousness Positioning Superpower.

Wisely using that superpower is essential for you to progress toward Spiritual Enlightenment. (Also, consciousness perspective you've received in this chapter can contribute toward solving a certain mystery we're exploring on the side — you know, the one related to Church-Wenters.)

Closing this chapter, let's acknowledge the open-hearted idealism of those who became involved in all that healing and worship and meditation.

However, since you're seeking Spiritual Enlightenment, rather than some cheap imitation, let's also call a spade a spade. What was lacking during the New Age Years and — for most spiritual seekers — what has been missing to this day?

Significant *discernment about vibrational frequencies.* That's what. Discernment matters. Speaking of which, these days do you often hear people brag or tweet about their "spiritual awakening"?

Misunderstand this and you'll never reach Enlightenment. Yes, you just read a big statement. It bears repeating:

Misunderstand spiritual awakening and you'll never reach Enlightenment.

In our next chapter, let's explore what "spiritual awakening" does (and doesn't) mean.

CHAPTER 5

Why Spiritual Awakening Is NOT Enlightenment

Before Enlightenment, a man has no real sense of self. Life in ignorance brings nothing but confusion about the self, causing us to live like the football of circumstances, kicked here and there.

Maharishi Mahesh Yogi, Enlightenment Teacher, speaking at a course in Poland Springs, Maine in 1969. (As recalled by Rose.)

Every experience of spiritual awakening strengthens our sense of self. As we continue to evolve spiritually, and especially once we cross the threshold of Enlightenment, each of us spontaneously lives with a sense of self that is constant, dependable, and true.

Rose Rosetree

During the Age of Faith, what did spiritual people seek? More faith! Sometimes they might also have sought approval for how well they obeyed "the teaching."

Whereas what matters most to us now, as spiritual seekers? Direct experience. Often, these days, a term for that is *spiritual awakening*.

As a Smart Spiritual Seeker, don't settle for that. You can pursue real-deal Enlightenment, which means so much more.

Pre- Shift, Was There Much Spiritual Awakening?

Probably not: During the Age of Faith, spiritual seekers would memorize scripture and follow their faith. Next to Godliness!

While today? Pious *content* no longer impresses most of us much; more likely we long for a *process*, the direct experience of God. Deep down, we yearn for a quiet moment of spiritual awakening, a taste of Heaven to quell our homesickness.

Although widely used as a synonym for Spiritual Enlightenment, "spiritual awakening" is different in many respects, as you'll be discovering in this chapter. Also, I'll introduce you to new concepts about discernment, a kind of discernment that's vital for today's spiritual seekers; preparing you for Part II, where you'll find many vivid examples of *authentic progress* toward Enlightenment versus *cheap imitations.*

In order to appreciate what's coming later, it's essential to keep reading now. So put on your counter-culture hat, if you own one. Maybe like a Robin Hood hat? And let's get going, Smart Spiritual Seeker.

Why Settle for Spiritual Awakening? Seek Enlightenment.

Smart Spiritual Seeker, sooner or later you might wonder, "Why doesn't today's Enlightenment Establishment offer *Age of Awakening* teachings about Spiritual Enlightenment?"

Differently put, why don't all of today's spiritual teachers and clergy explain how to benefit from humanity's new Consciousness Positioning Superpower?

Most commonly, the reason is simple: Sad to say, too many spiritual teachers are **Energetically Illiterate.** Physically, sure, they can tell their butts from their elbows. But energetically? Today's most professional spiritual teachers aren't yet knowledgeable in that way.

Despite being very learned about traditional Enlightenment teachings, or presenting a very photogenic appearance on YouTube, my colleagues keep on ignoring that Consciousness Positioning Superpower. And why?

Lack of energetic literacy, that's why. Far too many (otherwise lovely) spiritual teachers lack skills for tracking the consciousness lifestyles of their students. Think about that for a minute, Smart Spiritual Seeker. What is the *appropriate* expertise for today's spiritual teachers, how to steer an ox cart?

Let's not romanticize the provenance of Age of Faith teachings; these don't only predate cars and other technologies that we now find essential; in reality, those sweet old teachings predate modern dentistry, and even aspirin.

More up-to-date teachings can help seekers like you to fly forward in spiritual evolution... and also help you to land safely after each flight. In this Age of Awakening, that won't happen if your spiritual teacher lacks precision skills to research your consciousness.

I'd go so far as to say this. Every spiritual teacher in the Age of Awakening *must* develop expertise at today's literacy, energetic literacy, reading each student's chakra databanks.

But What ARE Chakra Databanks?

Smart Spiritual Seeker, here come seven essential facts about **Chakra Databanks**:

1. You've got a *Physical Body*, built at Human Vibrational Frequencies.
2. Around this human-type body you've got a set of *energy bodies*, full of information, each energy body larger than the one before.
3. Each of these energy bodies exists at an *Astral Vibrational Frequency*.
4. What is your *aura*? Quite simply, that means the full set of all your energy bodies, each one loaded with information about you.
5. Most of this info is encoded at an Astral Vibrational Frequency.
6. Deepest down you also have a presence (and info) at the *Divine Vibrational Frequency*.
7. *Aura reading* — energetic literacy — means downloading information from any human being's aura.

How, exactly, can you discern the most detailed knowledge about people's progress toward Enlightenment? By reading their *chakra databanks,* that's how.

> *Are you kidding? Shamanic healers and psychics have been seeing auras for 100,000 years at least. They don't mention Chakra Databanks.*
>
> *Fair enough — however, today's skills of energetic literacy go far beyond yesterday's version, which usually involves* **Seeing the Colours.** *Such a kindergarten level of skill, in my opinion, looking at auras as if visuals showed everything that mattered!*

While you're seeking Enlightenment in the Age of Awakening, it's optional for *you* to learn how to read your own chakra databanks. Surely though, this skill isn't optional, not for any ethical person today *who aims to serves as your spiritual teacher.*

Comparing Energetic Literacy to Word Literacy

Today's energetic literacy can definitely be compared to word literacy — since early model humans, living 100,000 years ago, sure didn't possess either kind of literacy.

Fast-forward, Smart Spiritual Seeker, and what will you find? As recently as 1800, most humans hadn't yet developed **Word Literacy.** Let's keep in mind, by 1800 the Psychic Barrier had grown relatively thin, despite continuing to grow thinner over the next 300+ years, before vanishing completely on December 21, 2012.

Good quality word literacy allows you to read this paragraph, right? As you may recall, word literacy is a skill, developed over time.

In order to read this paragraph fluently, first you played with alphabet blocks, then you sang the alphabet song, then you read your first little chapter book; over the years you continued developing skills until becoming a fluent reader.

Once word literacy is attained, those skills can serve you for the rest of your life.

Likewise, what happens after a person develops good skills for energetic literacy? Quite simply, you can read chakra databanks fluently, and read them for the rest of your life. However, before developing that degree of skill? Even the nicest, smartest spiritual teachers are lacking an indispensable skill.

Energetically Illiterate? That Explains a Lot

Let's face it. Energetic literacy is conspicuous by its absence in today's Enlightenment Establishment. Most of today's religious-and-spiritual influencers can't read even one chakra databank.

Back in the Age of Faith, who cared? Good skills weren't available yet; nor would they be for a long, long time — not until the Psychic Barrier was nearly gone.

Living now, when a Smart Spiritual Seeker like you can gain energetic literacy skills in a relatively short time, how stunning to realize this: Fact is, even the greatest Enlightenment Teachers of yore couldn't read chakra databanks.

I happen to know about the nadis, and how Vedic seers could read them many thousands of years before you, Rose Rosetree. What do you have to say to that?

Researching the nadis is not the same thing as reading chakra databanks. (Near the end of Part III, I'll go into some detail about this.)

For a practical response right now, chances are that you don't speak Vedic Sanskrit. Nor are you studying with the ancient sages for whom the *nadis* were a breakthrough discovery.

Ever since the Shift, chakra databanks have become the literacy equivalent of the nadis, only far more informative. Strangely enough,

I've known spiritual teachers who greatly respected the nadis, yet those same teachers couldn't be bothered with learning today's energetic literacy.

Granted, these sweet people enjoyed when we visited as friends, and every single one of them asked me to read their chakra databanks. When public facing, however, these spiritual experts withheld respect, and why? Because energetic literacy didn't exist in traditional spiritual teachings.

But how could it? How could any Age of Faith teacher have been familiar with a skill that was impossible before the Shift? Extraordinary though Jesus was, or Krishna (to many, an avatar), neither one talked about chakra databanks. We can, though.

Enlightenment Teachings Need to Catch up to NOW!

Even if otherwise magnificent, and fluent at today's Energy Talk, teachers from today's Enlightenment Establishment are energetically illiterate. Moreover, what else is outdated about the expertise of many of these spiritual teachers, despite the fact that they're all *living* in this new Age of Awakening?

Outdated Enlightenment Ideals, like the three coming up next in this chapter; these hoary, faith-soaked ideals are still being taught to today's spiritual seekers.

Typically, these aspirational ideals are dunked in sanctimony as well as belief. And the fact is, none of them may *ever* have worked terribly well, apart from inspiring more faith.

For sure, these Age of Faith relics won't help today's Enlightenment seekers. Oddly compatible with today's faddish enthusiasm over "spiritual awakening," these outdated ideals are pursued by many a spiritual seeker living after the Shift. Maybe even you?

Since this chapter aims to bring you discernment about spiritual awakening, let's consider these three ideals on their merits.

Our Program for Spiritual Enlightenment sure doesn't include a single one of them. Find out why not.

Outdated Ideal #1. Forgiveness

Striving to achieve **Forgiveness** could easily turn into a full-time job. To reach Enlightenment must you love your neighbor? Really? For instance, should monks and nuns manufacture loving feelings toward every annoying renunciate who happens to live under their roof?

Wait a minute, Smart Spiritual Seeker. Do you even live in a monastery?

Seeking Enlightenment in the Age of Awakening, you have no need to live like a monk or a nun. And, while we're at it, please don't fear that some nosy, judgmental version of God is constantly snooping around in your thoughts — perpetually testing you to decide if your emotions aren't "perfect enough."

What works better than forgiveness? With our Program for Spiritual Enlightenment, all you need is simple **Emotional Honesty**. Spontaneously feel what you feel, whether happy or sad, scared or angry, etc.

Buh-bye to any requirement that you plaster some bland, compassionate smile on your face, continually oozing forgiveness because otherwise... what? You won't be sufficiently holy?

Look, it's enough to do your reasonable best to act with basic good manners. Really, that's plenty.

Outdated Ideal #2. Purifying Yourself Like Crazy

Spiritual Purity involves making life choices as if you've got to keep scrubbing away at yourself, whether morally or financially or sexually.

Golly, another potential full-time job that is no longer necessary, if ever it was!

> For example, you really don't need to bother with self-imposed vows of poverty, chastity, or obedience.

- Nor, for that matter, need you strive for the waifish look of today's anorexic actresses, walking coat-hangers who are widely considered the ultimate in beauty and sexiness.
- As for meditating as much as possible? Wearing all-white clothing? Honestly, don't you already have enough to do?

Let's get real about what's needed for success at our Program for Spiritual Enlightenment. Do an appropriate amount-and-kind of Technique Time each day.

Yes, 20 daily minutes will be plenty.

You'll learn more about this in Part III. In advance, you might be interested to know that meditation may not be helpful any longer; ditto for other common religious practices that you may have learned along the way, purifying practices that are reputedly sacred.

For instance, have you ever taken Catholic communion? Beautiful: Except what about this part? Before partaking of the Eucharist, you're supposed to say prayerful words like these, along with the rest of the congregation:

"Lord, I am not worthy to receive you, but only say the word and I shall be healed."

If you find that sort of thing lovely, don't let me stop you. Otherwise you might choose to rethink that sort of approach as being exceedingly Age of Faith. Innumerable religious customs today are both lovely, obsolete, and optional.

Who can predict how many such customs will *survive* for long, now that we're all in the Age of Awakening?

Fortunately, as of this moment, there's no need for you to conjecture. Authorize yourself right now.

If you like, decide that you no longer need to apologize to your Creator for your supposedly being "impure" — as in "human." Up to you!

> **Outdated Ideal #3. EATING Pure**
>
> What's another way to keep busy while feeling terribly homesick for Heaven? Dietary *shoulds* and *should-nots* have been way popular. Traditionally, **Eating Pure** involved fasting, vegetarianism, maybe carrying a begging bowl.
>
> During the first decade of our Age of Awakening, purity trends for non-monks, **Householders**, have come to include juicing, eating raw, and veganism.
>
> Consciousness lifestyle research with energetic literacy reveals — uh-oh! Nearly nobody who "eats pure" is living in Spiritual Enlightenment. (For details, go to this post at my blog, the "Spiritual Enlightenment List." Feel free to contribute to our massive research project by nominating public figures who tout diet as the key to spiritual awakening, etc.)
>
> Meanwhile, are food austerities required for our Program for Spiritual Enlightenment? Definitely not; simply eat food that is reasonably healthy for your particular body.

Are You Getting the Picture?

Smart Spiritual Seeker, many Age of Faith customs have been designed to make a person more "spiritual." Yet they don't necessarily help the least bit for progressing toward Enlightenment.

Thank goodness, today's energetic literacy — not the pursuit of outdated ideals — has shaped our Program for Spiritual Enlightenment.

> Smart You, are you living on Earth as an incarnated human? This will never feel the same as living as an angel in a beautiful Heaven. But consider: That doesn't make human experience dirty, just different.

Take as long as you wish to consider all this, Smart Spiritual Seeker. Maybe snack on a "sinfully delicious" cookie, or have a good cry over all the unnecessary ways that you've been hassling yourself, as though you constantly had to fix yourself before God would find you acceptable.

On a brighter note, let's consider what Enlightenment actually is. If not involving emotional blandness, frequent self-scrubbing, and hunger... what is Enlightenment going to be like?

Honestly, there's no point to pursuing a goal if you're vague about it. You've learned a lot since our earliest chapters; now let's revisit this topic.

What IS Spiritual ENLIGHTENMENT?

Spiritual Enlightenment is a way of life, not merely a sweet experience or two. Ideally, once achieved, Enlightenment lasts for the rest of your life. Maybe you're wondering, what are its defining characteristics? Here are five of the most important things to know.

1. *Illusions* don't fool you anymore; at least, illusions don't fool you for long.
2. *Ever-fresh dawning of spiritual truth* can happen for you, gently surprising you many times each day, beautifully enhancing your regular human experiences.
3. In Enlightenment you're *using your full potential*, finding it easier than before to learn whatever you choose, whether for emotional growth, spiritual connection to the Divine, or simply to be of service to the people who matter to you. Why the accelerated learning? Simply put, you have much less inner resistance to life.
4. *A unified sense of self* pervades all your waking hours, quite different from everyday struggles to figure out, "Who am I?" (Or what Maharishi called the "football" experience — see again, the quote at the top of this chapter.) Pre-Enlightenment, we have a zillion ways to define ourselves, often depending on random things that other people say or do. Or tweet!
5. Compared to pre-Enlightenment, *God is more strongly present within you*. Strictly speaking, this is a matter of

degree, since every human alive possesses some underlying connection to the Divine. Wonderfully, in Enlightenment that subtle sense of connection becomes far stronger.

Quite possibly, Smart Spiritual Seeker, you could read this sort of description all day long, but would that move you into Enlightenment? Nah! Clarity will serve you better.

So Let's Add More Clarity about Spiritual AWAKENING

Thanks to the internet, idealized content about spiritual awakening has become popular clickbait, as if "Awakening" really meant something super-significant. For instance, Google just gave me 9 million hits on "spiritual awakening," versus 3 million for "Spiritual Enlightenment." Triple the popularity, but why?

Ever since the New Age Years, one crazy-popular trend has emerged, where "experts" will refer to **Spiritual Awakening** (or simply **Awakening**, for short) as though it's today's cooler way of talking about Spiritual Enlightenment.

> In truth, what is spiritual awakening? It's just an experience with more energetic intensity than whatever you're used to.

Quite likely you've enjoyed some of this by now, so you don't need me to tell you how encouraging it can feel.

For one thing, it's *inspiring* when your awareness expands beyond everyday sorrow, boredom, or even pretty-darned-good everyday happiness.

Sometimes an experience of spiritual awakening can make you feel as though you've touched the feet of God. Alternatively, you might feel spiritually big-big-big in an entirely new and unexpected way; as if galloping toward the destination where you most want to be.

Life-changing though spiritual awakening can seem, now hear this: In reality, an experience is just an experience, part of your progress toward Enlightenment, definitely not to be confused with arriving at your goal.

If you're wise, from now on...

Never Conflate Spiritual Awakening with Enlightenment

Sadly, many of today's spiritual teachers — knowingly or not — contribute to this mess. When did it all begin? As I recall, loose talk about spiritual awakening grew popular during the New Age Years, and who knows how long this nonsense will continue?

Specifically, which kind of *loose talk* do I mean? Conflating one enjoyable experience with a long-term way of living — is that even worthy of an intelligent teenager? Significant problems arise for every spiritual seeker who lowballs the concept of Spiritual Enlightenment. Please spread the word: Spiritual awakening is NOT Enlightenment.

Personally, here's how I learned the difference. For 16 years I taught Transcendental Meditation, adoring every word spoken by my guru at the time, Maharishi Mahesh Yogi. In retrospect, he ran a cult (among other problems). Nonetheless, he got some things right, including how he'd insist repeatedly that Enlightenment meant more than "flashy experiences."

These days any photogenic dilettante can gain credibility as a spiritual vlogger, etc. Over the years — like you, probably — I've encountered plenty of "experts" who prefer to curry favor with potential students by flattering them, even lying to them.

For instance, just today I googled, "Attend my nonduality retreat and gain spiritual awakening." How many hits? Wanna guess?

Shockingly, 125,000. Guaranteed "awakening" for the price of admission? P.T. Barnum would be proud.

Professionally, how did I learn that spiritual awakening is NOT Enlightenment? This education developed during some of my sessions with Energy Spirituality™ clients. Many spiritual seekers have come to me after being left both inspired and confused by an experience of spiritual awakening.

Also, some clients have come to me after attending nonduality retreats that threw their auras way out of whack; fortunately, I had the skills to help them regain a better balance.

Wait a minute. That sounds scary. How could spiritual awakening mess people up?

That excellent question deserves a thorough answer. Here it comes.

CONFUSION Can Result from Spiritual Awakening

Maybe it seems incredible how beautiful experiences of spiritual awakening could cause confusion, sometimes even wrecking a person's life. Yet this happens.

For example, consider some of the students who've come to me for sessions of Enlightenment Teaching. Often they made our appointments *after* quitting their jobs, or creating other drama, so utterly convinced they'd become that spiritually they "had arrived."

Many lovers of God, trusting in the power of their "spiritual awakening," convinced by "spiritual teachers" to make big changes to support their new realization; many of these believers have made drastic-and-unwise changes to their lives.

What was the common denominator? If ever you've felt homesick for Heaven, you can sympathize. Unless they follow teachings with a High Truth Value, enthusiastic seekers can trash whatever appears to stand in the way of more-more-more spiritual awakening.

Worst Case

Some of the spiritual awakening folks who've come to me for sessions — seekers whose auras were now seriously imbalanced — these good people considered themselves newly-minted experts, as if anointed by God to become Enlightenment Teachers.

Talk about the blind leading the blind! It was as if these well-meaning "experts," lurching through life with terribly messed-up auras, unencumbered by energetic literacy, should now influence others as wayshowers, maybe calling themselves "servant leaders."

More Responsibly

Other clients, believing they had awakened into Enlightenment, were somewhat more cautious. Although they yearned to "Do something beautiful for God," and start turning their lives upside-down, they took the simple precaution of a research session with me,

As it happens, Energy Spirituality™ skills include **Soul Thrill® Aura Research**, an advanced skill that's perfect for shedding light on potential choices. Dazzled by spiritual awakening, many seekers have asked to research the likely consequences of choices like these:

1. Quit my (materialistic) job.
2. Become a healer — with no need to take lessons.
3. Start eating vegan.
4. Live in a quiet place, far away from cities.
5. Publish a masterpiece spiritual guide, healing readers through the power of their personal story of awakening.

Meanwhile, what showed up in their Soul Thrill Aura Research? Any of the above-mentioned choices would have worsened the mess in their chakra databanks, not to mention the mess in their lives.

In general, as an Enlightenment Teacher, I've had many an opportunity to help clients *avoid* problems with integrating their cherished experiences of spiritual awakening.

(Good news for you, Smart Spiritual Seeker: Deeper into this program, I'll show you how easy it can be to responsibly integrate spiritual awakening, drama free.)

Important to note: For practical recommendations after a life-changing spiritual experience, there's no substitute for a personal session with a skilled Enlightenment Teacher. No book can provide that kind of individualized help.

However, in general terms, I can advance your understanding, including what comes next: True discernment about spiritual awakening must include knowing about this...

"Astral Flash," That's What

Smart Spiritual Seeker, by now you know some pro's and con's about spiritual awakening. But how much do you know about the related concept of **Astral Flash**?

If you haven't encountered this concept before, maybe that's because it's a term of art from Energy Spirituality™. Astral flash means an exciting kind of energy baked into certain experiences, *an energy which persuades you that something really important is happening.*

- On the positive side, that energy is about *process*, not *content*.
- But on the negative side, usually that energy is *astral*, not Divine.

Sometimes it's really exciting when, for any random reason, you position consciousness at an Astral Vibrational Frequency, and therefore feel impressed by astral flash. But please be reminded once again: Astral is not Divine. Consider astral flash to be the consciousness equivalent of pyrite, *fool's gold*.

Understandably, fooling around with astral flash can appeal to those of us who feel homesick for Heaven. But make no mistake: Astral flash is a *detour* on the road to Enlightenment, not worth confusing with a legitimate path, not if you're wise.

No repining! What if previously you've been caught up in astral flash? You can change, starting now.

Sometimes a word to the wise is enough. Definitely consider yourself warned, Smart Spiritual Seeker. Astral flash is addictive. The more you get, the more you'll want.

Regardless, no amount of astral flash can ever satisfy your longing for the Divine, which is why our Program for Spiritual Enlightenment includes protecting you from dependence on this cheap substitute.

When it comes to spiritual awakening, have you guessed yet? Sometimes it's simply an experience of astral flash. Yet there's another possibility too: You might be having a legitimately spiritual experience, a sweet moment with your consciousness positioned at the Divine Vibrational Frequency.

Most often, though, experiences labeled as "Big-Deal Spiritual Awakening" do involve astral flash. Discernment that you've gained in this chapter can protect you.

In Conclusion, for Now

Suppose that you *have* encountered some beautiful experiences of spiritual awakening. Then cherish them. Lovely!

Alternatively, suppose that you *haven't* had any flashy experiences of spiritual awakening? No worries: Maybe you just haven't needed them yet; maybe you'll never need them.

Many of my students in Enlightenment never had a single experience of spiritual awakening, nothing of the sort occurring until they gently slipped into Spiritual Enlightenment.

Enlightenment as a long-term way of life is *your* goal, right? Not just some flashy experiences, here or there.

> *But I have had some amazing experiences of spiritual awakening. What should that mean to me, long term?*
>
> *Simply that you've had some lovely experiences. Let that be good enough.*

Why do I urge you to take this approach? Because it can help you to progress toward Spiritual Enlightenment, the real deal. Meanwhile, any experience of spiritual awakening is lovely. Really, let that be good enough.

CHAPTER 6

Content or Process? Don't Be Fooled

Happiness cannot be traveled to, owned, earned, worn or consumed. Happiness is the spiritual experience of living every minute with love, grace, and gratitude.

Denis Waitley, Writer

In case you're wondering, living "with love, grace, and gratitude" is not called "Enlightenment." It's called mood-making. Thinking about positive ideas (content) *can actually hold you back from living your full potential in life* (a process).

Rose Rosetree

Ooh, the difference between **Content** and **Process** is such a major deal. At least if you're seeking Enlightenment. In this context, let's lead off with a tuneful example that may be familiar to you.

Sing along with me, if you like. (Otherwise, reading would be fine too.) And if you do prefer to sing, the tune comes from a great American spiritual, "I've Got a Robe."

Everybody talkin' 'bout Heaven ain't going there.

Now, substitute one word:

Everybody talkin' 'bout ENLIGHTENMENT ain't going there.

You see, random talk about *content* is cheap, whereas responsible talk about *process* counts as valuable. In this chapter you'll learn why. Let's start here.

Positioning Consciousness Is PROCESS, Not CONTENT.

Back in the Age of Faith, this distinction didn't matter so much. Walking-talking humans could do what? They could *pay attention.* Also, they could *direct attention.* However, they couldn't yet *position their consciousness.*

Already you've learned what makes that new ability possible. Smart Spiritual Seeker, you've got that nifty new Consciousness Positioning Superpower, which is good, because our Program for Spiritual Enlightenment depends upon using that constructively.

For that reason, it's essential to understand some new implications of what it means to position your consciousness.

As you know by now, the Psychic Barrier almost always prevented human beings from positioning consciousness away from Human Vibrational Frequencies. Granted, folks still *talked* about spiritual ideals. Usually this amounted to inspiring **Content**: Not direct experience, but pretty-pretty pictures.

You see, spiritual seekers would ponder high-sounding ideals, engaging in talk about them; often persuading themselves that they *lived* those pretty-pretty pictures. Only that was mood-making, which didn't help them to evolve spiritually.

No More Consolation Prizes, Okay?

Equating *content* with *process* is kind of old-fashioned, now that the Psychic Barrier is gone.

Still, that doesn't keep folks today from doing all they can to "be positive" or otherwise talk a good game, using spiritual content; as if mood-making were still the best option available to spiritual seekers.

No longer is this your best option, not now.

Seeking Enlightenment in the Age of Awakening, hello! You would waste your time, trying to fill your mind with positive ideals, such as this chapter's quote from that sweet writer of inspiring *content*, Denis Waitley.

Goodbye Psychic Barrier. Hello, Direct Experience

Today's Smart Spiritual Seekers need to understand that **Process** is the point of spiritual teachings, not *content*. *Process* means having a direct experience with your consciousness, a spontaneous experience, an up-close-and-personal experience.

Fortunately, *process*-type experiences add up... at least if you're seeking Enlightenment. Also fortunately, our Program for Spiritual Enlightenment will help you to avoid pretty-pretty side trips into *content* (i.e., mood-making).

Now let's continue to gain more clarity about *process* versus *content*. For that purpose, Smart Spiritual Seeker, I'm going to lead you through a pair of thought experiments.

Thought Experiment 1. During the Age of Faith

Suppose that churchgoer Jane is talking to her pastor, Rev. Sweeney. The year is 1995. Together they're discussing a Bible verse, which both of them believe to be "The Word of the Lord."

You see, the *content* of their conversation, the topic, is sacred, even considered Divinely dictated. By definition, this *content* is sacred compared to *content* about ordinary human things, such as fences or measles.

Of course, whenever people talk, unless they're mostly yawning, there's always going to be subject matter, or content. By contrast, how about the *process* of carrying out a conversation?

That's where positioning consciousness matters to us now. Smart Spiritual Seeker, you and I are living after the Shift, with no Psychic Barrier to limit the flow of our consciousness into different vibrational frequencies.

Nonetheless, our first thought experiment doesn't take place after the Shift. Let's imagine what it's like, having this conversation, either as Jane or the Rev., when it's happening *before* the

> Shift. Right now, the pastor is quoting Mark 12:30. Regarding *content*, he's reading aloud to Jane:
>
> "And thou shalt love the Lord thy God with all thy heart, and with all thy soul, and with all thy mind, and with all thy strength: this *is* the first commandment."
>
> Beautiful! Only, without knowing it, they're discussing this *content* as an idea, a belief, an ideal. Maybe they're hoping to gain more faith and apply it better through more understanding of that "first commandment."
>
> Whatever *is* occurring to each of these good people, what *isn't* happening? Neither one is experiencing anything akin to positioning consciousness at the Divine Vibrational Frequency.
>
> No *experience* in consciousness is transforming Jane's heart or mind or use of power. Likewise, what's happening to hardworking Rev. Sweeney, despite his conviction that he's always in close contact with God — after all, isn't he called "The Reverend"? Yes, he's mood-making too, just like Jane.
>
> In short, these faith-filled believers are discussing the idea of a sacred commandment. With all due respect, both of them are discussing *content*, not jump-starting personal experience (*process*) at the Divine Vibrational Frequency.

A Limited Standard for Spiritual Seeking

Thought experiment done, what did you notice? I hope you appreciated how, during the Age of Faith (even the New Age Years) there was a very limited standard for spiritual seeking.

During that Bible Study, the *content* was about God. But the *process* involved people who were paying attention to words, inspiring words; mere words, though; words experienced at a Human Vibrational Frequency.

However fervently they believed, however hard they tried, nothing about this conversation would blast through the Psychic Barrier's way of limiting these people's direct experience.

Both Jane and the Rev. were seeking to understand *content*. This didn't achieve what you and I can now do effortlessly, since it's now possible for people to move into a direct experience at the Divine Vibrational Frequency, a *process*.

Of course, this first thought experiment implied no insult to either sweet believer. Due to living pre-Shift, their consciousness was locked into Human Vibrational Frequencies; hardly anybody was positioning consciousness elsewhere (except for those who drank "spirits").

By Contrast, What Happens Now?

Underlying rules have changed, consciousness-wise. Ever since the Shift, oboy! Every split second that you're awake, the *process* of positioning your consciousness can change.

> At any given moment, while awake, human beings have always had consciousness. During the Age of Faith, folks could also pay attention or even direct attention. But that was all. Whereas now?

Living now, during your waking hours, you're often *positioning* consciousness, too. At any moment, yours could be at an Astral or Divine Vibrational Frequency, not necessarily one that is human at all.

Mind-boggling but true: Smart Spiritual Seeker, all your waking hours, minute by minute, people like you can effortlessly position consciousness at one vibrational frequency or another. You can and you do, even without trying. Practical takeaway: Whenever you speak to another person, don't assume that you know where anyone's consciousness is positioned.

Plus, Here's Another Amazing Concept

When two people are talking together, do you think they'll necessarily position consciousness at the same vibrational frequency? Nope.

Each person positions consciousness independently of anybody else. Same *content* being discussed by each person, yet everyone talking together could be having a different *process*, due to positioning consciousness at one of many possible vibrational frequencies.

Wouldn't that experience be determined by whatever the people were talking about?

Never assume a comfortable sameness, such as occurred during the Age of Faith. Also, might I suggest? Never waste your time looking for clues, or trying to figure out anybody's "wavelength" etc.

What if you're still curious? How, exactly, did Jane or Rev. Sweeney position their consciousness during Bible Study: for instance, last Saturday at 2:00 p.m.?

To find out, you can learn dedicated research skills: a considerably more advanced form of energetic literacy than simply reading somebody's chakra databanks from a photo.

Realistically speaking, good energetic literacy can be learned in a few months, studying part time; but be prepared to spend decades developing strong enough skills to learn a technique like Consciousness Positioning Consults®, expressly developed for precision discernment, in detail, about *who* is positioning consciousness *where*, and also informing you about the specific qualities of that person's subtle experience.

Lucky for you, this Enlightenment Teacher has spent those hours and decades, so let me share with you the kind of info one finds. Here's a typical example of what happens commonly now, given humanity's new superpower:

- Person A is positioning consciousness at a *Human* Vibrational Frequency.
- During that same conversation, Person B is positioning consciousness at an *Astral* Vibrational Frequency.

◞ Whereas Person C is positioning consciousness at the *Divine* Vibrational Frequency.

No kidding, this kind of mismatch happens daily to everyone. So how about this? Smart Spiritual Seeker, let's make the reality of this process more vivid by conducting a second thought experiment.

Thought Experiment 2. During the Age of Awakening

Smart Spiritual Seeker, let's imagine that Jane and the Reverend are having the exact same kind of conversation as in our first thought experiment; exchanging the exact same words about the exact same Bible verse. Only this second conversation happens today — a day which is occurring after the Shift on Dec. 21, 2012.

Sure, the *content* of this conversation is identical, right? But how about *process*, regarding each person's positioning of consciousness? That's going to be totally individual.

◞ Imagine that Jane is spontaneously positioning her consciousness at a MEDIUM *Astral* Vibrational Frequency.

◞ Meanwhile the Rev. is spontaneously positioning his consciousness at a MEDIUM *Human* Vibrational Frequency.

Would either of these faithful Christians consciously *know* how they are positioning consciousness? If asked, could they pinpoint the other speaker's consciousness positioning?

Nope and Nope

No wonder I wouldn't recommend that any of you try casually assessing this kind of thing in everyday life. (I sure don't.)

Whenever you talk with someone, it's plenty to have a conversation. Already you've heard the idea that specialized skills are needed for good quality consciousness detective work, but one thing more is required. In order to use a skill like Consciousness Positioning Consults®, guess what? This isn't casual, like picking up a vibe.

Researching anybody's positioning of consciousness is a skill, demanding your undivided attention. Thus, you'd do this kind of research on a separate occasion, never trying to research anybody's flow of consciousness... at the same time that you and others are talking together.

Look, you're human. Consequently, you can be in the *process* of carrying out a conversation OR you can be in the *process* of doing research into consciousness, but never both at once.

Despite being effortless, researching anybody's positioning of consciousness is completely different from casually checking out somebody's energies, or critiquing your friend's hairstyle, or privately reminiscing over the last time you had a sandwich made with mouthwatering cheese.

Either *skilled research* or *guessing about energies* would still count as Technique Time, which you'll learn more about in Part III.

Meanwhile, here's a bit more perspective for you as somebody seeking Enlightenment in the Age of Awakening. Two more reasons to avoid checking out people's energies while talking with them: First, the results won't be accurate; second, taking that extra Technique Time won't be good for you.

Weird! All the possibilities for consciousness positioning seem overwhelming. It's starting to seem like science fiction in everyday life. People today don't even know where the heck they're positioning their own consciousness?

Definitely not. Our new Consciousness Positioning Superpower works behind the scenes, working automatically.

But No Worries

Because our Program for Spiritual Enlightenment won't require that you monitor anyone's consciousness. Instead, you'll learn *practical knowledge-and-skills,* making it easy for you to use your superpower constructively, as you'll see in Part III. Never will I try to teach you how to purposely control where you position consciousness.

With a car or a bicycle you can physically shift gears, but is your awareness like a car or a bike? Of course not.

Smart Spiritual Seeker, it matters that you learn about having consciousness now, which is likely very different from what you'll hear from today's Enlightenment Establishment. What you're learning about in this chapter isn't merely *up to date* but also *a big deal.*

Pretty-pretty *content* won't take you where you want to go, not if your goal is the *process* of experiencing Spiritual Enlightenment.

A New Way of Thinking, Right?

Here on Planet Earth, in the Age of Awakening, up is still up; down is still down. Yet positioning of consciousness is no longer something that you can take for granted, especially if you're seeking Enlightenment.

Lacking discernment about that, spiritual side trips are surprisingly common. Expect to encounter some eye-opening examples in Part II.

Summing up What You've Learned So Far

Congratulations, Smart Spiritual Seeker, you have a lot to celebrate. By now:

1. You know the difference between *content* and *process* for spiritual seeking. (Although most people today don't; including the Enlightenment Establishment.)
2. You own the concept of positioning consciousness at either *Human, Astral, or Divine Vibrational Frequencies.* (Although most people today don't; including the Enlightenment Establishment.)

3. You appreciate that, living now, different people often share a conversation *while positioning their consciousness independently*. (Although most people today don't appreciate this, including the Enlightenment Establishment.)
4. And maybe most important of all, you understand how talking about godly *content* never guarantees the *process* of positioning consciousness beyond a Human Vibrational Frequency. (Even if most people today don't yet understand that difference.)
5. Although, mood-making may always appeal to you in a sentimental, wishey-hopey way… you're no longer living in the Age of Faith. Accept that you can do better than that, while seeking Enlightenment in the Age of Awakening.

Big Implications

Smart Spiritual Seeker, remember our Church-Wenters Mystery? To solve that, it's essential to distinguish *content* from *process*. Hello, religious authorities today often slip into a *process* of positioning their consciousness quite randomly. So too, renowned psychologists, yoga teachers, psychics, and growth seminar leaders.

Likewise it's true of today's upstanding members of the Enlightenment Establishment, who may appear like trustworthy authorities due to the wonderful *content* of their conversations.

But how about trusting them to help you evolve? Would that really be wise, until they know (at a minimum) what you've been learning here? This brings us to a final takeaway from this chapter.

Our Program for Spiritual Enlightenment is distinctive because you'll learn how to make good use of your Consciousness Positioning Superpower. Specific DOs and DON'Ts are a'coming. What you learn will involve both *content* and *process;* this will empower you to honor your free will in life, yet protect you from taking side trips.

Making wise choices that help you to evolve spiritually… isn't that one of the most delightful possibilities here at Earth School? Seems to this Enlightenment Teacher, you deserve that.

CHAPTER 7.

Energy Talk, A Seductive Substitute for Enlightenment

As a chef, I got into this because I love the creative energy and I love the science, but I also love to feed people and make them happy.

Christina Tosi, Chef

What accounts for the appeal of Energy Talk? Perhaps trying to prove how much you know about the spiritual nature of life. Ironically, a person who's really in Enlightenment has absolutely nothing to prove.

Rose Rosetree

When you think about it, isn't this obvious? Experiences of spiritual awakening are, quite simply, enjoyable experiences about energy.

By definition, that feeling of specialness excludes Human Vibrational Frequencies. Instead, the special feeling results from experiences at Astral or Divine Vibrational Frequencies; experiences where we've positioned our consciousness differently; common experiences now, given our new Consciousness Positioning Superpower.

In our last two chapters you learned that, despite feeling special, experiences of spiritual awakening aren't signs of Enlightenment. Congratulations, Smart Spiritual Seeker, on having survived this information, so rare and radically counter-culture, at least in these relatively early years of the Age of Awakening!

To reward you, let's explore something else related to spiritual awakening. In this chapter I'll help you gain clarity about a kind of conversation that happens ridiculously often now; in fact, just today, you've likely encountered many examples.

So Seductive, Today's Energy Talk

Whether you're visiting friends, watching the news, or streaming your favorite entertainment, you're likely hearing a lot of Energy Talk.

Instead of telling you about what happens to them in terms of human reality — WHO, WHAT, WHEN, and WHERE — energy enthusiasts slip into discussing something of far greater interest to them: Energies, that is; energies which are now available for anybody to notice. For instance, here come a few examples straight from my Facebook feed this morning:

1. *My morning contemplation: what is true intimacy? what is true communication? what does caring actually mean (behaviorally)? what IS truth? How do I meet someone with respect when our truths are so different?*
2. *Sunflowers follow the sun. But did you know? When it's cloudy and gray they face each other and share their energy. Imagine if we did this too.*
3. [Written while commenting at a Facebook friend's new cover photo] *It looks like Surrender to the Universe haha.*

> **Honestly, I've been waiting for you to get to the good part. As an Enlightenment Teacher, shouldn't you be talking about energies all the time?**
>
> *Quite the opposite!*

Given how much Energy Talk you're hearing on a regular basis, wouldn't it be smart to understand better what this kind of conversation actually MEANS?

> **That's simple. Using Energy Talk makes us more spiritual, right?**

> *Sure, you might get that idea, especially since talking this way has gone mainstream. Seductive though it seems, however, Energy Talk is psychic, not spiritual. It's astral, not Divine.*

Why make this distinction? It's vital for every Smart Spiritual Seeker. So let's begin to explore further what Energy Talk is... and isn't. Our next step is to add a spicy new idea to your (by-now familiar) concept of energy sensitivity.

New Age Leftovers

Learning about **New Age Leftovers** can prove very helpful for your Enlightenment path.

> Countless spiritual seekers, coming from all walks of life, are still partying as if it's 1980... or the other New Age Years. They're snacking on leftovers — beliefs and techniques that could be pretty stale by now.

Totally understandable, this snacking, given that most people living today don't yet know what you are about to learn: For starters, those years from 1980 until the Shift on Dec. 21, 2012; those New Age Years were transitional, rather than some ultimate destination for wisdom.

Ideas from that time aren't necessarily helpful any longer; and they're particularly unhelpful if you're seeking Spiritual Enlightenment. For starters...

Are You Proud of Being Energy Sensitive?

Between 1980 and the Shift, **Energy Sensitivity** emerged as a trend in pop culture; evidently, it's here to stay. As for how special that sensitivity makes any of us? That's debatable.

Starting in 1980, millions of spiritually-oriented people began to notice that they had energy sensitivity.

However, what didn't they notice? The cause — which was hidden, being unique and historic; a planetary cause rather than personal specialness; that cause was a *super-accelerated thinning of the Psychic Barrier.*

When the Shift occurred, that transition ended; by now the Psychic Barrier is no easier to locate than fragments of a burst balloon.

Of course, it's tricky to acknowledge this change, since the Psychic Barrier wasn't physical. While this existed, we couldn't sense it at any Human Vibrational Frequency. Rather, this was an abstract, causational structure at the Divine Vibrational Frequency.

Smart Spiritual Seeker, regarding the idea of New Age Leftovers, let's take it further; because what you're about to read next is essential for success at our Program for Spiritual Enlightenment.

What Is Energy Talk?

Once people began to gain energy sensitivity, what happened next? Millions of us began to speak fluent **Energy Talk**. Here's a summary of what that means:

1. Instead of talking about what they said and did *in reality...*
2. Folks emphasized *how they felt.* (Describing their own energies or emotions.)
3. Also, when they "told you about what happened" to them that day, *they began to substitute interpretations,* as if this were preferable to mere facts about human reality.
4. Further, many spiritual seekers took growth workshops or fell in love with Bible Study groups, both resources encouraging seekers to explore *"the real reason"* why people said things and did things.
5. Alternatively, many seekers would cook up their own special sauce for Energy Talk. So *uniquely important their energy insights seemed,* as if nobody else could equal their astounding brand of wisdom!

All this was kind of sweet, really. Except, what remains true to this day, regarding both energy sensitivity and Energy Talk?

Energy Talk may or may not involve "brilliant discoveries," but technically here's what is always involved, every single time: Shifting attention away from Human Vibrational Frequencies, then positioning consciousness at an Astral Vibrational Frequency.

Now that you've got the general concept, Smart Spiritual Seeker, let's start applying it.

Details matter here, in order for you to get results. Let's refine your understanding further, especially since we're aiming for real-life results in your day-to day.

Little Choices about Energy Talk Can Add Up

While you're seeking Enlightenment, smart choices can add up to success. Specifically, it can help you to recognize-and-then-avoid Energy Talk; that one change has greatly accelerated spiritual evolution for many of the students I've helped to move into Enlightenment.

But even when you're willing, pure willingness won't be enough. How can you *effectively* stop doing Energy Talk? Recognition skills help. Therefore, I invite you to play along with me, in this chapter and the next.

Together let's explore what, exactly, counts as Energy Talk; also, we'll practice how to substitute **Human-Type Language.** That is, using words that describe what happens in normal, human reality.

Our Framework for the Rest of this Chapter

Let's consider a fictional example, where you hear Ryan talking to his girlfriend Brittany. She asks him, "How was work today?" How does he answer?

Little does Ryan know that his response will illustrate differences between Human-Type Language and an Energy Talk translation of reality. Here comes a sample of each.

> **Human-Type Language from Ryan**
> *There were so many deadlines to meet, I had to eat lunch at my desk.*
>
> *Later that afternoon, my boss added another project to the pile he'd already given me.*
>
> *I had so much work to do: Three different reports, and all of them due by the end of the week.*
>
> **Energy Talk Translation of Reality from Ryan**
> *Work was a nightmare, like I was so overwhelmed.*
>
> *Then my boss, that narcissist — he had the nerve to pile on even more work.*
>
> *Can we smoke some weed now, Brittany? I've got to find a way to stop feeling so overwhelmed. I need to chill.*

Get the Diff?

Smart Spiritual Seeker, before reading further, let's think together for a moment. Lately, how have the people around you been talking?

"Energy Talk" gives you a specific concept for what has likely been going on right under your nose, except maybe you couldn't quite figure out what was causing that sickly sweet stink.

Consider: Haven't many people you know *stopped talking about human reality?* By which I mean, all too often, folks will skip right past telling you about the WHO, WHAT, WHERE, or WHEN. Instead, don't an awful lot of the people you know… mostly talk about the WHY? And that WHY involves their own subjective world of energy.

Especially True of People Today Who Are 30 Or Under

Granted, plenty of older folks are playing the same game, too. How about this? For the next day or so, take your own survey. On social media, as well as in person, after that conversation is over… take a quick moment to evaluate. Who just said what kind of thing?

Chapter 7. Energy Talk, a Seductive Substitute for Enlightenment

Before Energy Talk, it was normal for people to use human-type language:
- They'd have conversations with you about who said what and who did what. Remember?
- Whereas now... Do most of your friends do *Human* Talk?
- Or are they substituting *Energy* Talk, like, all about energies and feelings and beliefs.

For an extra Aha!s, did you ever notice how wonderful it's supposed to be... when friends are "Sharing" or "Reaching Out"?

Ooh, Sharing!

What does it indicate, how "*sharing*" has become a popular synonym for simply *talking* to people? In my view:

1. **Talking** means speaking out loud. Definitely Human Talk.
2. Alternatively, you might communicate via your favorite technology — like today's "**Shooting you an email**" or text.
3. By contrast, to me, **Sharing** implies that the literal words don't matter, being secondary to the speaker's intent to open up their deeper feelings and beliefs, treating others to that "precious gift."
4. While **Reaching Out** takes this one step further: "Hey, I'm not just sharing with you. Let's make a deeper connection."

Heck, Smart Spiritual Seekers, I'm tempted to comment further. What would be the ultimate in reaching out to total strangers and sharing?

Maybe soon we can switch over to telepathy? No longer needing to make those unevolved animal sounds???

Seriously, can you see how all this *reaching out and sharing* might normalize that New Age Leftover called Energy Talk?

In our next chapter you'll learn even more about Energy Talk, notably how this habit has caused many a spiritual seeker to misinterpret what they care about most.

CHAPTER 8.

Can You Recognize Energy Talk?

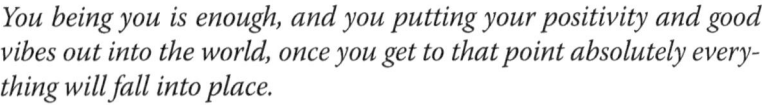

You being you is enough, and you putting your positivity and good vibes out into the world, once you get to that point absolutely everything will fall into place.

Lizzie Velásquez, Motivational Speaker

....

Informative conversation with another person, on any topic under the sun, never just falls into place because you're "being you." Nor is the point of any conversation to send people your vibes. Look, you went to a lot of trouble to learn how to talk. Please, keep on speaking Human-Type Language.

Rose Rosetree

....

By now you know a lot about Energy Talk, Smart Spiritual Seeker. But how well can you recognize it... when Energy Talk "falls into place" as part of a conversation?

Joke! Let's confine our recognition skills to recognizing Energy Talk if you *read* it or *hear* it. Trust me here: Recognizing Energy Talk can be a useful skill, and like developing any other skill in life, practice can help. Besides, I'm building some fun into the lighthearted exercise that follows in this chapter.

Let's explore 10 examples of Human-Type Language, followed by an Energy Talk version. For best results, don't just read these examples silently; read them aloud, maybe using a funny voice. Definitely don't skim over them — or skim-read any other part of this book, for that matter. Save skimming for clickbait articles on the internet, articles that mainly recycle what you already kinda know.

Chapter 8. Can You Recognize Energy Talk? 87

Distinguish HUMAN-Type Language from Energy Talk

In this exercise you'll find 10 questions, each one followed by an "answer" that's pure Energy Talk. Then the fun begins. Altogether, our learning sequence for each of "Discussion Topics" will go like this:

1. Naming a human-type problem, summarized as a question in *Human-Type Language*.
2. One possible answer, quoting a public figure who's using *Energy Talk*.
3. An alternative answer, from Enlightenment Teacher, Rose Rosetree. Yes, I'll be using *Human-Type Language* to discuss a human-type problem.
4. *YOUR answer.* Sure, make one up. Say it loud and proud, Smart Spiritual Seeker. Then write it down.
5. Reread your answer. Could you fine tune this? Eventually I'd like you to give an answer in *Human-Type Language*. What if, looking over your answer, oops! You realize those words are in Energy Talk? Then say a re-do, translating what you've just said into the more humanly relevant type of language.

For extra fun try to guess which public figure will be quoted in each of our 10 examples. If you decide to play, you'll find the correct answers at the end of this chapter. In advance, here's the cast of characters.

Quotes from Which Public Figure?

Smart Spiritual Seeker, you'll be reading words of wisdom from these famous influencers:

1. Billy Graham
2. Colm Wilkinson
3. Doreen Virtue
4. Joel Osteen
5. Joseph Campbell
6. Napoleon Hill
7. Norman Vincent Peale
8. Rainer Maria Rilke
9. Ryan Lochte
10. Sylvia Browne

Now let's get started.

Language Quiz: 10 Ways to Solve Human Problems

When folks talk about everyday problems, they're going to use language of some kind or other. But which kind of language, Human-Type Language or Energy Talk? Let's explore this with 10 examples.

Discussion #1. Q&A about Fights with Mom

A Question in Human-Type Language

Lately I've been having a lot of arguments with my mother. How do I make it stop?

A Public Figure's Advice in Energy Talk

I remember to breathe throughout the day. I remind myself that I can choose peace, no matter what is going on around me.

Whenever I desire, I can retreat to that quiet place within, simply by closing my eyes.

An Answer from Rose in Human-Type Language

Don't expect a quick one-size-fits all solution, but do find a way to problem-solve about those arguments.

Find something that you can do differently, something that makes sense to you; and something that's different from what you've been doing so far in the relationship with your mother.

YOUR Answer, in Human-Type Language

Discussion #2. Q&A about Physical Flab

A Question in Human-Type Language

My body has been getting pretty flabby lately. But I hate to exercise. Isn't there anything else I can do?

A Public Figure's Advice in Energy Talk

I listen to my spirit guide.

An Answer from Rose in Human-Type Language
Schedule time for exercise daily and do it, whether you're in the mood or not.

YOUR Answer, in Human-Type Language

Discussion #3. Q&A for More Money

A Question in Human-Type Language
Money is a problem, as usual. How can I make more money?

A Public Figure's Advice in Energy Talk
Think and grow rich.

An Answer from Rose in Human-Type Language
It may take a combination of practical approaches to meet your financial goals.

Many folks start improving their finances by learning how to budget, and then putting that into practice consistently. Budgeting may not be glamourous but it sure can help.

YOUR Answer, in Human-Type Language

Discussion #4. Q&A about Soul Mates

A Question in Human-Type Language
When am finally I going to find true love?

A Public Figure's Advice in Energy Talk
I believe that everyone has a soul mate, that they can spend the rest of their life together.

An Answer from Rose in Human-Type Language
Seeking more friendships might help you. This can improve your social life and stretch your social skills.

In addition, you'll relieve some of the pressure you may be putting on yourself (and life) to deliver you one official "soul mate" who meets most of your needs in life.

YOUR Answer, in Human-Type Language

Discussion #5. Q&A for Planning a Vacay

A Question in Human-Type Language
I'm planning to take a vacation next year. Any suggestions where to go?

A Public Figure's Advice in Energy Talk
The only journey is the one within.

An Answer from Rose in Human-Type Language
Start by taking a good, realistic look at your budget.

How much do you plan to spend on this vacation? Find options within this price range. Make a list. Then choose your favorite option from this list.

YOUR Answer, in Human-Type Language

Discussion #6. Q&A about Hating My Job

A Question in Human-Type Language
Isn't it terrible how I hate my job?

A Public Figure's Advice in Energy Talk
We must let go of the life we have planned, so as to accept the one that is waiting for us.

An Answer from Rose in Human-Type Language
Keep your job while you look for a better job.

> *Definitely start saving for retirement. Only, might I suggest? Begin by paying off all your credit card debt.*
>
> **YOUR Answer, in Human-Type Language**
>
>
> **Discussion #8. Q&A for Moving Up**
>
> **A Question in Human-Type Language**
> *I wish I lived in a nicer apartment. But what can I do? It's hopeless.*
>
> **A Public Figure's Advice in Energy Talk**
> *Change your thoughts and you change your world.*
>
> **An Answer from Rose in Human-Type Language**
> *Find out how much time you have left on the lease to your current apartment. Make practical plans to move somewhere better, right after your current lease expires.*
>
> **YOUR Answer, in Human-Type Language**
>
>
> **Discussion #9. Q&A for Seeing the Christ in Others**
>
> **A Question in Human-Type Language**
> *For years I've been working really hard to try and see the Christ in everyone. Honestly, I'm not having any results at all. How can I become more spiritual?*
>
> **A Public Figure's Advice in Energy Talk**
> *When you focus on being a blessing, God makes sure that you are always blessed in abundance.*
>
> **An Answer from Rose in Human-Type Language**
> *No single religious or spiritual path is guaranteed to help you forever. If you're not getting good results from trying to see the Christ in others, maybe it's time to find a new path.*

> *Find an approach that works for you now. After you find that new option, stop what you've been doing before, and start your new path. Give it a chance to make a significant difference.*
>
> *To be clear, our Program for Spiritual Enlightenment is not a path, a religion, or a way of life. It's simply a program designed to help you effectively move toward Enlightenment.*
>
> **YOUR Answer, in Human-Type Language**
>
>
> **Discussion #10. Q&A about How Time is Flying**
>
> **A Question in Human-Type Language**
> *Time is passing by and what do I have to show for it? Is there anything I can do to improve my life?*
>
> **A Public Figure's Advice in Energy Talk**
> *For myself, personally, I am never really aware of timing or anything because I am passionate about what I do, so I have found that if you really love what you do, then time flies.*
>
> **An Answer from Rose in Human-Type Language**
> *Find a good goal-setting program and stick with it for six weeks. If you like the results, keep it up. Setting goals effectively can give a direction to time.*
>
> **YOUR Answer, in Human-Type Language**

Now, What's Next?

Smart Spiritual Seeker, thanks for playing this language game with examples about solving human problems. What *won't* come next? For the rest of this book, I won't be giving you any more exercises like the one you just did.

So why did I make an exception for this chapter?

It's important that you can easily recognize Energy Talk. Follow through from now on.

If you're the one who's speaking, resist the temptation to do Energy Talk. Restate what you have to say in Human-Type Language. Now you've had practice at doing just that.

Avoiding Energy Talk is essential for success at our Program for Spiritual Enlightenment; practicing your skills for recognition and translation can pay off for you big-time, long term.

Maybe you're wondering, what's next? In our next chapter I'll be likening *energy sensitivity* and *Energy Talk* to.... *puberty*.

Before you turn the page, on your own, why do you think there might be a connection?

Quote Sources for Quiz Answers

1. Doreen Virtue
2. Sylvia Browne
3. Napoleon Hill
4. Ryan Lochte
5. Rainer Maria Rilke
6. Joseph Campbell
7. Billy Graham
8. Norman Vincent Peale
9. Joel Osteen
10. Colm Wilkinson

CHAPTER 9.

Like Puberty, Except about Energy

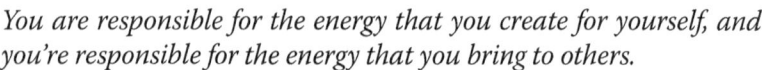

You are responsible for the energy that you create for yourself, and you're responsible for the energy that you bring to others.
Oprah Winfrey, Major Influencer During the New Age Years
....

In practical terms, you're only responsible for what you say and do. Beware frittering away this precious lifetime by trying to make it all about energy. You asked for a human life, and now you've got one.
Rose Rosetree
....

Smart Spiritual Seeker, ack! Surely you remember puberty. Without it you couldn't have an adult sex life now. Like me, though, you might feel very relieved that puberty is over, since those years were hardly a highlight of your life.

Do you recall the violent crushing? How mysterious feelings surged through you? That familiar body of yours was changing, to put it mildly. Like that, all that happened to you during puberty was so strange — weird and yet, somehow, universally human.

Socially, you needed friends desperately, right? Especially you needed them to share stories about your emerging worldview, since so many things were *obviously* sexual. Like, how can other people not talk about sex constantly?

Let's face it, Smart Spiritual Seeker, teenage years mean noticing *sexual everything*. Talking about it like crazy. Giggling about it.

Eventually, though, you did move into adulthood. Since then, ideally, you've been enjoying your sex life just fine. (Enjoying it for the most part, at least.)

By now, *discovering sex* no longer feels "Like, my entire life." For one thing, you're into this Program for Spiritual Enlightenment. For another, you no longer need to talk constantly about sex-and-crushing: **Puberty Talk.**

Overall, aren't you relieved that most of your waking hours are no longer complicated by figuring out some *hidden sexual subtext?* For most of us past puberty, interest in sex becomes better integrated into our lives. Maybe something more like this:

> **There's a time and a place for sex in my life; but that time isn't all-my-waking-hours, and that place isn't everywhere-I-go.**

All that said....

How Is Puberty Talk Like Energy Talk?

Have you made the connection yet, Smart Spiritual Seeker? Back in the day, Puberty Talk wasn't merely normal. It was necessary.

In retrospect, all that sex-on-the-brain was totally necessary, because puberty isn't just about learning *content*; along the way we encounter plenty of *process*, because puberty prepares us for sexual experiences as adults.

After completing those confusing teen years, we've gained a certain clarity: Puberty was something we had to go through, a **Standard Human Transition**, not meant to become a main goal in life.

Smart Spiritual Seeker, understanding this personal history can equip you to understand a comparably baffling experience, one that humanity's been going through collectively ever since the New Age Years. What did you, and your fellow humans, go through pre-Shift? That felt as deeply personal as when your sex organs grew and your armpits began to stink. But this was just a stage.

Pretty much like encountering the hormones of puberty that surge through an adolescent, hello! Ever since 1980, humanity has been adjusting to an exponential thinning of the Psychic Barrier, an adjustment that has clobbered us all, and not only teenagers.

In retrospect this global transition has messed with the minds of nearly all human adults, regardless of age. We spiritual seekers have been in the forefront of noticing, caring, trying our hardest to figure out "What the Bleep Do We Know!?"

Just standard human transitions! Despite feeling awkward at the time, ultimately these can enrich our lives. Annoying though our teenage years may have been sometimes (or for some of us, constantly), looking back, wasn't it all worthwhile?

A mature sexuality can enrich life immeasurably. Actually, having successfully undergone puberty might also be required as a prerequisite for attaining Enlightenment.

Let me assure you, our Program for Spiritual Enlightenment won't demand that you spend five hours a day naked, grunting away at Tantra Yoga. By all means, keep your clothes on. And what else might you find reassuring?

Standard Human Transitions Aren't Spiritually Significant

Holding onto standard transitional experiences shouldn't be considered a legitimate "path" for seeking Enlightenment.

- Defining "love" exactly as you did when 16 years old isn't really "The Ultimate."
- Likewise, energy sensitivity and Energy Talk felt really special at first, but this was just a stage.
- Unless we're encouraged to remain stuck in the past, we can move on from all that energy jazz. It will stop feeling like such a big deal, which is good.

From a historical perspective, noticing energy in everyday life is merely transitional. How so?

Smart Spiritual Seeker, **Transitional** means preparing for something new. For instance, teenage crushing is an unsettling-yet-thrilling prelude to what love can mean for mature adults.

Likewise, humanity's Energy Talk has held great appeal for millions caught up in transition during the Oprah Years, those New Age

Years. Glad to say, the rest of this chapter aims to liberate you from this transitional stage. And since you're a seeker of spiritual truth, what you're about to read... just might rock your world.

More than most seekers today, you already know a lot regarding your new Consciousness Positioning Superpower. Now let's explore what, exactly, this new superpower has to do with energy sensitivity and Energy Talk.

Technically, those New Age Years of transition are over, right? Technically, as of December 21, 2012, the Psychic Barrier disappeared, allowing humanity to begin the adventure of living in this new era, the Age of Awakening.

Obviously, we have transitioned into something, but what?

....

Now is a superb time to pursue Spiritual Enlightenment. Compared with seeking Enlightenment in the Age of Faith, you're far more likely to succeed.

....

For that you can thank your new Consciousness Positioning Superpower. Although subtle, it's just as real as pubic hair.

Please forgive my gross comparison. But it did grab your attention, right? Even more important, that comparison may have reminded you to think about this collective transition specifically and *humanly*... unlike many trendy conversations now about "Vibrations rising" and "Preparing for Ascension." (Neither of which theories is true, incidentally.)

More about What Changed for Keeps

After the Psychic Barrier disappeared, all humans — yes, including you — all of us began to experience a *process*.

This intermittent process allows us to travel in consciousness, spontaneously traveling away from Human Vibrational Frequencies; traveling in consciousness in a way that most often positions consciousness at an Astral Vibrational Frequency.

Long-shot unlikely, though possible, occasionally you might be positioning your consciousness at the Divine Vibrational Frequency, so I'll mention that for the sake of completeness. Yet almost always, what happens to people is simply **Astral Travel**.

Of course, I'm not using that term in the Age of Faith way, what pioneering consciousness teacher Robert Monroe dubbed "out-of-body experience."

> By contrast, what often happens randomly to you and me in this Age of Awakening? Only our consciousness does the traveling; there's no swapping out physical bodies for an astral physique.

What you'll be learning in Part II (coming up soon) is far less dramatic than looking down from the ceiling as you think, "How interesting. That's my physical body down there, and it's laying in bed."

Commonly, given that we're living post-Shift, we position only our consciousness in an astral direction. Furthermore, that consciousness travel is so subtle, we don't see ourselves doing a thing.

Since today's new version of astral travel can last just a split second, and that process involves consciousness only, of course it seems as if nobody has gone anywhere.

At least, it seems that way until you learn advanced skills of energetic literacy, such as doing Consciousness Positioning Consults®, in which case you can pinpoint the vibrational frequency where the person's consciousness is positioned at any particular moment.

Otherwise, lacking that kind of skill? Few people know that today's astral travel (in consciousness) happens to them; let alone that it likely happens many times each day.

Ironically, Smart Spiritual Seeker, this likely happens to every single person you hear using Energy Talk.

Most likely, this subtle form of astral travel happens to plenty of other folks, too, even if they don't happen to do a lot of Energy Talk.

Get the picture? What makes it possible for us to do this everyday version of astral travel? It's nothing less than our new Consciousness Positioning Superpower.

Such a Mysterious Superpower!

Everyday astral travel is more than mysterious and new. It's tremendously significant, especially if you're seeking Enlightenment in the Age of Awakening. Seems to me, this merits a dedicated term of art. So let's start referring to what you're now learning about as **Invisible Astral Travel.**

Why invisible? Because it's unlikely that a psychic or clairvoyant would see you stepping out of your physical body and taking one or more light bodies for a ride.

And why doesn't invisible astral travel show to most clairvoyants? Because it's personal, not energetic: People are simply positioning their consciousness.

If a psychic can't see it, should this invisible version still count as astral travel in consciousness?

Sure can. And does. Since you're seeking Enlightenment in this Age of Awakening.

Here's an idea to bring home this latest big concept. In a previous chapter, you've already done a couple of thought experiments.

Now let's explore a new one, designed to illustrate the human difference between what matters to Age of Awakening people like you and me, contrasting with what counted as significant back in the Age of Faith.

Quite a Personal Thought Experiment. Be Brave.

Smart Spiritual Seeker, please think back to the oldest family member or neighbor you've known well, maybe a grandparent or even a great-great-grand. For easy reference, I'll use a placeholder name, Shirley.

Now, imagine that you've just suffered a big romantic breakup, so you decide to tell Shirley your tale of woe. Of course, you're expecting that nice Shirley to sympathetically understand your feelings.

It might be especially comforting if Shirley could tell you how she was feeling your energy, so that she could appreciate how terribly you had been wronged.

Disappointingly, though, Shirley takes an old-school approach. Smart Spiritual Seeker, what I'm about to describe will be familiar to you if you've ever tried to talk inner experience with an old-timer... somebody born and raised in that previous era, 100 years or more before the Shift.

Suppose that you're describing your feelings, ever hopeful that Shirley will sympathize. Only she doesn't seem to get what you're talking about. So you go into more and more detail, longing for her to validate how you've been wronged and how awful it feels.

What if, eventually, you asked Shirley in so many words, "When are you going to validate my experience?"

This sweet old-timer might tell you something like this: "What's with this 'validate'? Back in my day, nobody had time for that nonsense."

Probably, though, you don't think of asking a direct question like that. Probably this particular *generational* difference — really an *earlier era* difference — never occurs to you.

All you're thinking is, "Shirley is nice. And she's wise. Once she understands what I'm trying to tell her, I know she'll be able to comfort me."

Only what happens when Shirley finally does speak up? Uncomprehendingly, she looks at you coldly, as though alarmed at how you're making a big fuss over nothing.

"You keep complaining that your feelings are hurt. Show me the bruises," says Shirley.

What Counted as Valid Then, Versus Now?

You see, Smart Spiritual Seeker, living now, when your feelings are hurt, you don't have to show physical bruises.

Why would that be necessary when you're in serious emotional pain? Seems like your energies are all "drained"? Most of your friends would have no trouble whatsoever with getting how you're in pain, inner pain, real pain.

In a nutshell, that's the diff between now and then. Greater consciousness freedom during the New Age Years, even more so after the Shift — this has altered how people understand what matters in life.

Folks like Shirley, born at least 100 years before the Shift, may love you tremendously; yet it's unlikely that they'll sympathize in the way that you might expect.

Living as Shirley has, born before 1912, who had time for pop psychology? It hadn't been invented yet. Faith was the likely answer to relationship woes, faith plus "Get back to work."

Maybe Shirley would sing, "Home Sweet Home" or "Gimme That Old Time Religion."

Hardly What You're Used to These Days, Is It?

Pre-Shift, how much energy sensitivity used to be available? Quite an easy statistic that would be to calculate: For almost all human beings from the Age of Faith, the answer would be *zilch*.

Back when the Psychic Barrier was firmly in place, everyday experience was *locked* into Human Vibrational Frequencies. Whatever happened in objective reality, that was what mattered; as for inner experience, that seldom mattered nearly as much.

Fast-forward to now, with our altogether new Consciousness Positioning Superpower. Seems to me, it's high time we updated our understanding of many things, including what we've been discussing in this chapter.

Nearly everyone now does a ton of invisible astral travel, unlike before the Shift, when precious few people could do astral travel of any kind during their waking hours.

Only visionary outliers, like Robert Monroe or certain yogis from the East, had the capacity to do the more literal version, astral travel complete with out-of-body experience; *astral flashier* travel, to use a term you now recognize; also astral travel that's far clunkier than today's easy-peasy, super-speedy, invisible astral travel.

Living now, Smart Spiritual Seeker, we're fully capable of positioning consciousness in a way that brings us the very different, and natural, experience of today's new invisible astral travel.

And man oh man, will you be reading many examples of this, once we complete our Part I! Before then, let's be sure to touch on this last thing…

One Additional Consciousness Fact of Life

Concerning today's invisible astral travel….

What else makes this so impossible to pin down, consciously? It's the sheer effortlessness.

Smart Spiritual Seeker, it's vital for you to appreciate how radically effortless it is, using this new Consciousness Positioning Superpower; a capacity of yours that demands zero pushing, no straining in any way whatsoever; never requiring that you concentrate or squint or make the least bit of effort.

Just how effortless is this new freedom to position our consciousness? Totally! None of the trips you make in consciousness is harder than routinely blinking your eyes.

Keep in mind, though, how that very effortlessness can lead to problems. Although we won't consciously know what we're doing, we might use that super-easy superpower hundreds of times every day, which is way too much for those of us who are seeking Enlightenment.

Of course, one of my goals is to help you to habitually use your superpower *on purpose* and *productively*, and mostly not use it at all. As our chapers unfold you'll come to appreciate how this change is essential for seeking Enlightenment in the Age of Awakening.

Right now we're still laying the groundwork for understanding, so I can teach you properly in Part III. But in case you're the slightest bit worried at this point, please hear this:

Once you learn what to do — and yes, as you keep learning about our Program for Spiritual Enlightenment, I'll explain all the simple DOs and DON'Ts — the more you learn, the gladder you'll be... that wisely positioning your consciousness will take no effort whatsoever.

Seriously! No more effort than you had to make this morning, just so that you could go through your day smelling like a grownup.

And it gets better. Know that you can trust this amazing new superpower of yours. Bringing back the analogy about adjusting to puberty, by now you may have begun to relax about both types of standard human transition. Honestly do you feel weird every morning because you no longer smell like a sweet-and-innocent first grader?

Likewise, what if you've been caught up in humanity's energy sensitivity transition, and maybe you've been using a lot of Energy Talk?

At first you may feel a bit nostalgic, but soon enough you'll leave that behind. Meanwhile, soul-thrilling knowledge awaits you, since you'll learn how to mobilize that superpower far more productively than any Energy Talk conversations you've ever had.

Congratulations, Smart Spiritual Seeker!

Congratulations because you're now completing Part I of our Program for Spiritual Enlightenment, having learned a great many concepts worthy of a **Thought Leader** like you, one of the first to recognize useful truths that are new for humanity.

In terms of consciousness, Robert Monroe was a thought leader. He published *Journeys Out of the Body* in 1972, publishing it eight years before the New Age Years and 40 years before the Shift.

Smart Spiritual Seeker, I wouldn't say you've done the *hardest* part of our program, since none of it requires effort. Yet Part I may well have tested your patience.

Some of my students are so eager to gain Enlightenment, they'd rather race ahead to learn what to do, not really caring if they understand a thing, so long as they can feel something exciting.

If you think about that, how much sense would that make? Thanks for not taking a *just-do-it* approach, which might have worked fine in the Age of Faith, back when understanding was optional and obedience was the gold standard for religion and spirituality.

Humanity's gold standard has changed; now it's the Age of Awakening, no longer an Age of Obeying. Thinking will prove indispensable for you, helping you to make the easy choices built into this Program for Spiritual Enlightenment.

Smart Spiritual Seeker, yes, you're graduating from Part I. What will be your graduation gift?

You're going to build on what you've learned so far. Progressing through Parts II and III, expect your chosen spiritual path to become more meaningful than ever before, more *humanly real* to you.

Say goodbye, if you like, to "Me so small. Life so big."

PART II

What the Enlightenment Establishment... Overlooked

So much about spiritual seeking has changed since the Age of Awakening began. Yet you sure wouldn't know that from following today's big-and-profitable Enlightenment Establishment. In this group I include:

- The Growth Seminar Establishment
- All of America's famed televangelists
- And every personal development influencer on YouTube

How could so many spiritual experts have overlooked something so important? Who knows for sure?

For many, one reason might be how these teachers have *personally* been going through the same "standard human transition" as you, being no different from other mortals, and they're stuck in believing that Energy Talk is The Way.

Back in Part I you learned about that. Also you read that noticing energy might be called spiritual awakening, but hey... Now that we're in Part II, I'll put this Energy Talk idea more bluntly: Playing around with energies won't help a single sweet soul to move into Enlightenment.

Now, Smart Spiritual Seeker, let's take your practical education further. This time, instead of exploring the topic of puberty, let's do something even bolder. Let's talk pregnancy.

What to Expect When You're Expecting

Have you ever had a baby? If not, don't you have at least one friend who's gone through pregnancy? Either way, then, you've probably known women who read books like this one, *What to Expect When You're Expecting*.

Bestselling authors Heidi Murkoff and Sharon Mazel have written a fabulously useful book to help expectant mothers. Incidentally, this modern classic was published during the New Age Years, back in 1984, beautifully combining practicalities with valued qualities of sensitivity and caring.

Of course, if pregnant, you're wise to read a book like *What to Expect*. Back when I was pregnant, I gobbled up that book as if it were chocolate ice cream. Some days, I enjoyed both the book and the ice cream. All those practical recommendations and reassurances — yum!

- However, after my son was born, did I keep on consulting that book?
- How about all the pregnant women *you've* known?
- After they became mothers, was it a page-turner for them, re-reading *What to Expect When You're Expecting*?

Or, as new mothers, did these women have more urgent things to do? As you may know, new mothers often feel overwhelmed by caring for a glorious, fresh-from-God, tiny person; somebody often found screaming or pooping or both; a frighteningly vulnerable animal in their care; namely, a baby!

By definition, pregnancy is a time of transition. Once pregnancy ends, that transitional time is over, right? Having already given birth, a new mother had better start taking care of her baby, not keep on reliving those glory days of morning sickness.

Enough said. Rather than our thinking further about pregnancy, either, let's shift over to the point of this chapter's new analogy, which compares pregnancy to the transitional New Age Years: pregnancy, not puberty. (If anything, pregnancy is even more freaky weird.)

Instead of a Baby, We've All Got a Brand-New Era on Earth

Psychic Barrier gone, transition over, all of us are living in this new Age of Awakening. Sadly, how much accurate knowledge do most people have yet, regarding how to live successfully now?

You know, zilch. Instead, folks are doing the equivalent of favorite pregnancy techniques, enthusiastically snacking on New Age Leftovers; in many cases, beautiful spiritual seekers are gaining few results beyond the placebo effect; yet they don't know what else to do, except to work harder than ever at the usual; many beautiful spiritual seekers are exhausting themselves by working heroically hard at their favorite-but-obsolete practices.

Historians of the future may scratch their heads in frustration, struggling to comprehend humanity's near-total ignorance about the Shift, even a decade after it happened. Won't they wonder why it took us so long to get a clue?

Those historians may be fascinated by the great improvement that we humans eventually achieved, once we finally reached a tipping point of knowledge; and then finally millions of people began to purposely use humanity's new Consciousness Positioning Superpower; using it purposely and wisely.

Maybe historians will say this: *In the early years of the Age of Awakening, many ordinary people became thought leaders. After moving into Enlightenment, they began to use their full potential in life. So unexpected, so brave!*

Accelerated emotional growth and spiritual awakening can became quite effortless, once we're doing this Program for Spiritual Enlightenment; of that I'm sure, having seen rapid evolution in so many of my students.

Remarkably, Smart Spiritual Seeker (and perhaps for the first time in human history) effective pursuit of Enlightenment need not become a full-time job.

Quite possibly, in just one generation, millions of Smart Spiritual Seekers will become... Enlightenment Finders.

CHAPTER 10

Humanity's Superhero Story

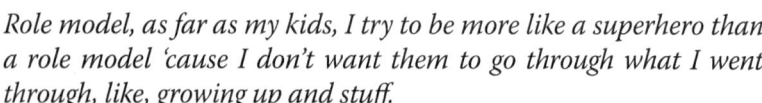

Role model, as far as my kids, I try to be more like a superhero than a role model 'cause I don't want them to go through what I went through, like, growing up and stuff.

21 Savage, Rapper

....

In real life, gaining today's Consciousness Positioning Superpower does not allow us to opt out of human living. Our superpower can help us greatly, but only if we develop a delightful default, positioning our consciousness at Human Vibrational Frequencies.

-Rose Rosetree

....

Smart Spiritual Seeker, let's talk superhero movies. Ever since "Spider-Man" appeared in 1962, superhero movies have taught the public about ordinary people who became superheroes.

For instance, as a teenager, fictional Peter Parker lived like an awkward every-boy. After an accident gave him superpowers, some confused experimentation followed.

Surprisingly or not, being given a superpower doesn't mean the same thing as knowing how to use it.

Eventually, Spiderman did master his new set of superpowers, so he could proceed to save the world — or, at least, become a powerful force for good.

In a way, you're like teenage Peter Parker, discovering *how* and *when* and *when not* to cling to walls.

All of us humans alive at this time are in the process of learning something comparable, only what's involved is not our physical bodies but how we use our consciousness.

Growing up, Smart Spiritual Seeker, sometimes you may have felt like an awkward every-person yourself. Even so, if you lived during the New Age Years, you joined millions in going through a historically unique, collective awakening to energy sensitivity.

So extremely awkward, then puberty-like, then pregnancy-like, for many of us! Whatever happened to you during the New Age Years, did it prepare you to master the full superpower that you'd receive after the Shift? Hardly!

No Wonder, New Age Fads Still Might Appeal to You

Just between you and me, what (if any) was your experience during the New Age Years? When the stirrings of energy sensitivity grew within you, did this feel like discovering your own personal talent or even a spiritual calling?

- Perhaps that new sensitivity inspired you to meditate or learn healing; alternatively, you might have become more deeply involved in religion, joining an active Bible Study group; perhaps you began to experiment, getting together with fellow worshipers as you earnestly attempted to See the Christ in everyone.
- Alternatively, a newfound fascination with energy might have caused you to listen to channeled teachings, or pursue Law of Attraction; maybe you booked a standing appointment for psychic readings, or you'd make a "sacred" ritual of daily communing with your spirit guides.
- Equally possible, following Oprah Winfrey's lead, you credentialled yourself as your own therapist, routinely asking, "How does that make me feel?"

Smart Spiritual Seeker, you might have pursued approaches like all of these and more, practices that might not have been *called* "New Age" at the time, yet they were popularized *during* the New Age Years; fascinating explorations with an added allure — that special feeling aroused by exponential thinning of the Psychic Barrier.

Back then, millions of us found inspiration by following a new spiritual or psychological path, or through joining a new church. No way did we think of that analogy I presented to you at the opening of this Part II. Honestly, who thought this?

"*Gaaa, it's as if we're all pregnant.*"

The Shift Is a Huge Consciousness Event to Understand

Many a spiritual seeker isn't particularly curious about the significance of the Shift, being more like a follower than a leader.

By contrast, thought leaders like you aren't intimidated by exploring something that big, so great is your desire to gain authentic self-actualization.

Eventually others may follow your lead; meanwhile, please don't wait for them. Since you're seeking Enlightenment now, I'm here to step up as someone who can help you to see what's happening now, during these early years of the Age of Awakening,

Granted, I'm not claiming that nobody can move into Enlightenment by continuing to snack on New Age Leftovers, or by dutifully following traditional practices from deeper into the Age of Faith.

However, my research does suggest that all of us *are* living post-Shift — know it or not, like it or not. For this reason it's unlikely that followers of Age of Faith teachings will receive the results they've been promised.

In this Part II, our priority is to develop more understanding about what does work, really works now. What can help you to succeed at attaining Spiritual Enlightenment?

My spiritual teacher often tells me, what is closest to the truth lasts longest. Why stop trusting in the traditional teachings?

Because the rules have changed, that's why. Now is a different era, a subtly different era in human history. Seeking Enlightenment now demands up-to-date knowledge.

Even the wisest Age of Faith teachers couldn't prepare us to evolve spiritually in the Age of Awakening. A momentous change to human consciousness on Earth — nothing less — has begun.

In case you're wondering, this change has nothing to do with vibrations rising or some cosmic kind of ascension. What matters is this: How you and other spiritual seekers have been given a paradigm-shifting change, subtly altering how your consciousness works.

Nothing Less

Compared to consciousness limitations during the Age of Faith, you've received something quietly amazing. Since the Shift you and I, and all the people you know, we've all begun to do something breathtakingly new; although — for even the wisest among us — what we gained wasn't the least bit obvious.

Wouldn't the Shift have been easier for us all if, Peter Parker-style, we had simply discovered that we could cling to walls: physically positioning ourselves, that is, on physical walls? Only that would be crude by comparison.

Hence, the *abstract*-seeming name for what you've received: Neither Spidey-Sense nor Superhuman Strength nor That Wall-Clingy Weird Thing. What you got was this oddly intangible ability called a "Consciousness Positioning Superpower."

Yet, for seeking Enlightenment in the Age of Awakening, nothing could serve you better, provided that you learn some indispensable skills.

Unless You Use that Superpower Wisely, You'll Struggle

You and every other human alive: All of us are facing such a superpower-struggle! Frankly, it's astounding, how much we can miss — and mess up — while learning to purposely use our new capacity.

For instance, most of us have no clue how much invisible astral travel we're doing each day, randomly positioning consciousness away from Human Vibrational Frequencies. Rest assured, this

Program for Spiritual Enlightenment will include how to avoid those potentially confusing side trips. But before you learn the specific DOs and DON'Ts in this program, it's vitally important that we consider the WHEREs.

Yes, the WHEREs

You see, Smart Spiritual Seeker, an up-to-date education is beginning for you, leading to knowledge of different WHEREs for positioning your consciousness. Very likely, you've already experienced different vibrational frequencies as an abstract *process*; now it's time to humanly understand the related *content*.

> *Three types of vibrational frequency; yeah, yeah — you told us about that already. When will we get to the good part?*
>
> *True, Human, Astral, and Divine Vibrational Frequencies were sketched out for you in Part I. Now, Part II will teach you more about them, far more. Systematic teaching is what you're receiving here, necessary knowledge for seeking Enlightenment. For that reason, we can't afford to "save time" by skimming over those WHEREs.*

Given how important this knowledge can be for you, and how subtle it is, who can best help you to gain this intellectual understanding? These WHEREs being so abstract, who can describe them in a humanly-relatable way, so that consciousness positioning becomes *relevant* to your everyday life?

Absolutely, let's give credit to today's brilliant neuroscientists and psychologists; however, let's also be clear that, despite all their credentials, they lack good skills of energetic literacy.

How long will it take before experts like these develop the skills needed to give you a straight answer, a practical answer, about where you might be positioning your consciousness today? Or how that might feel! Look, you might have to wait hundreds of years before scientifically trained experts can tell you all this.

Fortunately, off the academic grid (as it were), I've been developing precision skills to help you to understand these WHEREs, developing these skills for decades; for that reason, our Part II can provide exactly the relevant kind of education. Together with me, you'll be exploring this knowledge in chapters that follow, chapters essential for your success at our Program for Spiritual Enlightenment.

Utterly fascinating knowledge, and useful: Together we're about to explore different ways to position consciousness; a knowledge unlike anything you're used to hearing from scientists and also wholly unlike whatever you might be told by professional intuitives, with their indiscriminate preference for energy *anything*. Learn from an Enlightenment Teacher who isn't a psychic any more than she's a neuroscientist.

Incidentally, what if you're curious to learn more about my standing to conduct this leading-edge, post-Shift, research into consciousness? Search around at my blog, *Deeper Perception Made Practical*. You'll find plenty to satisfy you. Meanwhile…

Here's to Our Learning Adventure!

Becoming a thought leader in the Age of Awakening? That's not necessarily easy. However, I think you're wise in your insistent desire to understand, "What the Bleep is happening with my consciousness?"

Really, how many folks do you know who *care to explore the truth* about what their consciousness is actually doing now, in contrast to all the traditional supposed-to's? Take your own survey of those supposed-to's, along the lines of "Seeking Enlightenment, if you meditate long enough, you'll be filled with perpetual bliss."

In reality, when you're seeking Enlightenment in the Age of Awakening, what would make things a whole lot easier for you? If only members of the Enlightenment Establishment would update their knowledge, and also develop essential skills of energetic literacy. (Since they can.)

With that update, spiritual teachers could easily discern which students are evolving beautifully, versus the many taking a spiritual side trip. Members of today's Enlightenment Establishment, otherwise so learned, can't read so much as a single chakra databank. Sadly, this personal choice will limit more than their personal knowledge; indirectly, energetic illiteracy lets down their trusting students.

Smart Spiritual Seeker, Take Your Own Survey

Among all the spiritual teachers and influencers in your life, which of them knows about your new Consciousness Positioning Superpower? In your survey, sure, include intuitives and psychics, neuroscientists and psychologists, yoga teachers and Tai Chi masters, meditation experts, nonduality teachers, vloggers, and more.

Also do you remember how, in the background, we're still solving the Church-Wenters Mystery? Definitely expand your survey to include popular pastors, plus all these other good people: faithful churchgoers, wise church-wenters; also the interesting individuals who wear crosses as a political statement that's religious-but-not-spiritual.

> **Today's invisible astral travel is done while you're still in your human body. Realistically speaking, neither you nor others will seem to have changed, since physical *content* about folks in the room remains identical. Only the *process* of living-and-learning will change.**

Such a thrilling prospect for us thought leaders, getting to explore this everyday kind of consciousness adventure! The combo of your persistence and passion; your willingness to develop discernment; and your strength to grow as a thought leader — all this can help you.

Every human on earth with normal mental functioning can aspire to spiritual awakening and more… with your Consciousness Positioning Superpower at the ready to help.

But make no mistake, that superpower alone won't bring you to Spiritual Enlightenment. Let me show you what can.

CHAPTER 11

Defy the Allure of the Astral

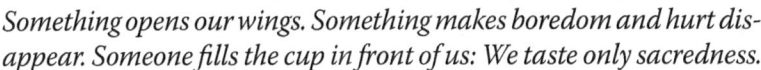

Something opens our wings. Something makes boredom and hurt disappear. Someone fills the cup in front of us: We taste only sacredness.

Rumi, Sufi Mystic in the 13th Century

....

Living in the 13th century, Rumi could write so innocently. He had no need to question the source of his treasured experiences. But living now? We'd better learn how to distinguish astral from Divine.

Rose Rosetree

....

Today's Smart Spiritual Seeker must defy the allure of the astral. In this chapter you'll learn three essential concepts, all directly related to what may be happening to you on a daily basis.

Even if you've spent years studying spiritual teachings, religious teachings, psychological development, and/or psychic development, guess what? Despite seeking God or your Higher Self, very likely you're often positioning your consciousness at an Astral Vibrational Frequency.

Maybe all three concepts in this chapter will be news to you. For sure, gaining clarity about them all… can help you to defy the allure of the astral, *essential knowledge for seeking Enlightenment in the Age of Awakening.*

First, "Normal Human" Can Be an Illusion

When you position consciousness at an Astral Vibrational Frequency, will your experience seem different from normal? That is, **Normal** like *normal for a human being.* The answer is no, not usually, not now that we're living in the Age of Awakening.

Typically, when you're experience life at an *Astral* Vibrational Frequency... it will feel like life at a *Human* Vibrational Frequency... only somewhat improved.

This holds true especially if your consciousness *naturally* shifts into experience at a LOW Astral Vibrational Frequency. "Naturally" means, no beer required, nor any other recreational substance.

Picture this situation. You haven't indulged in any kind of booze, yet somehow you're feeling slightly more special; as if you're really onto something; like you're having a really good day, or somehow you've become extra-friendly; a rosy glow may even be in the background of your experience, as if you've become wiser than usual.

Caution though: Astral Vibrational Frequencies aren't your native consciousness habitat. Keep in mind, you're a human, not a discarnate spirit. Unfortunately, some of my first-time clients are spending seven hours or more, every day, with their consciousness positioned at astral energy.

Smart Spiritual Seeker, have you put this together yet? When people folks enjoy the *content* of Energy Talk, usually the *process* involves positioning consciousness in the astral.

Although this Process Feels Normally Human, Oops!

Whenever we position consciousness at an Astral Vibrational Frequency, here's one difference. To our perception, human-type *objective reality* doesn't exist. Instead, we notice only energies, astral energies; these seem "real" but aren't.

Granted, Energy Talk feels totally normal to many people you know, for instance, your friend Marie. And why does this version of life feel so normal to her?

1. Because her consciousness is often positioned at an Astral Vibrational Frequency.
2. Yet it feels like a Human Vibrational Frequency... only slightly improved.

3. Another factor: Marie's Consciousness Positioning Superpower makes this invisible kind of astral travel ridiculously easy to do, totally effortless.

But easy or not... Intentional or not... For Marie and also for you... This kind of hobby...

This Hobby Would MISUSE Our New Superpower

Randomly positioning your consciousness at an Astral Vibrational Frequency? It won't help you one bit, not if you're aiming for Spiritual Enlightenment. Fortunately, our program will help you to cut way down on these counterproductive happenings; and achieve this spontaneously, without forcing.

Meanwhile, our goal in this chapter is simply to understand how astral positioning of consciousness *can seem totally normal.* Good to know!

Essential Astral Concept #1.

The lower an Astral Vibrational Frequency, the more normal it feels. LOW astral frequencies feel especially familiar.

Mysterious, don't you think? Yet true.

Of course, astral side trips can have great allure for additional reasons. Let's stare this next concept right in its sneaky little face. (If it actually had a face, which technically it doesn't, being just a concept.)

Second, Pseudo-Sacredness

Take a deep breath, Smart Spiritual Seeker, and get ready to flex some discernment muscle. We're about to smash a way-popular illusion in mainstream culture. So far you've been learning that Astral Vibrational Frequencies feel normal and human, but now let's refine that idea.

Both LOW and MEDIUM Astral Vibrational Frequencies feel quite normal.

However, that's not the case for HIGH Astral Vibrational Frequencies; usually these do feel somewhat different from normal. Commonly, folks refer to HIGH astral experiences as being "spiritual." Specifically:

- Maybe they'll call it being inspired by "Spirit."
- Or they'll say, "I'm plugged into The Universe!"
- Other times, folks will share inspiring messages from astral spirits, calling those discarnate beings "angels" or "God's messengers."

Pseudo-Sacredness Need Not Impress You

Hey, Smart Spiritual Seeker, our second Essential Astral Concept warns you about pseudo-sacredness.

Essential Astral Concept #2

Astral Vibrational Frequencies are totally different from The Divine Vibrational Frequency. So don't confuse them simply because both feel "special."

To be clear, astral entities aren't God. Nor do they qualify as "God's messengers" — no more than humanly incarnated folks, like you or I, have earned the right to call ourselves "God's messengers."

Omnipotent, omniscient, omnipresent God does not really require messengers.

To spell out the particulars, soon I'll introduce you to Earth School's Non-Human Cast of Characters. Before then, let's turn to our final Essential Astral Concept. Like the preceding two, this one is important to understand; it will help you to succeed at our Program for Spiritual Enlightenment.

Don't Assume that Astral Beings Represent God.

Make no mistake, Smart Spiritual Seeker. No discarnate astral being deserves to be called "God's messenger." Nor "a sacred angel." Etc.

First of all, *astral* beings are definitely not *human* beings. Granted, due to their astral nature, discarnate spirits may seem impressively exotic, quite tantalizing to those who feel homesick for Heaven.

However, no *astral* being is necessarily as spiritually evolved as *human* you. Sure, they're unencumbered by low-slow Human Vibrational Frequencies. Beyond that? Don't assume that having a discarnate body... makes these beings wiser than you, or purer of heart.

Quite a mistake that would be! No doubt, you'll learn more on this theme as you keep reading Parts II and III. For now, it's enough to understand this next point.

Essential Astral Concept #3

Astral beings may seem mysterious and powerful, even "very evolved." Yet that's debatable. For sure, astral sure doesn't mean Divine.

Now for a Quiz: Astral or Divine?

This quiz can take your understanding further. All three concepts you've learned in this chapter will make more sense after you've taken this next quiz, having gained new clarity about which kinds of beings have which kinds of bodies. Smart Spiritual Seeker, please take the following quiz.

Quiz about Beings Who Aren't Human

Keep reading and you'll find seven different categories of beings who are not human (like you). And I'm not just talking theory here. On any given day, you might encounter several types of **Non-Human**

Beings, thanks to your Consciousness Positioning Superpower. Smart Spiritual Seeker, why not know who's who?

Every *human* alive exists at a Human Vibrational Frequency. While every other kind of being, every single *non-human being*, exists and thinks and speaks at a particular vibrational frequency, and it ain't human.

For example, every *non-human being* has a body. Calling that an "energy body" won't be precise enough to help you much. I'm going to give you a list of seven different types of non-human being. Beyond not being human, this kind of being is either astral or Divine.

> Please answer one question at a time. QUIZ ANSWERS will follow. Now, let your Quiz Begin.

Quiz QUESTIONS: Astral or Divine?

Smart Spiritual Seeker, I'm going to list seven different types of being who are not human. Your job will be to decide which kind of being is which: Astral being or Divine Being?

Don't rush through this quiz. Also, for best results, say your answers out loud.

#1. God

Examples being: Almighty Father-Mother God, The Holy Spirit, The Intelligence that Rules the Universe.

Do you have a favorite in this category?

Astral or Divine?

#2. Ascended Masters, Gods and Goddesses

Examples being: Jesus, Buddha, Kwan Yin, St. Germain.

Do you have a favorite in this category?

Astral or Divine?

#3. Archangels

Examples being: Archangel Michael, Archangel Gabriel.
 Do you have a favorite in this category?
 Astral or Divine?

#4. Seraphim, Cherubim, Thrones

Examples being certain old hymns and classical arias, like "Let the Bright Seraphim." (Hear that aria performed via YouTube.com and it could inspire you for hours.)
 Do you have a favorite in this category?
 Astral or Divine?

#5. Stuck Spirits

Most commonly they're known as "ghosts." For example, you might remember the Ghost of Christmas Past in *A Christmas Carol* by Charles Dickens.
 Do you have a favorite in this category?
 Astral or Divine?

#6. Extra Terrestrial Entities (ETs)

Maybe you've seen a classic movie about them: "E.T. the Extra-Terrestrial," the blockbuster movie which was released during the New Age Years.

Of course, in that fictional story the ET character was played by a puppet; technically that puppet existed at a Human Vibrational Frequency, which is definitely not true about real ETs.

 Do you have a favorite in this category?
 Astral or Divine?

#7. Astral Entities

Many astral entities became famous during the New Age Years, such as Abraham (channeled by Esther-Hicks).

> Do you have a favorite in this category? Astral or Divine?
>
> **Quiz QUESTIONS Complete!**
> ....

Quiz ANSWERS: Beings Who Aren't Human

You deserve some answers, Smart Spiritual Seeker, since I'd like to help you to graduate from sweetsie-weetsie, mushy thinking that's all too common today regarding non-human beings. Answers here can help you to make wise choices.

#1. God: DIVINE

What could be more Divine? Nothing, nobody.

Technically, terms like *God, The Holy Spirit,* and *The Love that Rules the Universe* — they're names for the **Impersonal Aspect of God,** "impersonal" since God has no identifiable body.

Despite being impersonal in that sense, what do folks in Spiritual Enlightenment discover about God? That answer is personal. Isn't it understandable that individuals in Enlightenment could have very individual experiences indeed?

You, for instance. In Enlightenment you may discover that God becomes more real to you than ever, real in the very most personal way. One way of describing this is to call God, "Nearer than the nearest and dearer than the dearest."

#2. Ascended Masters, Gods, and Goddesses: DIVINE

In order to qualify as an **Ascended Master,** that eternal soul must have lived on Earth at least once (living in a human embodiment), and also have gained the equivalent of Spiritual Enlightenment.

Most are not nearly as famous as Jesus or Buddha, Kwan Yin or St. Germain. Granted, there may well be other Ascended

Masters who are equally famous for their leadership at learning planets beyond Earth School. I'm no expert on that.

However much you love Divine Beings, their job is not to rescue you from living as a human. Self-actualization begins with a willingness to be human, then do what is yours to do.

#3. Archangels: DIVINE

For practical purposes, such as learning Energy Spirituality™ skills to cocreate with the Divine, might I suggest? Choose from one of these four **Archangels** only: Archangel Michael, Archangel Raphael, Archangel Gabriel, or Archangel Uriel.

But aren't there plenty of other Archangels who could help me?

Maybe. During the New Age Years, it was trendy to take an interest in "angels and archangels." Altogether different kinds of beings -- they barely belong in the same sentence.

Confusingly, America's most influential New Age psychic was angel expert Doreen Virtue. From my perspective, she mostly sold toys for psychic development, like "Archangel Oracle Cards", freely mixing up angels and archangels.

#4. Seraphim, Cherubim, Thrones: DIVINE

Certainly, **Seraphs** etc. do exist. In my experience, these are high-level Divine Beings, mainly involved in behind-the-scenes work involving causation and other *process*-type functions. Seldom do these high-level beings get involved directly in helping humans (unlike Archangels and Ascended Masters). Actually, you'll seldom encounter any Seraphs at all.

Even if you do take time to research angelology, or listen to classical arias like Handel's aforementioned masterpiece, "Let the Bright Seraphim" — hello! Hobbies like these won't help you to attain Enlightenment; no more than collecting baseball cards would make you a fabulous pitcher.

Speaking of distractions that have no place in our Program for Spiritual Enlightenment, some teachers with really messed-up consciousness lifestyles have gone wild in this Age of Awakening, urging their followers to live in the **Fifth Dimension**, etc.

Advocates of living in the Fifth Dimension are currently popular, in some circles anyway. Typically, these influencers claim that various space beings are guiding them, as if these beings were really Seraphim and the like.

- Such a false claim! According to some research I've done to help clients, the wise-and-kindly "5-D Advanced Beings" are simply unscrupulous ETs.
- As for the trusting seekers following 5-D instructions, poor kids; they develop really messed-up consciousness lifestyles.
- Regarding ETs, just keep reading. Quiz ANSWER #6 is coming soon in this chapter.

#5. Ghosts, Stuck Spirits: ASTRAL

Surely you've heard of **Ghosts**, Smart Spiritual Seeker. After a human physically dies, sometimes that person's aura remains stuck for a while, stuck here on Earth. (Hence my preferred term for ghosts, **Stuck Spirits**.)

Although Stuck Spirits may sometimes hang around humans, *human nature* can't rub off on a ghost.

Before the physical body died, Stuck Spirits *used to be* human, but following physical death, that's no longer true. Fact is, having your own working, breathing, physical body is a requirement for living at Human Vibrational Frequencies.

Many psychics think it's snobby to think that ghosts can't do things that people can do. Couldn't ghosts be really be wiser and more spiritual than humans, since we're earthbound, trapped in our bodies? Couldn't that be true?

Here's the truth about ghosts: They're **Discarnate Spirits** *— living in astral bodies, with no further connection to their human-type bodies, now dead. Never expect human wisdom from these astrals.*

Speaking of which, Stuck Spirits can't see us. They just read our auras. *Traditionally* these discarnates can't make contact with us at Human Vibrational Frequencies either, except for psychics who've learned how to position consciousness at a discarnate being's Astral Vibrational Frequency.

But now? With your new superpower, you might see or sense them. Some might try to entice you by claiming to be God's messenger, but don't believe it.

Every Stuck Spirit is astral; consequently, each one has a strong personal agenda (unlike Divine Beings or human beings who are living in Enlightenment).

In short, Stuck Spirits aren't at all trustworthy. Considering them to be wise advice-givers? Count that as a major mistake.

#6. Extra Terrestrial Entities (ETs): Astral

Smart Spiritual Seeker, both you and I have signed a personal Life Contract before we could live here on Earth as humans; by contrast, **ETs** have signed up to incarnate in a different world from Earth, some astral world (of which there are many).

Ever since the Psychic Barrier left this planet, it's become super-easy for ETs to come to Earth; unfortunately, many choose to develop a relationship with energy sensitive humans. Know any, by chance?

In these early years of the Age of Awakening, it's common for **Opportunistic ETs** to seek to influence humans. Like other astral spirits, they may claim superior wisdom, or represent themselves as Divine Beings. Any such claims would be a lie.

#7. Astral Entities: ASTRAL

Also common in these early years of the Age of Awakening: Many **Astral Entities** come to this planet, attempting to influence human beings. Often, they're known as **Angels**, which is a romantic term for any soul in an astral body.

Astral entities work with psychics, mediums, and channelers. Like astral entities, both ETs and ghosts can easily become involved with people today, especially those human beings who pursue psychic development.

In these early years of the Age of Awakening, people who do a lot of Energy Talk may be partial to astral spirits, considering them to be "sacred" and "wise." That would be a mistake. If you're really seeking Enlightenment, don't hang out with discarnates.

Speaking of which... Although angels have quite a reputation for sweetness and light, many are quite the opposite. Whatever the intent of any discarnates who provide "guidance" to humans, what is definitely true?

- Not that they're wiser or more evolved than you. Hardly!
- Nor that their intentions are pure as fresh snow.
- Merely how they live in an *astral body*, rather than the kind of *flesh-and-blood body* you happen to have.

From now on, feel free to wear that body of yours with a certain spiritual pride. Although you may not look like a famous supermodel, guess what? Your human body is the envy of many a discarnate being.

Quiz ANSWERS Complete!

....

Congratulations on Finishing this Quiz

Maybe you'd like to take a break for a moment. For instance, Smart Spiritual Seeker, you might do a congratulatory dance — like an Irish jig, some salsa, or a bit of ballet — any dance form that doesn't require hovering.

In Conclusion

Please don't think for a minute that any astral being is "of God." After all, you're a SMART Spiritual Seeker, right?

In this chapter you've liberated yourself from three common misunderstandings about astral beings; knowledge that frees you up to learn more, unsentimentally learn more, learn more about what astral experiences are really like.

Also you've wised up about seven different kinds of non-human being. Good to know!

In our next chapter we'll explore what it's like for human beings when we position our consciousness at an Astral Vibrational Frequency. Will different astral frequencies be pretty much alike? Hardly.

Let's begin by (safely) exploring the kind of Astral Vibrational Frequency that is closest to any Human Vibrational Frequency. Which would that be???

CHAPTER 12.

Super-Comfy LOW Astral Vibrational Frequencies

> *If a girl is smiling and is bringing positive energy and she's happy, that's what I notice right away — and her teeth.*
>
> **Chandler Parsons, Professional Basketball Player**

> *Energy sensitive people often feel special when they talk about energy. What's missing is discernment about whether that Energy Talk helps or hinders their spiritual growth.*
>
> *Ironically, what's also missing? Discernment about which type of energy is being noticed: Often any random form of astral energy is considered superior to human wisdom, but why?*
>
> **Rose Rosetree**

Smart Spiritual Seeker, let's recap what you've learned so far. Your Consciousness Positioning Superpower allows you to do something amazing yet easy: position your consciousness at a vibrational frequency that isn't human at all.

Living in this still-new Age of Awakening, knowledge — or *content* — about such experience is lagging far behind our *process*-related, spontaneous experiences.

No wonder smart people like Chandler Parsons can feel as though big-deal knowledge involves distinguishing "positive" energy from "negative" energy. In this chapter you'll begin to develop more precise knowledge, related to useful concepts, all designed to educate you in a practical way.

Chapter 12. Super-Comfy LOW Astral Vibrational Frequencies

What's it like, positioning consciousness at one type of vibrational frequency rather than another? In this chapter we'll begin by exploring LOW Astral Vibrational Frequencies.

For a Smart Spiritual Seeker, this kind of knowledge is hardly optional. Seeking Enlightenment in the Age of Awakening demands far more precision than the kind of Energy Talk that's so common today.

Positioning Consciousness Is Subtle, Mysterious

To gain clarity, let's explore your *process* of having experiences, related to where your consciousness is positioned. Already you know better than to be fooled by mistaking *content* for *process*. Now let's take your understanding further.

Very likely, positioning consciousness is subtler than you expect. Importantly, this positioning doesn't show. Our eyes show us plenty of important things, but not that.

Smart Spiritual Seeker, this absence of visual cues has big implications. Sure, it makes sense how positioning consciousness is subtle, being an inner kind of experience. But don't you also assume that *you still ought to be able to see it somehow?*

For example, what if you're hanging out with your friend Nick, and he's doing something different with positioning his consciousness? If the two of you were in some TV show, special music would start playing in the background, and that would clue you in. "Ooh, Nick is tripping around, moving in his consciousness."

Only, in real life, where's that music? Where are your visuals?

Consciously we can't tell. Only energetic literacy skills will reveal this... provided that we're taking some time to actively research what's happening with Nick's consciousness.

Taking this example further, suppose that you're visiting your friend Nick and he looks totally normal. And you're not picking up any kind of a weird vibe, either. Then isn't it safe to assume that his consciousness must be positioned at a Human Vibrational Frequency?

Not Really

Fasten your seatbelt, Smart Spiritual Seeker. I'm here to help you explore, in detail, what is happening with people like your friend Nick. Of course, this kind of thing can happen with you, too.

Discernment about different experiences of consciousness — that's the purpose of Part II, knowledge that can blow your mind because....

In the Age of Awakening our everyday human experience, often involves positioning consciousness at a vibrational frequency that is NOT human.

Truth! Although *you're still human*, your awareness will often explore *something not human*. If you have no idea this is happening, does it matter? Sure does, since you're seeking Enlightenment.

Here's an example that aims to make this concept more concrete. Let's say that your Aunt Wilma usually lives in Cincinnati, Ohio. Only now she's taking a trip to New York, where she visits your apartment. Aunt Wilma tells you, "Gee, things sure are different here."

Alternatively, she might not notice much at all, apart from the obvious tourist sights outside your window. What if you asked Aunt Wilma outright, "Being here, do you find that things seem different?"

Imagine your aunt's face taking on a worldly-wise expression. Smiling sweetly, she says, "Nothing important is different. People are people, wherever you go."

Either way — whether or not Aunt Wilma notices much — her experience definitely counts as New York-ish. My question to you is this. Sure, Aunt Wilma is physically in New York. Does that mean she notices much about being there?

Not necessarily. Likewise, something similar could be true of you, Smart Spiritual Seeker, except that you're learning how to appreciate how more could be happening than meets the eye.

So Together Let's Have a Think about Consciousness

Seeking Enlightenment in the Age of Awakening, it's essential to learn what really could be happening in consciousness, especially *your consciousness*.

So Together Let's Have a Think about Consciousness

Some of my British clients have taught me this great expression, *have a think*. Together, now, let's have a think about your own consciousness.

> **Anybody seeking Enlightenment in the Age of Awakening needs new ways to understand consciousness. Since human consciousness now moves in new ways, seeking Enlightenment hinges on *what we do* with that consciousness of ours.**

To summarize key ideas that you've already learned:

1. Whenever you're awake, you experience life through your *consciousness*.
2. Since you're living in the Age of Awakening, whenever you're awake, your consciousness will be positioned at *one* particular-and-unique vibrational frequency.
3. That means, you have *only one* positioning of consciousness at any given time.

Such a relief, right? Never will learning about this topic have to feel like a super-complicated mess, due to your having multiple positionings at once.

Rest assured we can keep this topic manageable, subtle but manageable. Smart Spiritual Seeker, you can definitely learn all you need to know about this topic, so essential for seeking Enlightenment.

In this chapter and the rest of Part II, you'll be learning *content* about one particular vibrational frequency at a time; just useful info, not having to experience any of this as a *process*.

You could say, you'll simply be learning…

Consciousness Whats???

Smart Spiritual Seeker, let's start exploring some **Consciousness Facts of Life,** not concerning the birds and the bees, but about ways of being human post-Shift.

Such a superb adventure hidden in plain sight! Very likely, every day of your life, for years now, you've been positioning your consciousness at different vibrational frequencies. For example:

- One minute your consciousness is positioned at a Human Vibrational Frequency.
- Next minute, you begin positioning your consciousness — super-effortlessly, and with zero fanfare — at a LOW Astral Vibrational Frequency.

What would that be like? For starters...

How Does It Feel?

Suppose that're hanging out with your friend Nick, and both of you have spontaneously positioned your consciousness at a comfortably LOW Astral Vibrational Frequency.

During one sample minute, you might feel one or more of the following:

1. *Pleasurably* down to earth.
2. Like you're *accepting yourself* a bit more easily than usual.
3. Feeling as if you're definitely made of flesh-and-blood, *and your physical body* happens to be doing great.
4. Maybe you're also feeling *extra-attractive.*
5. Possibly you're even feeling *sexier than usual.*
6. A casual observer might also call you *"very relaxed,"* as if somehow you've figured out a special knack for that.
7. While speaking, it's so easy to *express yourself.*
8. Also, it's as though *you understand other people* a little better. Awesome you!

9. For sure, whichever people you're sharing this moment with? (In our example here, that would be Nick.) So nice, and *definitely on your wavelength!*
10. Altogether, it's as though you're *feeling no pain*, only a mild form of satisfaction.

How Can Your Consciousness Get Positioned There?

Since we're all living in the Age of Awakening, positioning consciousness at a LOW Astral Vibrational Frequency has become ridiculously easy. Any of the following options, and more, can make it happen. No guarantees, though, because different people react differently to different activities (and, when relevant, different intoxicants).

1. *Drinking beer.* Consciousness positioning changes due to any kind of beer, whether super-expensive or cheap.
2. Going on guided *Ayahuasca* tours.
3. Watching what I call **Angel Porn**. (Namely, reading about angels; using angel cards, etc.)
4. Listening to podcasts about *near-death experiences.*
5. Random *daydreaming.*
6. Indulging in *detailed fantasies* about fame, sweet revenge, etc. Also included would be pornography and video games spiced up with cruelty.
7. Watching gritty *reality shows* or *soap operas.*
8. *Dream-boarding,* once you're good at it.
9. Participating in a *drumming* circle.
10. Doing *Mindfulness Meditation.*

Starting to Make Sense Yet — Human-Type Sense?

Whatever prompts this kind of invisible astral travel, it's super-easy to do. Probably you feel normal; that is, feeling like yourself, very human, comfortably human; just that you happen to feel extra-good somehow.

Definitely it's unlikely that you'll feel as though you have positioned consciousness anywhere. After all, don't you still feel like yourself? Sure you do; that kind of consciousness travel comes with the territory of living on Earth now, in the Age of Awakening.

Quite possibly, LOW astral experience can include wishing that you could feel this way always, akin to having magic in the air. And what if you're hanging out with other people at the time, folks doing the same kind of thing as you? Somehow, all of those folks might seem extra-pleasant, maybe kind of familiar.

So what if you've only just met these people, like strangers at a bar? Who thinks about positioning consciousness? You might simply think, "I really lucked out: What a fabulously friendly, super-nice group!"

Subtle But Familiar

What I've described so far is way subtle, of course. Long before the Shift on Dec. 21, 2012, sometimes you might have just clicked with a group of strangers; only back then there wasn't much spontaneous astral positioning of consciousness.

> *Rose, how can you possibly give us a detailed picture of what's going on within a person?*
>
> *Good question! Trust me, Smart Spiritual Seeker, I've thought long and hard about how to communicate the quality of something this subtle — the positioning of consciousness at different vibrational frequencies. How to describe this in human terms?*

Eventually, I figured out how to do that. In our next chapter I'll explain; following that, Part II will be crammed with juicy details about subtle experiences of consciousness. When you're ready, when you're set, let's go!

CHAPTER 13.

Snapshots of Consciousness: Innovation for Smart Spiritual Seekers

Anyone who devotes time and attention to what makes people tick, to me, is a smart person.

Actor and Activist Ron Silver

Worthwhile though it is to seek a better understanding of people, which approach are you going to take? The "Whatever" approach? Aiming for significant clarity, we can benefit from skills — ideally, precision skills — like researching a person's chakra databanks.

Rose Rosetree

No matter how many pictures you've got on your phone right now, I'm pretty sure that you've never seen this new kind of snapshot. With your life already so photo-rich, why am I bothering to bring up this energetic literacy specialty called "**Snapshots of Consciousness**"?

Here's why. These snapshots aim to reveal how someone is experiencing consciousness, akin to a snapshot that shows you how people look physically.

When the truth we're seeking is discernment about consciousness, this new kind of snapshot is just the thing; so let's use this chapter and the next to properly introduce you to this leading-edge application of energetic literacy.

Basically, a snapshot of consciousness describes in relatable words: What is it like when a person positions consciousness at a Human, Astral, or Divine Vibrational Frequency? By now you're starting to appreciate how helpful this kind of knowledge can be, given that you're seeking Enlightenment in the Age of Awakening.

Yes, You'll Succeed More — Which Is the Point

Seeking Enlightenment is a big deal, not some cute little fad, akin to showing the world how spiritually cool you are... by wearing a Lululemon yoga outfit.

Back in the Age of Faith, spiritual seeking was serious. Many took vows as renunciates. They'd wear the special garb to signify their religious commitment — like a Catholic priest's white collar, a Franciscan nun's black-and-white habit, the saffron robe of a sanyasi.

How about devout individuals who couldn't officially "give their lives to God"? Many lived "ordinary" lives, garbed in ordinary clothing; yet they longed for spiritual purity, striving for ever more faith, aiming for surrender; and without necessarily making a show of religiosity, these seekers of truth tried hard to follow the rules of their religion.

Since you're living in a different era, and the Age of Awakening is still very new, let me ask you this. As a Smart Spiritual Seeker, what would be your equivalent way to show spiritual devotion?

Seems to me, the true picture would show in your aura, not your clothing; specifically, your spiritual commitment would show in how you position consciousness during your waking hours.

Of course, that doesn't really show — except, hello! It does now, for those who've gained good skills of energetic literacy.

What's the most reliable way to tell how you (or anybody) is doing on a spiritual path? Simply put, you take a snapshot of consciousness. Or else you let a person who's developed that skill... take that snapshot for you and then share the findings.

What a Privilege It Is, Seeking Enlightenment NOW!

We're capable of much faster spiritual evolution, compared to the Age of Faith. Equally magnificent is how our spiritual growth is supplemented by pursuing worthy human-type goals in life. Unlike the extreme difficulty of seeking sainthood or Enlightenment during the Age of Faith, now we can pursue our spiritual goals just part time. And we can succeed.

Really, it's astounding how little we have to do, compared to spiritual seekers of yore. When rightly used, our Consciousness Positioning Superpower will speed you on your way.

Smart Spiritual Seeker, if I know you, yes! You're game to read this pretty accessible book and then faithfully spend 20 minutes a day, following our Program for Spiritual Enlightenment, knowing that you can then progress powerfully — no orangey sanyasi robes needed.

In order to help you succeed, our snapshots of consciousness will help you to develop discernment about the *sacred exploration of a spiritual seeker.*

While reading the snapshots of consciousness that follow in Part II, please don't expect so see anything fancy. In fact, don't expect to literally see a thing — except for the words you'll be reading. Actually, authentic spiritual growth never needs to involve seeing a thing.

Although I refer to "snapshots" of consciousness, what you'll be reading are more like concept-pictures, humanly relatable descriptions about ways to position consciousness.

I've never heard of such a thing. Weird! Are these snapshots supposed to be a different approach to Enlightenment teaching?

In a way — mostly these snapshots can empower you and help to protect you, as somebody seeking Enlightenment now; these concept-pictures will fit right in as practical background for our Program for Spiritual Enlightenment.

Enlightenment Isn't a Theory But an Experience

And you know why that is, don't you, Smart Spiritual Seeker?

Theories, ideas, dogma, scripture reading — all of that counts as *content*. No amount of theoretical learning will bring you the *process* of living in Enlightenment, nor the human experience of using your full potential in life.

Today's nonduality teachers, meditation teachers, awakening teachers, preachers and others... far too many of them teach what they love, what they were taught, as if still living in the Age of Faith. Usually, members of the Enlightenment Establishment do their job by sharing sacred *content*, all that God talk or Energy Talk; as if there were just two alternatives:

Either you're into worldly things. Or else you can follow the "teachings," which allow you to pursue God. Only, hello! If you're homesick for Heaven, *content* is no longer enough. As a Smart Spiritual Seeker, you deserve a direct experience of the Divine (*process*).

Meanwhile, too many spiritual teachers lack discernment about where students take those traditional teachings, positioning consciousness at an unhelpful WHERE. Energetically illiterate, too many spiritual teachers inadvertently lead their students on side trips into astral experiences.

Spiritual Side Trips?

Today they're so much more common than you might expect. (This you'll be learning in detail during most of our Part II.) **Spiritual Side Trips** involve positioning consciousness at some random Astral Vibrational Frequency; doing this off and on, all day long.

Compounding that problem, the culture of spiritual teaching often romanticizes Enlightenment as though it solved all human problems.

Especially popular are inspiring stories about seekers who have *attained* Enlightenment. Sounds great, except these pretty stories only help with mood-making; they won't *help you progress* toward Enlightenment; not necessarily; not now; not in my opinion, anyway.

You see, in the Age of Awakening, we spiritual teachers can't do our jobs properly without energetic literacy, not if we aim to help students who've got today's new Consciousness Positioning Superpower — which means every single student, right?

As a practical matter, spiritual seekers need to know the truth about how they might be positioning their consciousness. Answers show clearly in chakra databanks; snapshots of consciousness communicate that, and don't you deserve to know what's what?

- Imagine the mess if a trusted Enlightenment Teacher were to regale you with pretty-pretty "Enlightenment" tales that are really about astral experiences — and thus, as far away from Divine as could be.
- Actually, you don't have to imagine this mess happening. Since, I assure you, it already is.

When reading our upcoming snapshots of consciousness, what will help you the most? Don't skim through it, like passively scrolling through pictures on mobile phones, where you can instantly get the point; where the truth is obvious for all to see, right there on the screen.

Regular photos may entertain us without being the least bit relevant to exploring anything conceptually new or spiritually valuable; whereas these snapshots are extremely relevant to your seeking Enlightenment.

How to Benefit Most from Snapshots of Consciousness

Two simple steps sum it up:

1. Smart Spiritual Seeker, read through the words slowly, rather than skim-reading.
2. After you read, think a bit about what it would mean for you, if *you* were the person whose chakra databank had that particular size and quality.

Really, that's all there is to it. Adding what you've gained in this chapter, you're pretty well prepared by now, having gained a ton of discernment about *process*, rather than *content*, especially when it comes to where spiritual seekers are positioning consciousness.

Besides that, remember the ongoing mystery that we're solving in the background? That Church-Wenters Mystery just might involve some religious teachers and church members who have something not-so-great that shows in their snapshots of consciousness.

> ***Sorry, but I don't get the connection yet. Why does it matter where pastors might go in their invisible astral travel? Isn't their job mainly preaching and teaching?***
>
> *Not now, not in the Age of Awakening. Where religious teachers position their consciousness isn't only personal; this has professional relevance, since that leader's work aims to help followers attain important spiritual ideals.*

Imagine the confusion if:

- Unknowingly, preachers habitually experienced life at an Astral Vibrational Frequency — *process*.
- Yet those very same leaders were preaching their *content* as if personally connected with the Divine, swooningly-lusciously connected; all the while taking a spiritual side trip.

Tricky business, sorting out which is which! Our snapshots of consciousness can bring you discernment about people in many professions, people you meet every day, helping you to stop assuming that "Everyone is just like me."

Sadly, when it comes to seeking Enlightenment, many of the people you meet are like walking-talking examples of what NOT to do with your Consciousness Positioning Superpower.

Lacking discernment, you could fool yourself; or others might inadvertently try to fool you. In order to protect yourself, let me help you to gain discernment. Knowing what's what, and where's where:

All this is necessary for Seeking Enlightenment in the Age of Awakening. Why settle for anything less than making authentic progress?

Smart Spiritual Seeker, it's not asking too much for you to demand real progress along your path, rather than unknowingly taking spiritual side trips.

Too many seekers today limit themselves by treasuring some warm-fuzzy feeling that comes from doing what "everyone says" is The Way.

Does popular mean **High Truth Value**? (That term of art means a high degree of clarity and integrity.)

High Truth Value can become your standard for discernment while seeking that deeply fulfilling goal, Spiritual Enlightenment.

In Conclusion

You're ready to go, ready to read about those snapshots; maybe you're as eager as I am to start teaching you about these different ways of positioning consciousness.

But have you ever heard the saying, "God is in the details"? In our next chapter I'm going to introduce you to some very important details about the kind of info contained in any snapshot of consciousness.

Rather than racing ahead, next I'll help you wrap your *conscious-and-human mind* around specific ways that your fellow seekers are exploring everyday life. You see, through these snapshots, the truth of a person's abstract experience of consciousness will be described in Human-Type Language.

Why can this kind of knowledge help you? Mostly because, Smart Spiritual Seeker, you're not merely a theory. Nor is Enlightenment merely some grand theory.

What you learn next can help to bring the *process* of living in Enlightenment down to earth... in a way that just might be new to you.

CHAPTER 14.

Snapshots for SOPHISTICATED Spiritual Seekers

The audience today has heard every joke. They know every plot. They know where you're going before you even start.

That's a tough audience to surprise, and a tough audience to write for. It's much more competitive now, because the audience is so much more — I want to say "sophisticated."

Betty White, Popular Entertainer for Six Decades

....

SOPHISTICATED about consciousness and energy? If you're seeking Enlightenment now, protect yourself by developing a more sophisticated kind of discernment about that.

Of course, the discernment in this chapter has nothing to do with all the sophistication you may have gained from binge-watching "Friends" or other show biz favorites.

Rose Rosetree

....

Which *human-type insights* will be most useful for discerning how somebody positions consciousness? Expect to learn so much about that in this chapter. Benefit from how I've been refining energetic literacy skills, exploring auras just about every day of my life, for decades.

As my student, you won't be required to put in all those thousands of hours; this short chapter will ground you in the human relevance of aura-level insights. Which qualities of awareness are most relevant to pursuing Enlightenment? The answer might surprise you. But first things first. I'd like to answer a practical question about snapshots of consciousness.

How Exactly?

How exactly do I create these snapshots? First I locate a photo of somebody with a particular kind of consciousness positioning. Then, to prepare a snapshot of consciousness, I'll systematically research-and-describe five different chakra databanks.

For our last two snapshots of consciousness in Part II, I'll add one more, a sixth chakra databank at the Third Eye Chakra. When we get there, I'll let you know which one (and why it's relevant).

Help, I'm still kind of fuzzy about chakra databanks. Can you explain them better?

Definitely possible! In the Age of Awakening, every Smart Spiritual Seeker needs to know about chakra databanks.

Build upon What You Know So Far

Maybe you remember how, back in Part I, I introduced you to chakra databanks? Now let's build upon that, point by point:

1. *Your aura* is loaded with information about your emotional and spiritual development.
2. With **Stage 1 Energetic Literacy**, people generalize about a person's *entire aura*.
3. Although doing that can feel good, it's merely a form of Energy Talk; since the literacy skill is so limited, *accuracy will be limited too.*
4. Accurate information about auras is especially concentrated in **Chakras**. Generally, these are located in front of your body.
5. When people gain enough skill to do Chakra Readings, that counts as **Stage 2 Energetic Literacy**.

6. Granted, generalizing about chakras *feels good to do*; for sure, this is more sophisticated than generalizing with Stage 1 Energetic Literacy.
7. Unfortunately, Stage 2 happens to provide *a ridiculously limited amount of information*; at least if you aim to learn about anything as important as Spiritual Enlightenment.
8. Fortunately for us, every chakra contains 50 different chakra databanks.
9. Smart Spiritual Seeker, once you develop the skill to research any chakra databank you choose, ta da! You've attained **Stage 3 Energetic Literacy,** also known as **Good Quality Aura Reading.**
10. In short, you're **Energetically Literate.** Meaning that, just as with word literacy, you're free to read whatever you like.

Which kind of learning are we talking about, though, once a person has attained good quality aura reading? Names of chakra databanks summarize the topic area; each name for a chakra databank is like the title for a different book of life, one that you can open up and read.

Maybe it's because I don't know any other spiritual teachers who talk about chakra databanks. But I figure, if this were really important, wouldn't all of them be writing about these databanks?

Look, *this* Enlightenment Teacher isn't qualified to explain why other teachers do what they do, so I'll rephrase your question into something that I *can* answer.

What's So Important about Chakra Databanks?

Understandable though this question is — and it's a good one — consider this. Future generations born in the Age of Awakening will probably laugh at such a question. (Good naturedly, I hope.)

After all, wouldn't you giggle a bit if somebody asked you a similar question about word literacy: "What's the big deal about reading sentences and paragraphs? I'm satisfied chatting with my friends about the shapes of letters, like how A is different from B or C. That's plenty satisfying."

Smart Spiritual Seeker, once you develop Stage 3 Energetic Literacy, whenever you research a chakra databank, you can learn information that's highly specific, deeply personal, accurate, and up-to-date.

To understand even more, once again, let's go point-by-point.

1. *Each chakra databank has a name*, the name of something important to humans like us. In our snapshots of consciousness, I'll always supply the name of a particular chakra databank before telling you what I find.
2. Every chakra in a person's aura *contains 50 chakra databanks*.
3. To picture one these, *imagine a slim tube of energy*. In your mind's eye, you might imagine this like a straw, only filled with information rather than ginger ale, etc.
4. Deep within each chakra databank is a Divine-level **Gift of the Soul**. Unchanging for a human being's entire lifetime, what's encoded there is the person's pure potential; always inspiring, and as beautifully individual as a fingerprint.
5. Mostly, though, information in chakra databanks changes second by second. I like to call this *"the business end"* of a chakra databank. Meaning, it's the practical part.
6. For example, every chakra databank contains a **Symbolic Size**. This reveals how actively that particular aspect of life is working... at that particular time.
7. In addition, chakra databanks also contain a **Quality**, which provides equally useful insights, as you'll soon see for yourself.
8. In our snapshots of consciousness, every time that I report on a chakra databank, I'll tell you about both; first the symbolic size AND then the quality. *Together they're a fascinating source of info*, more informative than either symbolic size or quality... alone.

9. Once you develop skills for Stage 3 Energetic Literacy, *you can research chakra databanks on yourself.* Also, you can research them on any person who's physically present with you. Probably, though, *you'll mostly be reading auras on people from their photographs.* (Here I mean regular photographs, such as those you can find on your phone or the internet.)
10. None of the information from chakra databanks involves **Mind Reading**, or spilling the beans about a person's conscious thoughts.
11. By contrast, our snapshots of consciousness will tell you what's happening with the person's *subconscious* mind, corresponding to *astral components of an aura.*
12. Finally, please keep in mind this important point: Each snapshot of consciousness comes from researching *one* photograph of *one* particular individual… at *one* particular time. When researching any chakra databank, I'll answer this question to the best of my ability, "What was happening with that person's consciousness, during the split-second when the photo was taken?"

Important points all, despite hardly being common knowledge in society now. To see what I mean, just google "Chakra Databanks" with your favorite search engine. How many people today are publishing this kind of research? (The answer might surprise you.)

> **All this is new to me. Looks exciting. What if I'd like to see some examples of reading chakra databanks?**
>
> An excellent free resource is my blog, *Deeper Perception Made Practical.* Search *there* on "Chakra Databanks." Unlike searching on the internet, at my blog you'll find hundreds of aura readings of public figures, articles brimming with juicy details.

All that said, snapshots of consciousness contain a highly specific, dedicated array of chakra databanks.

Which Chakra Databanks, Exactly?

Smart Spiritual Seeker, I'm so excited to be introducing you to five chakra databanks in particular. Together that full set counts as the minimum for a snapshot of consciousness. Here's your list.

1. Root Chakra Databank for Presence in the Room

How is the person *living socially*? Of course, that means living at the time of the photograph.

At this particular time, in general, what it's like being that person? Also, what kind of a statement, energetically, does that person's presence make to others?

2. Root Chakra Databank for Connection to Objective Reality

How does the person *notice* human-type objective reality? Actually, to what degree is that person even paying attention?

Of course, this can be fascinating.

> Especially interesting for our purposes here, remember: People can only notice objective reality when their consciousness is positioned at a Human Vibrational Frequency. During an Astral or Divine experience, they're *substituting an energy version* of a person or thing; an energy version that the person considers humanly real. But isn't.

Incidentally, in our next chapter, you'll learn more about objective reality versus the subjective kind; this form of discernment being useful for smashing illusions while you seek Enlightenment.

3. Belly Chakra Databank for Sexual Self-Esteem

Feeling attractive, even sexy? How much?

Many chakra databanks reveal sexual secrets, so why am I choosing to include this particular one? Surprisingly or not, how we feel about ourselves sexually matters a great deal... when we're seeking Enlightenment.

At least, that's true now that we're living in the Age of Awakening, when it's no longer necessary to take Age of Faith-style vows of celibacy. But you don't need me to tell you that sexual self-esteem is pretty darned important — and revealing! Hey, what if you always want to read about this databank first? Go for it.

4. Heart Chakra Databank for Emotional Receiving

Feeling loved? Or perhaps disrespected? Willing to accept kindness from strangers?

You get the idea: When it comes to emotional receiving, whatever shows at this chakra databank... is going to be intensely human.

From your own personal experience, Smart Spiritual Seeker, you know that *emotions* can change second by second. Moreover, by now you know that *chakra databanks* also can change second by second.

> But maybe you've never before thought about this: What happens emotionally if somebody's consciousness is *positioned away from Human Vibrational Frequencies?* Pretty revealing — as you'll see.

5. Third Eye Chakra Databank for Connection to Psychic Guidance

How comfortable is this person with receiving information from astral beings? That's the topic of this chakra databank.

Psychic Guidance means being influenced (subconsciously or consciously) by discarnate spirits; whether they're called spirit guides, Spirit, angels, guardian angels, ETs, ghosts, advanced beings, helpers, "God's messengers," or anything else.

Have you ever seen the old-time religious pictures with Everyman being influenced by astral beings? An angel hovers over one of Everyman's shoulders, while a devil hovers over Everyman's other shoulder; both of these astral beings are whispering advice.

Devil is a religiously-flavored term for astral spirits, and a scary one at that. However, there's a huge range of astral beings. (Remember our Quiz about *Beings Who Aren't Human*? You took that quiz back in Chapter 10. Take another peek, if you like.)

I wondered when you were going to bring up Satan, the Devil. Can you tell us more?

Sure can.

Snapshots of Consciousness Never Reveal "The Devil"

Religious traditions that speak of good Angels versus Devils are thousands of years old. Makes sense, since fears of Satan, etc., developed when? Back in the Age of Faith, that's when.

Smart Spiritual Seeker, as you know by now, religious fears were prevalent when human consciousness was locked into Human Vibrational Frequencies; fear of devils would fit right in with other heavy beliefs that were common during that Age of Faith.

Living in the Age of Awakening, though, phew! Humanity is capable of far more nuance, although some of you Smart Spiritual Seekers may prefer to keep believing in traditional "Fear of the Devil." This belief won't keep you from seeking Enlightenment; I include my point of view only in case it's helpful to some of you readers who might not have known that such beliefs are optional.

For sure, today's psychics take considerable interest in spirits of one kind or another. By contrast, Energy Spirituality™ emphasizes your human resourcefulness rather than astral anything.

Look, if we aim to understand what's happening with a person's consciousness, it's essential to include this fifth chakra databank in our snapshot, since this databank reveals the degree to which a person is being influenced by discarnate beings. Among other things, this chakra databank can answer two practical questions:

1. At the time of this snapshot of consciousness, was that person being influenced by discarnate beings?
2. And if so, how so?

Important to know, Smart Spiritual Seeker: Whenever your consciousness is positioned at a Human Vibrational Frequency, the answer is decidedly NOT.

You're NOT likely to be influenced by discarnate spirits. Pretty essential for those of us who care about Spiritual Enlightenment!

By Now You've Read a Lot. And Learned a Lot

Thanks for educating yourself through this chapter and the previous one. Now we're ready to rock-and-roll.

Smart Spiritual Seeker, coming next is our first official snapshot of consciousness.

CHAPTER 15.

Learn More About a LOW Astral Vibrational Frequency

*They who **drink** beer will **think** beer.*

Washington Irving, Short Story Writer

Beer doesn't only relax you. It doesn't merely provide you with a fine, substantial belly. Drinking beer is a common way to position your consciousness at a LOW Vibrational Frequency.

Rose Rosetree

Smart Spiritual Seeker, meet Nicholas. And I mean, really meet him.

In this chapter he'll star in a snapshot of consciousness that aims to convey what it's like for him to have consciousness positioned at a LOW Astral Vibrational Frequency.

Researching the array selected expressly for our snapshots of consciousness, you'll learn about super-abstract qualities of his subconscious experience. During the Age of Faith, clarity about this positioning of consciousness would have been quite impossible. But now? Decide for yourself what's possible, what's valuable.

How Does It Feel, Being Nicholas at the Time of His Photo?

That is to say, what's it like, living with consciousness positioned LOW-astrally? Nicholas still looks human, and is human, which gives rise to a tricky situation.

Know it or not, there can be quite a consciousness contrast between what we *expect* our inner experience to be — versus what consciousness *actually is doing*. Again, invisible astral travel is both common and effortless.

> In my experience, the following snapshot of consciousness is typical of consciousness positioned at a LOW Astral Vibrational Frequency, amounting to a relatively mild variation on how to see life.

Smart Spiritual Seeker, keep reading the snapshots in our Part II and you may be surprised, how experiences at higher Astral Vibrational Frequencies become progressively stranger and stranger.

What you're about to read in this chapter may seem pretty mild... until you get to the fourth and fifth chakra databanks of our set. Even then, none of this will seem dramatic, compared with what you'd see in a horror movie.

Practically speaking, this first snapshot of consciousness will likely seem mild, compared with what you'll find in later chapters, as we explore snapshots taken at ever higher Astral Vibrational Frequencies.

Also worth noting: At the time of this snapshot of consciousness, Nicholas believes himself to be noticing, "Life as it is." Having downed a few beers, he may feel pleasantly sloshed. That's all. Probably this next part never occurs to him: Every person he talks with is actually a different version of that individual.

- No longer is Nick making contact with the ordinary version, experienced at a Human Vibrational Frequency.
- Instead, he's visiting with a version (tucked within that same person's aura) at a LOW Astral Vibrational Frequency.

No, none of this is science fiction; more like the fascinating play of consciousness for all of us human beings living now. Lest all this seem abstract, how about this? One chakra databank at a time, we'll bring home the consciousness truth of Nick's LOW astral experience.

1. Nicholas's Root Chakra Databank for Presence in the Room

Symbolic Size

Out to the moon. Over-functioning: Trillions of miles

Quality

Aware of life at a LOW Astral Vibrational Frequency: With consciousness positioned here, it's as though Nicholas feels comfortably spaced out, yet also perfectly normal. Actually, this version is an upgrade, compared with this man's usual awkward experience of life when consciousness is positioned at a Human Vibrational Frequency.

2. Nicholas's Root Chakra Databank for Connection to Objective Reality

Symbolic Size

2 inches. Almost completely shut down.

Quality

"I don't need to know or care where I am. It feels good now, that's all; like I'm in my happy place."

3. Nicholas's Belly Chakra Databank for Sexual Self-Esteem

Symbolic Size

45 feet. Within normal range.

Quality

Feeling more studly than usual.

4. Nicholas's Heart Chakra Databank for Emotional Receiving

Symbolic Size

1/8 inch. Flatlines.

Quality

"I have everything I need; it comes from everywhere."

Smart Spiritual Seeker, have you noticed how this symbolic *size* was shut down? That's what's meant by "flatlines" when used as a size descriptor for a chakra databank. Next, the *quality* of that same databank gives us a second clue.

Unbeknownst to Nicholas, his emotions aren't functioning normally. "It comes from everywhere" refers to how he's noticing energies, not any authentic kind of human emotion.

But doesn't it strike Nicholas as weird if he can't notice human feelings? How could he not notice that energies are different from regular emotions?

Since the Shift, countless people have begun to confuse energies with emotions. This confusion can reflect astral positioning of consciousness at different chakra databanks.

In reality, of course, there are important differences between noticing human emotions versus noticing energies.

5. Nicholas's Third Eye Chakra Databank for Connection to Psychic Guidance

Symbolic Size

30 feet. Within normal range.

Quality

Feeling pleasantly aroused psychically, at that LOW Astral Vibrational Frequency, Nicholas feels high, "spiritually" high.

(Only he isn't having a *spiritual* experience at all. He's having an *astral* experience. Smart Spiritual Seeker, by now it can be simple for you to make this distinction, but Nicholas sure doesn't.)

How I Interpret this Snapshot of Consciousness

Overall, Nicholas feels normal. With his conscious mind, he might describe himself as "pleasantly buzzed." However, we've gained perspective on his subconscious and energetic experience, a perspective more directly related to the truth of his consciousness positioning.

Smart Spiritual Seeker, perhaps it's dawning on you with increasing clarity: Every spiritual teacher today must guide each student's experience of consciousness.

How can it not be a job requirement to help students succeed in that way? In my view, every Enlightenment Teacher must develop skill at researching chakra databanks. Otherwise, all we can do is conjecture. Since I do have good skills with energetic literacy, let me warn you: Smart Spiritual Seeker, not all LOW Astral Vibrational Frequencies feel as pleasant as drinking some fabulous beer.

Fortunately for Nicholas, this snapshot of consciousness reveals that he's having a pleasant type of astral experience. To him, this feels normal — except for feeling slightly better than usual (when his consciousness is positioned at any Human Vibrational Frequency).

Once again, Smart Spiritual Seeker, it's worth noting how effortlessly these shifts happen now, whether due to a recreational substance or related to that irrepressible Consciousness Positioning Superpower.

Developing a Hankering for One Vibrational Frequency

According to my research, it's common for someone like Nicholas to develop the habit of positioning his consciousness at *one particular*

Astral Vibrational Frequency. With repetition, this LOW Astral Vibrational Frequency becomes his new normal, like buying a second home in the country.

Over time a person can turn a favorite Astral Vibrational Frequency into a default for everyday living. This would be akin to moving to that home in the country as a primary residence. Smart Spiritual Seeker, if we're literally talking real estate, that change of address might seem like a swankier upgrade, an improvement to how Nicholas lives.

Only here we're talking consciousness, not real estate — and not necessarily LOW Astral experience from drinking beer, either.

Powered by our new Consciousness Positioning Superpower, folks can habitually experience life with a natural "high" --no substances required. For instance, this happens as an unintended outcome of doing mindfulness meditation.

However, calling this a "high" might make it seem desirable, like an improvement over ordinary human life. It isn't.

In case you're wondering, this kind of "high" should never be confused with Enlightenment. Such an illusion!

In our next chapter we'll explore more useful knowledge concerning spiritual illusions, only we'll hardly take a traditional approach to this topic.

Ironically, many of today's worst illusions for spiritual seekers… come from today's Enlightenment Establishment.

CHAPTER 16.

Overcome Spiritual Illusions

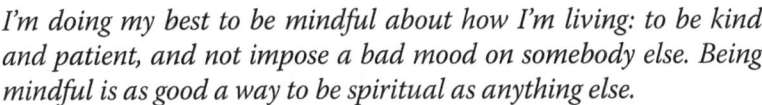

I'm doing my best to be mindful about how I'm living: to be kind and patient, and not impose a bad mood on somebody else. Being mindful is as good a way to be spiritual as anything else.

Deirdre O'Kane, Comedian

....

Mindfulness is one of today's most popular illusions. I agree with Deirdre that following one idealistic illusion is as good a way to "be spiritual" as pursuing any other illusion.

Use your precious time for that, though, only if you don't care about attaining Enlightenment. This you can't reach by seeking to perfect... feel-good illusions.

Rose Rosetree

....

Fresh from exploring our first snapshot of consciousness, yes! Smart Spiritual Seeker, you've begun to see how inner experience changes when a person positions consciousness at a LOW Astral Vibrational Frequency.

Sometimes this process happens as a result of drinking beer but, what happens more often these days? The process occurs substance-free, related to human choices we make, plus the impact of our new Consciousness Positioning Superpower.

Ever since the Shift, invisible astral travel has been done by open-hearted spiritual seekers; happening off-and-on, astral positioning of consciousness randomly mixed in with experiences at Human Vibrational Frequencies. Related to this problem are many other illusions, new ones. You deserve to be warned about all four of today's biggest spiritual illusions.

> *But nonduality teachers tell us that every single thing on earth is an illusion. Why should any of these illusions matter more than others?*
>
> *Because you're seeking Enlightenment now, in the Age of Awakening. I have yet to meet a nonduality teacher who even recognizes that something significant happened with the Shift, let alone has learned good skills of energetic literacy. How can such a teacher be qualified to advise today's spiritual seekers?*

Spiritual evolution is slowed — not hastened — by pursuing illusions, and are there ever plenty of them now! The purpose of this chapter is to protect your progress through a practical education in today's **Spiritual Illusions.** Most are new; not problematic during the Age of Faith, but quite distracting now.

Spiritual illusions and confusions can stall our authentic progress, until we're running full-speed ahead... in a wrong direction that feels very much like a right direction.

Look, trusting your feelings is fine... provided that first you've established some understandings to safely structure your progress. Keep reading to educate yourself about many popular illusions, most of which aren't recognized yet by today's Enlightenment Establishment.

> *How can that be? I think of statues I've seen of Buddha, so wise and so jolly, knowing everything about Enlightenment.*
>
> *During the Age of Faith, you might have been encouraged to love a religious statue or painting, then expecting Jesus or Buddha (or others) to protect you. But you'll be a far better Christian or Buddhist if you stop believing in statues. Talk about illusions!*

A human being made that statue; it's a physical object that exists at a Human Vibrational Frequency. Since you're seeking Enlightenment, it can help you to consider that statue to be beautiful *content,* as distinct from some magical *process*, regardless of whatever you've been told.

Only with magical thinking from the Age of Faith would looking at a statue of Buddha mean that he's watching over you, ever-available to bring you help. Look, that's sweet, like playing with dolls. But in reality, Buddha is like Jesus and other Divine Beings. They're available to help you directly, here and now, once you learn effective skills for cocreating with them.

Otherwise, "being spiritual" by gazing at your favorite statue, or making the sign of the cross? Most likely, that will send you on a bit of a spiritual side trip to an Astral Vibrational Frequency.

But who would purposely choose to take a spiritual side trip?

*Exactly nobody. At least no dedicated spiritual seeker I've ever met. Keep in mind, even when today's side trips occur **accidentally**, they still bring consequences.*

Accidental or not, these side trips are surprisingly common. Smart Spiritual Seeker, one of my goals in this book is to help you to make wise choices. Let's take a tour of three way popular kinds of illusion.

> **FIRST, Maya and Other Old-Fashioned Illusions**
>
> Traditionally, spiritual teachers are known for discoursing on illusions, right? For instance, in the Age of Faith, old-time gurus would teach about **Maya,** a traditional word for spiritual illusions. Likewise, Western religious teachers would warn the faithful about illusions leading to Satan and Hell.
>
> Understandably (and unfortunately) many in today's Enlightenment Establishment still repeat these outdated ideas.
>
> In my opinion, it's very Age of Faithey, telling believers this kind of *content* about illusions; teachings that are emotionally comforting yet otherwise unhelpful; as if grand spiritual illusions were really the causes of all real-life suffering.

Supposedly, "Once you learn about this kind of illusion, you'll go free; all unpleasantness will cease." Alternatively, "Once you purify enough to move into Enlightenment, life's illusions will no longer separate you from God."

SECOND, Religious Illusions

Countless *religious believers* have been taught to think, "The Devil made you do it."

How were believers supposed to counter that illusion?

- Pray for protection.
- Beg God for forgiveness.
- Define God as "A jealous God." So "Become a good, God-fearing believer."

Believing that God wants your fear? Surely that's an illusion.

Likewise, does God possesses some magical *power to forgive you*, which will remove the consequences of your mistakes? That's another illusion.

Expecting God to *protect you* is actually pretty insulting to everybody concerned, since God gave every human a brain and a heart, allowing each of us to make wise choices.

In the Age of Awakening, keep what you love about your religion. But consider discarding obsolete illusions.

THIRD, Enlightenment Teaching Illusions

Traditionally, it has been considered helpful to teach high-sounding theories to Enlightenment seekers, intricate theories such as, "The illusion of darkness exists so that we can learn the true nature of Divine Love."

How, exactly, were believers supposed to benefit from all that illusion-talk? "When you feel bad, know those feelings are just the illusion of darkness. Meditate more."

> Much like religious believers, Age of Faith Enlightenment seekers have been urged to detach themselves from reality, as if that *process* would really prove helpful.
> Long story short, pre-Shift, religious and spiritual illusions might have brought comfort when folks felt homesick for Heaven. But that happy mood came at a price. For example...

Age of Faith Seekers Were Supposed to Doubt Themselves

Under the circumstances, why wouldn't believers learn Catholic guilt, Jewish guilt, Buddhist guilt, Muslim guilt, etc.? Traditional teachings taught seekers to fear illusions.

As a result, spiritual seekers were kept busy with doing what they were told. Intentionally or not, too many religious authorities made trusting souls *dependent*.

But now that we're in the Age of Awakening? Hello, **Spiritual Self-Authority**! That means trusting in what seems true to you.

Today's spiritual teachers can bring you clarity, while helping you to *free yourself up* from illusions. In fact, our Program for Spiritual Enlightenment aims to strengthen your confidence in yourself, while balancing that with reliable knowledge.

Living now, evolving as a Smart Spiritual Seeker, you can safely believe in yourself. However, today's spiritual teachers have a duty to help you overcome today's illusions and, thus, empower you to *steer yourself* in the right direction.

Fact is, since the Shift, spiritual illusions have multiplied like crazy. Many a true believer is working harder than ever... without much discernment, or gaining many real results outside of mood-making.

For example, countless well-meaning folks are working ridiculously hard for one reason that few people dare to admit in public.

Everybody's an Authority Now. (And That's Not Good)

Courageous-and-brilliant religious reformers like Martin Luther... never could have seen it coming. Hundreds of years after the bold

Protestant Reformation, humanity would go through the New Age Years.

Thinning of the Psychic Barrier was accelerating by the day; consequently, people began to access energy on their own, a *process* that resulted in some pretty wacky improvised *content*.

For example, you may remember when the experience of energy sensitivity started to wake up within millions of spiritual seekers. How to make sense out of this *process*? New Age leaders created appealing-appalling *content*, like "Everybody is my mirror" and "Everybody can be a spiritual teacher."

High on their new energy sensitivity, thrilled to be doing Energy Talk, many an otherwise intelligent seeker fell into line and got busy. For instance:

- Trying to grow spiritually by "Learning about what I need to heal" from total strangers.
- Also, we began listening to advice from every random person within earshot.

Before the transitional New Age Years, farther back into the Age of Faith, who was one's source of guidance? The faithful turned to a credentialed member of the spiritual teacher establishment.

Whereas now? Spiritual advice is everywhere, with total strangers "sharing of their wisdom" and getting into the act of advising others on how to "be spiritual." Check out social media and you'll see exactly what I mean.

Or, heck, just reread the quote at the start of this chapter. Does being *kind and patient* really seem like important advice to follow if you're "a spiritual person"?

Hint: Do you have unlimited time every day for spiritual busywork?

> From what I've seen as an Enlightenment Teacher, God doesn't hand out Enlightenment based on who could win a blue ribbon for patience.

In Truth, Dedicated Spiritual Teachers Are Not Hobbyists

No ethical Enlightenment teacher will simply fling around quotes, like offering quickie spiritual tips on Twitter; tips which, zap! Supposedly this is all a person needs to slip into Enlightenment?

Incidentally, what kind of "program" is being offered by folks like that sweet Deirdre O'Kane? Sure, it sounds "spiritual" to "be kind and patient." But beware.

Countless spiritual seekers are frittering away their lives by "being good," earnestly following whatever offhand advice comes their way. Might I suggest? See questionable advice for what it is.

> **Following random advice in order to progress spiritually? That could be the worst spiritual illusion of them all.**

Too many of today's sweet seekers believe that the more tips they follow, and the harder they work, the more they're evolving spiritually. Such an illusion! Yes, an illusion.

Finally, Smart Spiritual Seeker, know that many of today's illusions are unprecedented, leading to spiritual side trips. Speaking of which, let's debunk one last kind of illusion.

FOURTH, New Illusions Related to Consciousness

This category comprises new spiritual illusions related to experiences of consciousness.

As I see it, Smart Spiritual Seeker, these newest illusions began during the transitional New Age Years and are picking up momentum in collective consciousness.

Most likely, brief experiences at higher vibrational frequencies began as a *process*; later, folks improvised reasonable-sounding *content* to explain it.

But there's a simple way to avoid believing in all these new distractions. Did you know this?

Many illusions arise when folks substitute subjective reality for objective reality, and vice versa. So let's get clear about this twofold nature of human reality.

Hello, OBJECTIVE Reality

Here at Earth School, **Objective Reality** is hugely important for experience at Human Vibrational Frequencies. Objective reality includes:

- People, how they look and where they are located physically
- Animals, vegetables, minerals
- Clothes and furniture
- Physical objects of all kinds
- And whether any of them changes position

Also Included

The following aspects of objective reality also are worth noticing:

- Who is *talking*
- Who *says* what kind of thing
- What *moves,* any which way — whether an animal, plant, or some inanimate object

In addition, objective reality includes facts, figures, statistics.

Basically, objective reality includes anything that would show in a YouTube video. Equally important, but totally different, is what?

SUBJECTIVE Reality, Hello

Smart Spiritual Seeker, **Subjective Reality** doesn't show in the same way as objective reality. Although just as real, at Human Vibrational Frequencies the quality of subjective reality is different.

This more personal kind of reality involves your thoughts and feelings; specifically, involving your *surface-level thoughts and feelings*, such as noticing whether you happen to feel happy, sad, scared, or angry.

For perspective, note this. Whenever your consciousness is positioned at a Human Vibrational Frequency, you can notice either objective reality OR subjective reality.

By contrast, when your consciousness is positioned at any Astral or Divine Vibrational Frequency, you can ONLY notice a subjective kind of reality, an energy that is not human at all.

But hey, before we continue, please make sure your seatbelt is still fastened tightly. Ready? Then let's accelerate.

Don't Confuse Subjective and Objective Realities

In the opinion of this Enlightenment Teacher, which are the most influential illusions right now that limit spiritual seekers? These illusions result from confusing SUBJECTIVE reality with OBJECTIVE reality, Energy Talk being only one popular example.

Without warning, folks are doing invisible astral travel (*process*), then generating nice-sounding ideas that are supposed to apply to human life (*content*).

Here's an example, Smart Spiritual Seeker. Ever hear that "Thoughts are things"?

> Please, do yourself a favor. Stop believing that nonsense.
> Thoughts are not things. Thoughts are *subjective*. Things are *objective*.

In human reality, thoughts are definitely not things. Unless you prefer to live in a dreamworld — and, thus, disallow progressing toward Spiritual Enlightenment — please cut that out.

Likewise, don't talk about energies as though they were real-life objective reality, or anything else existing at a Human Vibrational Frequency.

Phew! Maybe Intense, But Good to Know

Quite some chapter, Smart Spiritual Seeker! Congratulations on all the illusion-spotting you've learned to do here.

The rest of our chapters in Part II will educate you further about experiences at different Astral and Divine Vibrational Frequencies. Let's start with learning about one that's pleasantly intoxicating.

And yes, this next way to position your consciousness is usually a big waste of your precious time.

CHAPTER 17.

Pleasantly Intoxicating MEDIUM Astral Vibrational Frequencies

I think hard drugs are disgusting. But I must say, I think marijuana is pretty lightweight.

Linda McCartney, Photographer

....

For most people, marijuana positions consciousness at a MEDIUM Astral Vibrational Frequency. By contrast, cocaine positions consciousness at a HIGH Astral Vibrational Frequency.

If you're seeking Enlightenment, make no mistake: All recreational drugs are heavyweight ways to disconnect from Human Vibrational Frequencies.

Rose Rosetree

....

Yes, marijuana usually positions consciousness at a MEDIUM Astral Vibrational Frequency. How many kinds of vibrational frequencies are we talking about here, under that general category?

Many thousands: The same would be true if we were considering HIGH or LOW Astral Vibrational Frequencies.

Wrap your head around this. Wow, could be mind-blowing! Smart Spiritual Seeker, of course Human and Astral Vibrational Frequencies are ridiculously abundant.

For instance, what if you were studying biology? Quite early on you'd learn that mammals count as different from reptiles. But would that be all you needed to know?

"Hey, I'm a mammal." Would knowing that mean you had no further need to learn about different kinds of mammals? Or would it be enough for you to consider yourself pretty similar to a tiger, a puppy, or a rat? Probably not; altogether there are 5,000 *different species* of mammal on Earth, humans being just one of them.

Nonetheless, when compared with the wider array of Astral Vibrational Frequencies, all the Human Vibrational Frequencies might seem like a modest collection. How ridiculous, then, when folks who do Energy Talk… proudly lump together all that is *astral* or *Divine*, and this is supposed to be super-special; maybe also, "of God."

You can do better, Smart Spiritual Seeker, and frankly you'll need to; at least, if you're seeking Enlightenment in the Age of Awakening. To move forward without taking side trips, it's essential for you to know more, for instance, about MEDIUM Astral Vibrational Frequencies.

Strangely, most of today's spiritual teachers don't yet know what you're about to learn; they're fluent speakers of Divine *content…* while unintentionally leading their students into a random kind of astral *process*.

How can a spiritual seeker like me ever tell the difference?

Fortunately, for practical purposes it's enough to recognize three — just three — overall categories of astral experience; plus, we need to know how to distinguish them from what counts as Divine. Definitely a manageable project!

MEDIUM Astral Vibrational Frequencies, for instance, come with their own distinctive set of illusions-and-confusions. To begin…

How Does It Feel?

Boldly, let's put human flesh on the bones of the MEDIUM astral experience. Just imagine this, Smart Spiritual Seeker. You're hanging out with your adventurous buddy Stephanie. This time, both of you have spontaneously positioned your awareness at a MEDIUM Astral Vibrational Frequency.

How does it feel? One or more of the following might apply.

1. Blissed out, as though "Blissy" is your middle name, describing your *authentic* self.
2. Worries about your weight and appearance dissolve, allowing you to *feel effortlessly gorgeous*.
3. Lighthearted — that seems like the only possible way to feel, as if *everybody ought to be able to live like this, always.*
4. Joy and laughter can overcome you at any time, until *you're giggling with glee*, like a kid.
5. *Brilliant ideas, dazzling creativity*? Somehow, these miracles of insight start happening within you spontaneously; with amazing perceptions dazzling your awareness; fantastically exciting, your every thought is like the world's most colorful butterflies.
6. At times, you're *really getting into color*, as if discovering it for the first time.
7. Sense of hearing deepens too, almost as if you've *grown ears within your ears*.
8. Ordinary touch seems so pitiful compared with what you've got now: *magical* touch, revealing more than you ever dreamed possible.
9. Your senses of *taste and smell and energy...* both separately and also together, your senses can turn downright trippy.
10. *Developing "the munchies"* is a distinct possibility.

How Can Your Consciousness Get Positioned There?

Pretty darned easily, that's how. Given your Consciousness Positioning Superpower, sometimes you might briefly move into this kind of playground experience.

But what's very unlikely? Prior to reading this chapter, it's unlikely that you'd make a realistic assessment, such as, "I've just done something that positioned my consciousness at a MEDIUM Astral Vibrational Frequency."

More likely, you would feel like your usual self — that same person you've always been — only now you're discovering the *real* meaning of life, or *THE* Path, *True* Guidance, how meditation is *supposed* to feel, etc.

Common Ways to Position Consciousness at MEDIUM Astral

With the list that follows, I'm not suggesting one-size-fits-all reactions; the truth is more like what some car ads proclaim about fuel economy: "Your actual mileage may vary."

For instance, one's experience at a MEDIUM Astral Vibrational Frequency would most likely feel enjoyable, verging on surreal. Yet the possibility exists — as with any astral-type experience — that it might also feel more like a nightmare; a bad trip; like a dream you can't wake up from, and it's terrifyingly vivid.

Although the quality of MEDIUM astral-type experiences may not be within your control, what is? Doing any of the following behaviors, most likely, will position your consciousness off-and-on at a MEDIUM Astral Vibrational Frequency. (Up to you to just say no!)

1. Watching *pornography*; happy porn, without cruelty or violence, more like an elaborate sexual fantasy.
2. *Getting a reading* from an experienced psychic.
3. Doing *your own angel card reading* (or Tarot, etc.), and this time it feels as though the cards are taking over, transporting you to the Other Side.
4. During *a group meditation*, it seems as though everybody is feeling the very same thing, and "It's just got to be God."
5. Participating in *a Reiki share*, you begin to put your hands on somebody else's very trippy energy.

6. Teaming up with *a spirit guide*, you're receiving "important" Messages.
7. While *attending a nonduality retreat* (because you're seeking darshan from people who are supposedly Awakened), you open yourself up until the silence around you starts to buzz and shine. Suddenly it feels like, "I'm there!"
8. At church, it's a special occasion, because you're being *slain in the spirit*.
9. Smoking *marijuana*.
10. Drinking *good quality wine*: Ah, it's the good life, and you totally deserve this; everyone does!

You get the idea, Smart Spiritual Seeker. Sometimes this kind of experience is vivid enough for you to tell that you're having "an experience."

Yet it's also possible to dip in-and-out of a quick astral experience, due to your effortless Consciousness Positioning Superpower.

Fortunately, our Program for Spiritual Enlightenment can protect you both ways. Keep reading and you'll learn useful skills for seeking Enlightenment in the Age of Awakening. Even if, like Paul McCartney's wife Linda, in the past you've concluded that weed was no prob.

Linda concluded this based on what? Her vision as a photographer; her wisdom status due to being married to a Beatle; or simply her society's prevailing lack of energetic literacy?

Look, as long as we're questioning misunderstandings that often lead to spiritual side trips...

Let's Dispel Some Illusions about Psychological Work

Why would illusions from pop psychology fit in perfectly with our exploration of MEDIUM Astral Vibrational Frequencies? To begin answering that question, let's clarify this:

What counts as your **Subconscious Mind?** It's deeply inner thoughts and feelings.

- In *psychological* terms, you might value subconscious experience as more important than ordinary thinking.
- In *metaphysical* parlance, subconscious experience means positioning your consciousness at an astral level of life.
- Two sides of one coin — both terms can be used to describe the same subconscious experience.

> Smart Spiritual Seeker, this has huge implications, right? When I first realized this equivalence — how *subconscious* equals *astral* — it rocked my world for a week.

Now that we're living in the Age of Awakening, this equivalence takes on even more significance. Both terms, *subconscious* and *astral*, involve positioning consciousness away from Human Vibrational Frequencies.

And Speaking of SUBCONSCIOUS Reality...

Let's refine a useful concept from our last chapter? Remember the distinction we made between objective reality and the subjective kind? Both are found at Human Vibrational Frequencies. Well, might some MEDIUM astral experiences count as *objective* too?

MEDIUM and HIGH astral experiences can become startlingly vivid, sometimes appearing to be totally real, surreal even; more solid than solid, like monumental truths of objective reality.

Only that's the very definition of a **Hallucination,** right? Picture, for instance, a hilarious moment while your friend Dean is stoned on grass; to him it might seem as though his left hand is having a heated debate with his right hand, both hands talking away!

But hello! However vivid astral experiences may feel, every perception counts as subjective rather than objective.

Definitely that's true of every single thing that a person notices with consciousness positioned at a MEDIUM Astral Vibrational Frequency; psychological work included. For instance, Susie might be working on herself psychologically, analyzing some trauma from five years ago, when it feels to her like, "I'm really getting somewhere."

Only where, in reality, is that "somewhere"? Reno? The North Pole? Nope. Susie might be positioning consciousness at a MEDIUM Astral Vibrational Frequency.

But isn't the point of doing psychological work to help you to find a deeper truth? Something real. Something more real than you've understood before.

Maybe. Sometimes. Nonetheless... Here's what matters for sure.

Seeking Enlightenment? Let These Illusions Go

No matter how much you might love doing **Psychological Work,** it involves positioning consciousness *away* from objective reality.

- Before the Shift, a lot of psychological work may have been done at a Human Vibrational Frequency, where folks would theorize about subconscious experiences (*content*), while not having those experiences directly (*process*).

- However, since the Shift, psychological work often positions consciousness ever-deeper into subconscious-and-astral experience, producing a high that can become quite addictive.

Lacking energetic literacy, who can discern what is happening to Susie's or Dean's awareness?

When they're having experiences that feel so real and important, even sacred, who can tell if this is simply a spiritual side trip?

Mainstream society gives that job to psychologists. Can we really count on mental health professionals for discernment about this kind of thing?

Look, Psychology Is Designed as a Science

When you think about it, scientific sophistication is perfectly compatible with *energetic illiteracy*. But how well can psychologists tell where clients position their consciousness, or what the spiritual consequences might be? Lacking good skills of energetic literacy, frankly, they can't.

Even psychologists in Enlightenment (and there are some) don't have training as Enlightenment teachers.

But neuroscience maps consciousness, no?

Elegant though neuroscience can be, mapping which parts of your brain light up during particular moments? This bears little relevance to preventing everyday consciousness side trips.

For Sure, Psychological Work Impacts Your Consciousness

And not always impacting your consciousness as you've been led to believe! Even when your goal is to do some sensible, productive work on yourself, your consciousness will be off and running… away from Human Vibrational Frequencies.

- "Analyzing yourself psychologically?" That describes *content*.
- How about *process*? Technically, you'll likely land at an Astral Vibrational Frequency.

In case you're wondering, this astral positioning occurs whether you're in session with a professional therapist or else you're on your own, trying to "be your own therapist."

For example, picture that you've just revisited an incident from your childhood, a very traumatic argument that took place when you were seven years old. Though it's extremely uncomfortable, you're willing to probe away, believing in the power of therapy to help you; believing that the more painful your experience, the more you'll "heal."

Not necessarily so — an opinion I've formed after researching chakra databanks of many psychotherapists, as well as others who routinely explore clients psychologically.

Remember the idea of "consciousness lifestyles"? When we explore this further in Part III, be on the lookout for a particular messed-up consciousness lifestyle, one that results directly from doing too much psychological work.

Meanwhile, Smart Spiritual Seeker, let's explore another cause of spiritual side trips, a common problem related to MEDIUM astral positioning of consciousness

Which Lovers of God Could See This Problem Coming?

Thus far in our explorations together, you've learned that astral is not Divine. In theory, at least, you've learned this. However, if your consciousness moves into experience at a MEDIUM Astral Vibrational Frequency, guess what? Usually it *feels* sacred, not astral:

- Possibly, you feel *spiritually blessed.*
- Or you're loving the energy, and definitely feel *in the presence of God.*
- Alternatively, suppose that you've paid to attend a meditation retreat, and here's how you interpret your MEDIUM astral experience: *Oooh, I'm starting to feel detached from everything, a sure sign that I've Awakened."*

Of course, your personal language for astral experiences can be phrased altogether differently from what I've provided here.

The point is, can you recognize having experiences with the heightened sense of "reality" that I'm describing here?

So where does illusion come in? Special feelings don't necessarily mean "Truth." More like, "All this is just so astral."

You Can Live Fine without MEDIUM Astral Illusions

That's the main thing you need to know. Pursuing psychological work feels good, but remember this saying:

"You're free to buy anything you like at God's store. Just remember, you'll have to pay the price."

Smart Spiritual Seeker, thanks for spending some time to order to learn from this chapter. The knowledge you're gaining can help you to appreciate our simple Program for Spiritual Enlightenment, rather than aiming for something with "really exciting energy."

Our next chapter will put icing on the cake of your MEDIUM astral knowledge. When you read our next snapshot of consciousness, you'll gain extra discernment, a discernment that — for the purpose of seeking Enlightenment — matters as much as knowing that humans, puppies, and rats are not interchangeable, even if all of us are mammals.

Similarly, astral experiences are not Divine, simply because we can relate to both as "energy."

Summing up what You've Learned in this Chapter

Smart Spiritual Seeker, dare to recognize the truth value of these counterculture ideas:

1. What some folks might call, "Feeling relaxed and mellow" is NOT Spiritual Enlightenment.
2. Casually positioning consciousness at an Astral Vibrational Frequency doesn't make a person "evolved." (Ironically, this way of dipping into energy awareness can halt — not hasten — that person's spiritual evolution.)
3. What if being relaxed and/or mellow has been your highest ideal? You're welcome to find yourself a new ideal, one that's more worthy of you.
4. After this lifetime, when you're an *astral* being living in a heaven, you'll be plenty relaxed and mellow. For now, make hay while the sun shines, evolving spiritually like a *human*.

5. In truth, the meaning of life is not enhanced by living like a stoner — either with drugs or through superpower misuse, haphazardly positioning consciousness at a MEDIUM Astral Vibrational Frequency.

Of course, there are definite differences between Enlightenment versus positioning consciousness at some random Astral Vibrational Frequency. Undesirable consequences from doing the latter will worsen if a person lingers there for long periods of time every day.

Through snapshots of consciousness, you're gaining discernment about different forms of astral distraction. Our first of these snapshots introduced you to the quality of Nicholas's LOW astral-type experience. Next chapter, we'll explore our second snapshot of consciousness. This one's about Stephanie. Currently she's in love with that MEDIUM astral kind of experience.

Physically, does Stephanie look normal? Sure. However, physical appearance doesn't reveal what happens in a person's consciousness — so don't expect your phone to deliver notifications with that sort of information.

Are you curious, then? What will you discover about illusions related to positioning consciousness at a MEDIUM Astral Vibrational Frequency?

And has the kind of thing going on with Stephanie... been happening to you lately?

CHAPTER 18.

Learn More about A MEDIUM Astral Vibrational Frequency

Heaven... I'm in Heaven.
And my heart beats so that I can hardly speak.
And I seem to find the happiness I seek
When we're out together dancing cheek to cheek.

Irving Berlin, Songwriter, "Cheek to Cheek"

In the Age of Awakening, falling in love can mean spontaneously positioning consciousness where? Often one sweetly positions consciousness at a MEDIUM Astral Vibrational Frequency.

What a feeling! But hello, what happens at a time of infatuation? That experience may not be as Divine as it seems. Your crush hasn't necessarily been sent by God. I think Irving Berlin had it right when he compared falling in love to being "in Heaven" — an astral world.

Rose Rosetree

Is there really much difference between positioning consciousness at a MEDIUM Vibrational Frequency, versus LOW or HIGH Astral Vibrational Frequencies?

Oh yes! In this chapter you'll learn how this particular difference can add up to a pretty big deal — even though your new Consciousness Positioning Superpower can take you there effortlessly, as always.

Smart Spiritual Seeker, allow me to introduce you to our second snapshot of consciousness.

How Does It Feel?

Suppose that you're hanging out with your buddy Stephanie; both of you having positioned your consciousness at a MEDIUM Astral Vibrational Frequency. Whether you're sharing some excellent wine, or a joint... or else the shift in consciousness is due to a breathwork class you both took... or for some other reason. Whatever!

By now, you're both feeling a similar high. And since you've taken a fine photo of Stephanie at the time, easy-peasy! Of course, this Enlightenment Teacher can use that photo as the basis for a snapshot of consciousness.

How does it feel to be Stephanie right now? For one thing, she's wearing sunglasses to protect her newly sensitive eyes. Inwardly her experience feels intense in a familiar way; it's a MEDIUM-level, astral kind of high. Now let's explore the details.

Stephanie's Snapshot of Consciousness

Smart Spiritual Seeker, here's a tip for getting the most out of any snapshot of consciousness: Remember to read it as though it's happening to *you*, not some *weirdly different other* person.

Not that I'm recommending you smoke marijuana, far from it. However, if (for any reason) your consciousness has ever spent even a few minutes while positioned at this same vibrational frequency, then your past experience *might* be similar.

1. Stephanie's Root Chakra Databank for Presence in the Room

Symbolic Size

Out to the moon. (Trillions of miles.) Over-functioning.

Quality

Once again, Stephanie's back on **The Energy Ride**.

Note to you Smart Spiritual Seekers: Stephanie happens to be a pothead, and like many with this hobby, she probably has a pet name for being back THERE. For this snapshot of consciousness about Stephanie, I'll approximate her pet name for this by referring to "The Energy Ride."

Stephanie never knows exactly where The Energy Ride will take her, or how weird she'll feel later, after getting off the high.

All she knows for sure is how thrilling it feels, and how authentic *she* feels, whenever she gets to ride on that energy. It's almost as if God has promised her that riding this way... will teach her the meaning of life.

2. Stephanie's Root Chakra Databank for Connection to Objective Reality

Symbolic Size

14 feet. (On the small side of normal for Stephanie — her normal at the time of this photo.)

Quality

The texture of physical objects has changed, which is one of the ways she can tell that she's THERE. While taking The Energy Ride, Stephanie can touch ordinary things, like a wall; only now she's able to touch things with her "entire self."

Simply by moving her eyes to take a look, she'll travel inside that person or thing, traveling as deeply as she wishes to go, exploring-exploring-exploring.

If Stephanie can remember to move her head, she'll pop out of that adventure; then she can go on to her next one.

Granted, Stephanie doesn't always remember to steer the headlight of her eyes; often she'll keep on noticing the same kind of thing for quite a while.

But as far as she's concerned, whenever she spaces out, lost in a sort of *cosmic beauty trance*, that's only because "I'm supposed to be learning about life right where I am, now-now-now. Everything feels perfect."

3. Stephanie's Belly Chakra Databank for Sexual Self-Esteem

Symbolic Size

2 inches. (Close to shut down for Stephanie, at the time of this photo.)

Quality

Sexual self-esteem comes easy. Actually, Stephanie has no immediate need to get physical with anyone in particular, and why not?

Because she's already feeling the best kind of sexual pleasure; even though she isn't specifically interested in touching anybody right now.

Whatever! In the background, it's still happening: Basically, the skin all over Stephanie's body has turned into one huge erogenous zone for touching the *mystery of life*.

Granted, ever since her teenage years, Stephanie hasn't usually felt sexy enough; sometimes she's even doubted whether she was a good-enough lover.

But now it's different, as though God — or an angel or somebody else very sacred — is telling her The Truth: How totally loveable she is.

By taking The Energy Ride, Stephanie is learning how to feel this good about herself all the time. (Or so she believes.)

4. Stephanie's Heart Chakra Databank for Emotional Receiving

Symbolic Size

Out to the moon. Over-functioning.

Quality

To be honest, right now Stephanie feels like a goddess, like she's become a Cosmic Earth Mother.

Basically, everybody-who's-anybody loves her, which is what she deserves. Graciously Stephanie loves everybody back. That's because she's pure goodness, which happens to be one of the reasons why she is so loveable to everyone else.

Doing nothing at all except being herself, right now Stephanie feels like a huge bouquet of bright shiny balloons, all different colors. So loved and free — which is such a wonderful way to feel!

Weirdly, though, Stephanie kind-of-notices something else. It's in the background, a different kind of feeling, a detachment from any emotion whatsoever. Almost as though she were a *burst* balloon; like a limp, damp, little, dark green fragment of popped balloon.

Very confusing! What with that?

Of course, Stephanie knows that things don't have to make sense when she's high… which is good because sometimes they don't.

To be honest, in the background Stephanie is feeling detached from all people; and that's okay, because she's far too spiritually beautiful for them to appreciate her nearly enough.

5. Stephanie's Third Eye Chakra Databank for Connection to Psychic Guidance

Symbolic Size

75 feet. Somewhat over-functioning.

Quality

This time about 80 of *THEM* are there with her, sitting together, and they're having a kind of picnic. All of them are sitting right there in her mind's eye: Stephanie's cute name for them is **The Wise Guys.**

Again, Smart Spiritual Seeker, folks tend to make up their own special pet names for astral entities, when encountering them often, due to astral consciousness positioning. With repeat experience, such as smoking weed as often as once a year, the presence of discarnate beings within chakra databanks can become very vivid.

Back when Stephanie got stoned the first few times, The Wise Guys didn't come in yet. More recently they do; although their appearance is never predictable. Actually, this figures. The Wise Guys are very important.

Obviously, they decide among themselves which ones will appear at any given time; by now, quite a few "sit in her presence" every time she's stoned. (Very flattering!)

Sometimes all they do is keep her company, which helps Stephanie overcome how she usually feels in her heart of hearts, which is kind of lonely. Other times, like right now, they're whispering special messages, Secrets of Life.

Stephanie appreciates how it's a big honor whenever they come to her, sharing all this. Quite honestly, hanging out with The Wise Guys has recently become her favorite part of getting high.

Somehow Stephanie has this feeling — not exactly sure how she got it, but that's okay — Stephanie has this feeling like God has given her a certain kind of promise: When she's learned enough from The Wise Guys, she can hang out her shingle as a prophetess... or maybe a great healer... or else a world-famous actress.

They're training her for sure. One of these days she'll be able to quit her stupid job and make her life much more important.

How I Interpret this Snapshot of Consciousness

First of all, Smart Spiritual Seeker, Stephanie's relationship with those Wise Guys may have surprised you a bit. Who are they, really? And what does it mean that, technically, they've taken up residence in some of Stephanie's personal, private chakra databanks?

During my sessions with clients, before the Shift, seldom would I encounter that sort of intrusion; yet ever since the Shift, this problem has become increasingly common. Although I don't know everything about it, I do know some things. Here's my current understanding of what's happening with Stephanie.

As you may remember from Chapter 11, astral beings are discarnate spirits, living in astral bodies. This contrasts with human-type bodies, like those we've been given for attending Earth School. Astral beings can easily play around with the aura of any human being who's open to their "guidance." Sounds icky, right? Smart Spiritual Seeker, maybe you're wondering, how can that be allowed to happen?

For context, do you recall what you've learned about the Psychic Barrier? Then you remember how that barrier left for good on December 21, 2012. Once that happened, what was the biggest benefit for you personally, Smart Spiritual Seeker?

The answer would be: your new Consciousness Positioning Superpower. (Soon you'll see how that superpower is going to prove really-really helpful for seeking Enlightenment.) However, it's important for you to know something else that changed with that Shift, something not so lovely.

Building upon What You Already Know

Back in Chapter 11, I introduced you to several different kinds of discarnate beings. Ones at Astral Vibrational Frequencies sometimes like to play around with humans, making us dance (usually figuratively, but sometimes also literally).

In addition, Smart Spiritual Seeker, here's something new. Pre-Shift, the now-disappeared Psychic Barrier used to serve as a kind of keep out sign — akin to an electric fence. In a way, this simplified experience for us humans. Astral entities and ETs couldn't come to Earth for fun whenever they liked.

But Now? Here's the Shocking Truth

After that cosmic keep out sign disappeared, it became super-easy for random astral beings to visit Earth and then play around with anybody they liked… at least, anybody who was interested.

- Back when the Psychic Barrier existed, ghosts had a much harder time getting involved in people's lives.
- But now? **Opportunistic Astral Beings** can easily stick to the *outside* of people's auras. Totally unscrupulous, these astrals know little about being human, yet give advice freely.
- Some opportunistic entities have even developed various arrangements for living inside people's auras.

Most commonly, opportunistic astral beings find it easy to influence us humans whenever we do what? Whenever we regularly position consciousness at a MEDIUM or HIGH Astral Vibrational Frequency.

And Guess What Else? (Shocking But True)

In what context are people vulnerable to astral influences? Smoking weed is just one possibility. For more examples, revisit our last chapter, particularly the list of 10 "Common Ways to Position Consciousness at MEDIUM Astral."

Quite possibly, you might do any of those 10 activities regularly, and thus have developed your own inner language for The Energy Ride.

In which case, please stop interpreting these experiences as "spiritual." Whichever activity results in repositioning your consciousness, it's tempting to believe that you're receiving something pretty darned great. Common misinterpretations include receiving:

1. Wisdom from *your spirit guide*.
2. Answers to your prayers, directly from *Jesus*.
3. Healing assistance from *Spirit* for doing energy medicine.
4. Religious messages, inspired when you're listening to a sermon from *your favorite pastor*. (Remember, Smart Spiritual Seeker, in the background we're still putting together a solution to the Church-Wenters Mystery.)
5. Powerful insights from *your subconscious mind*, through doing brilliant psychological work on yourself.

So Much "Wisdom," Seemingly Divine, but Astral!

Post-Shift, no longer do seekers merely *take classes* or *read scripture*, etc. Given our new superpower, many such activities will also spontaneously position consciousness at a MEDIUM Astral Vibrational Frequency.

With the Psychic Barrier gone, millions of us can easily hear or feel "messages" from astral beings; namely, those who exist at the particular frequency where we've positioned our consciousness; beings who whisper to your subconscious mind; beings with no standards for truth-telling. They have no problem with claiming to be:

1. Your *spirit guide*.
2. Or *Jesus*.
3. Or *Spirit*, helping you heal.
4. Or *your own buried memories* that you're finally uncovering.
5. Or results from the *brilliant psychological healing* that you're giving yourself.

Only not really! Develop good energetic literacy and see for yourself.

Makes Discernment More Important than Ever, Right?

Yay, discernment! That's your protection, Smart Spiritual Seeker. Despite the icky news I've shared with you in this chapter, what's one advantage of following a well-designed Program for Spiritual Enlightenment? You can receive much-needed discernment; new kinds of discernment that are essential, seeking Enlightenment now, in the Age of Awakening.

Constructed with discernment, our program can help you avoid practices that open the door to entities messing with your mind (and aura). Sadly, your Enlightenment Teacher encounters this **Icky Astral Jazz** fairly often.

Simply put, discarnate beings aren't really Wise Ones. These opportunists always have their own agenda. Regardless of whichever lies they tell — yes, you read that right, *lies they tell* — hanging out with discarnates isn't helpful for seekers who feel homesick for Heaven.

Yet activities leading to MEDIUM astral positioning of consciousness seem to be especially appealing to seekers who aim for any of the following:

1. Emotional growth
2. Emotional stability
3. Psychological self-actualization
4. Psychological wholeness
5. Religious purity
6. Spiritual awakening
7. Or — you guessed it — Spiritual Enlightenment.

Smart Spiritual Seeker, no reason to feel discouraged: Just keep reading.

Please, No Worries

Did you find it weird and icky to read about Stephanie in all that detail? Sigh! I can relate. But please don't worry. When you combine our snapshots of consciousness with reliable knowledge about relevant skills that are truly constructive for spiritual evolution, relax! You're helping yourself to move toward Enlightenment... full speed ahead.

With Stephanie's snapshot of consciousness, and more so with another one coming up soon about HIGH Astral Vibrational Positioning, a snapshot that's even ickier...

Simply reading our snapshots, as if they were happening to you, will provide all the detail you need in order to grasp what's involved.

We could say, I did this kind of research — *process* — so that you wouldn't have to; all you encountered in this chapter was *content*. Reading about entities won't cause them to stick to your aura. Hey, if MEDIUM Astral seemed a bit weird to you, next you'll (safely) learn about HIGH Astral. Definitely weirder — maybe get up and take a stretch, then sit down and re-fasten your seatbelt.

CHAPTER 19

The False Grandeur Of HIGH Astral Vibrational Frequencies

We live in a fantasy world, a world of illusion. The great task in life is to find reality.

-Iris Murdoch, Novelist

Amazing Earth School can be a world of illusions or a world of reality. Which will it be for you?

The answer depends on your discernment, and then how you use your freedom of choice. Definitely you can give yourself a chance to pursue — and attain — Spiritual Enlightenment.

-Rose Rosetree

Experience at any HIGH Vibrational Frequency makes you feel *high as a kite*. You do know what that expression means, right?

Smart Spiritual Seeker, if ever you've flown a kite, hasn't it lifted up your heart? While holding the string of your gracefully-moving kite... that colorful kite can look more beautiful to you than any bird or rainbow. Maybe that kite can even cover up your view of the sun and, thus, seem bigger than the sun.

But "high as a kite" doesn't quite do justice to experience at a HIGH Astral Vibrational Frequency. When positioning consciousness there, it can feel as though you *own the sky*. No wonder people can equate this sense of grandeur with the Divine. Though, as you'll soon learn, the term *cheap substitute* would be more accurate.

How Does It Feel?

Boldly, let's put human flesh on the bones of this HIGH astral consciousness positioning. Once again, join me as we imagine together.

Suppose that you are hanging out with your adventurous buddy James. This time, both of you have spontaneously positioned your awareness at a HIGH Astral Vibrational Frequency.

One or more of the following might apply:

1. *You feel Godly*, maybe as promised by your religion.
2. You're feeling downright Lordly, like you've become *one of God's favorites*.
3. *Euphoria* seems to know no limits, and you feel as though it will last forever.
4. A *thrilling giddiness* demands that you develop an interesting kind of balance; otherwise you might feel quite detached from your body and surroundings.
5. As if from high, you look down on regular people. Maybe it seems as though you can *pull their marionette strings*.
6. People who aren't feeling *high* or *blessed* like you right now? Sad! They're missing the purpose of life.
7. Talking to these ordinary people would be such a comedown. It's clear to you how they're so messy and insecure, *ignorant of what's truly important*.
8. Why not simply call this "Feeling superior to all other people"? Because that wouldn't do justice to *the extraordinary-and-gorgeous specialness* of your every thought, every feeling.
9. However, with others who are on your wavelength? Talking to them, even if they're complete strangers, is such a pleasure. Any shyness evaporates; *you feel sure these people can tell how amazing you are.*
10. If other people would only do what you've done, they'd enjoy the same superior experience. *And it's so easy!*

Newfound Abilities

What else can happen when your consciousness is positioned at a HIGH Astral Vibrational Frequency? I've read some descriptions at websites and social media, where people describe feeling as though they've been given special new abilities, such as:

- Turning people into empaths.
- Discovering special powers for healing anybody they like. Maybe preforming miracles? (Like Jesus.)
- Now they can understand the speech of animals.

What Can Position Somebody's Consciousness There?

Overall, any of the following options might set off a HIGH astral positioning of consciousness. Here are some ways this might happen. (Below I'll use italics to suggest where you'd likely give credit.)

1. Being blessed by *a minister or other religious celebrity with special powers.* (Unbeknownst to you, this person is living with a messed-up consciousness lifestyle called Extreme Spiritual Addiction. All you know is, you've been waiting for that special feeling you always get, and now you're starting to feel it again.)

2. Having a reading with *an "amazing psychic"* who always makes you feel so special. (Unbeknownst to you, this person is living with the consciousness lifestyle of Extreme Spiritual Addiction. You've been waiting for that special feeling you always get, and now you're starting to feel it again.)

3. Taking *a growth seminar*, a really popular one attended by thousands. (Unbeknownst to the crowd, your famous teacher is living with the consciousness lifestyle of Extreme Spiritual Addiction. You've been waiting for that special feeling you always get, and now you're starting to feel it again.)

4. Attending *a nonduality retreat, or other meditation event,* hosted by a famous Enlightenment celebrity. (Unbeknownst to you, this person is living with the consciousness lifestyle of Extreme Spiritual Addiction. You've been waiting for that

special feeling you always get, and now you're starting to feel it again.)
5. Having the time of your life at *a rock concert or rave.* (Unbeknownst to you, the famous performers are living with the consciousness lifestyle of Extreme Spiritual Addiction. You've been waiting for that special feeling you always get, and now you're starting to feel it again.)
6. Getting high on *cocaine.*
7. Getting high on *crystal meth.*
8. Enjoying a contact high with *somebody else on cocaine or crystal meth.*

Worth Noting

Recreational drugs act as a gateway to fake-divine experience. In that context, *addiction* to these drugs can make more sense than ever.

Maybe that's NOT news to you. However, you might feel shocked by examples you've just read about being influenced by people in "Extreme Spiritual Addiction." Remember, please, that's an awful consciousness lifestyle, and an avoidable one. For now, you could think of this as a **Fake-Enlightenment** experience — falsely impressing other people as if it were authentic spiritual Enlightenment,

In Part III you'll learn more about today's range of consciousness lifestyles. Already, if you follow the Energy Spirituality™ blog, you may be somewhat familiar with problems coming from Extreme Spiritual Addiction. Gee, maybe this fake enlightenment weirdness can become a clue to help you solve the Church-Wenters Mystery!

Of course, meditation teachers and pastors are hardly the only influencers with this kind of problem.

Witness the story I'm about to share next. It highlights how confusion can arise when a trusted expert brings others a contact high, or appears to be "powerfully connected to God." Although, in reality, the trusting student is being impressed by a person in fake enlightenment.

A Shocking Teaching Tale

Smart Spiritual Seeker, I'm not going to drop the name of this psychic, except to assure you how influential she was; for instance, selling product like crazy wherever she went. Although never a fan, of course I was aware of her work.

What was evident from that work? Although famously clairvoyant, this famous psychic never got beyond Stage 1 Energetic Literacy. Her lack of accuracy as an aura reader helps explain why she regularly mixed up Astral and Divine Vibrational Frequencies; for instance, she told students that the astral beings who helped her... were Divine Beings.

Among this famous psychic's legions of fans and followers were two of my Energy Spirituality™ clients, Rachel and Justin. Separately, each one told me the same kind of "inspirational" story:

"While I was getting a reading with the Amazing Psychic, her Divine presence was so strong that I fainted."

Proof positive, to Rachel and Justin — proof at the time, anyway; proof it seemed to these trusting believers— that this Angel Expert was helping them to stand in the Presence of God.

Curious, I asked Rachel for permission to research what was going on with her consciousness at the time. Incidentally, several years later I researched the consciousness of an Exvangelical Christian who fainted while being "Slain in the Spirit." Same deal!

Before going into details, here's a question worth asking.

> *Does God really make people faint?*
>
> *Of course not. God helps people to wake up spiritually, not to pass out and temporarily lose consciousness.*

That said, what was happening, energetically? While in session with Rachel, the psychic was not positioning her consciousness at the Divine Vibrational Frequency.

More Specifically

By that time in her career, the famous psychic had been living for years in the consciousness lifestyle of Extreme Spiritual Addiction. As a result, discarnate spirits were firmly lodged in her chakra databanks. (Remember Smart Spiritual Seeker, you'll learn more about consciousness lifestyles in Part III.)

Given that psychic's extreme consciousness lifestyle, what happened when she began to give a "spiritual" reading to clients like Rachel and Justin?

The entire room filled up with opportunistic astral entities, some of whom started to infest Rachel's chakra databanks. When she lost consciousness, that served as a kind of protection, according to my research of an "energetic hologram" from that incident.

By fainting, Rachel stopped actively welcoming the "blessing" of what was happening. After she lost consciousness, phew! Her aura shut out the entities. By the time Rachel returned to reality, those entities had cleared out.

Reassuring to Know

Really, if you think about it, why would fainting — that is, temporarily losing consciousness — indicate a Divine blessing? Quite the opposite is true, I assure you. A major reason to seek Enlightenment is to become more awake inwardly, not to blank out.

Let's be clear. Contrary to some people's cherished beliefs, God doesn't take people over. Not while they're kneeling at the church altar. And not because psychics are channeling entities who are supposedly "Ascended Masters."

Smart Spiritual Seeker, by now you appreciate how claims like this amount to false advertising, right?

- *Ascended Masters*, like Jesus and Buddha, don't do **Channeling**, using human beings who are willing puppets; taking those channelers over in order to communicate astral messages at a Human Vibrational Frequency.

⁓ **Archangels** like Gabriel and Michael don't take people over for channeling, either. Period.

Granted, sometimes very aggressive astral beings do try to take human beings over... which I'd call yet one more reason to study with an Enlightenment Teacher who's not energetically *illiterate*.

A *spiritual teacher worth the name* must be able to distinguish astral from Divine; likewise, it helps to know how to facilitate personal **Sessions for Energy Healing,** using cocreation skills with the client's choice of Divine Being, cleaning up a spiritual seeker's aura, removing whichever variety of astral garbage is stuck there.

Speaking of which, Smart Spiritual Seekers, I think you're ready to gain a new-and-practical kind of discernment. After all, this topic is closely related to what you've been reading.

Understand Better Why "Astral Flash" Can Seem Divine

Smart Spiritual Seeker, in Chapter 5 you were introduced to **Astral Flash.** It's an exciting kind of energy baked into certain kinds of experience, *an energy which persuades you that something really important is happening.*

Let's build upon what you know so far by adding more advanced knowledge. When psychics and other influencers have messed-up consciousness lifestyles, astral flash is definitely a factor.

In my view, one reason for that Angel Expert's success was simply this: Her aura was loaded with astral beings at a HIGH Astral Vibrational Frequency. Automatically this brought a great deal of astral flash to her words and body language, as well as her aura.

How impressive is that kind of thing? Quite similar to a Las Vegas performer who wears outfits designed to be ridiculously eye-catching — think, "Clothing that's more like a costume, outrageously gaudy."

Many celebrities and influencers benefit from their Extreme Spiritual Addiction, since the resulting astral flash can amplify their success... success of a certain kind, at least; counter-productive for Enlightenment but appealing to children and other innocents.

By comparison, influencers don't seem nearly as exciting if their auras are only jumbled up with entities at MEDIUM Astral

Vibrational Frequencies. Even less alluring are auras where the astral-dazzle comes from beings at a LOW Astral Vibrational Frequency.

Seeking Enlightenment, Use Discernment

Smart Spiritual Seeker, your glorious new Consciousness Positioning Superpower can help you more when supplemented with the discernment that follows.

Of course, it won't be necessary for you, personally, to research the chakra databanks belonging to religious leaders, spiritual teachers, and the like.

Instead, this chapter has increased your *practical* human-type discernment. Sadly, in these early years of the Age of Awakening, many sweet seekers are easily fooled.

- Excitedly, they believe that fainting means: *How spiritually impressive that psychic or pastor is!*
- Rather than a smarter response, which would be: *Flee from that famous influencer's astral flash.*

From this chapter, one of your takeaways can be to question today's religion and spirituality, healing and meditation, and other forms of self-help. Because successful influencers often have auras loaded with unscrupulous astral beings, similar to the ones in that Angel Expert's aura.

Fact is, a high degree of astral flash brings fame to influencers, whether in the role of teacher or healer or pastor, etc. Even if these influencers happen to be sweet, well-meaning people, their advice will take you on a spiritual side trip.

Knowing *where not to go* can surely help you, even if this topic isn't as pleasant as dreaming about *where you'd like to be headed.*

Our next chapter will be helpful (even if somewhat sobering) since you'll be reading *content* about one person's *process* of having consciousness positioned at a HIGH Astral Vibrational Frequency.

Fear not. As always, when you read about a snapshot of consciousness, phew! This isn't a *process* that will cause you, personally, to duplicate that experience. Reading useful *content* is just reading.

CHAPTER 20.

Learn More about A HIGH Astral Vibrational Frequency

Illusion is needed to disguise the emptiness within.

Arthur Koestler, Author and Journalist

....

Which matters more to you, God or pretty illusions that you've been taught in God's name? (Or have you been clinging to the austere illusion of emptiness?) Consequences will flow from your choice.

Rose Rosetree

....

For our next snapshot of consciousness, you'll be learning about Rev. Carlton, an enormously influential pastor. You could say, he's gone off the deep end, the HIGH astral end, of the consciousness swimming pool.

As a result, he's living more like a puppet than like a person. Who runs him? Sadly, he shares his aura with a gang of astral beings. And it's not just any relatively low-key entities at LOW Astral Vibrational Frequencies, nor the crowd living at MEDIUM Frequencies.

Rather, Carlton collaborates daily with entities at a HIGH Astral Vibrational Frequency. They cause him to feel high as a kite, even "godly."

Does this consciousness lifestyle have a name? Yes, and by now you know it. That name is "Extreme Spiritual Addiction."

Look, I could have researched chakra databanks of a person with a nicer consciousness lifestyle, somebody photographed during a "fabulous meditation class" or receiving a "powerful" psychic reading.

Why did I choose somebody with a long-term experience of consciousness influenced like Carlton's? Because of one more spiritual illusion that I'd like to help you smash.

After the Age of Faith, "Surrender" Is No Longer Smart

Absolutely, surrender and obedience were highly respected during the Age of Faith. Think about your oldest relatives, those born toward the end of that long, long era.

Whatever faith they believed in, wasn't surrender considered the ultimate sign of goodness, spiritual goodness?

And not only in Western religions: Equally this has been true of Hinduism, Buddhism, and other Eastern religions where Enlightenment has been taught for thousands of years.

I remember Charlie, a friend of mine from the years I spent teaching Transcendental Meditation. Charlie could tell that he was drawing ever closer to Spiritual Enlightenment, so he decided to document his sacred transition by writing diary entries about his progressive willingness to relinquish his personal sense of self forever.

After he moved into **Traditional Enlightenment,** my friend shared that diary with me. How beautiful it was, how honest and loving! Charlie was surrendering all that remained of his personal ego.

Important to note, this kind of surrender doesn't apply to **Age of Awakening Enlightenment,** the newer kind available now. Indisputably, though, total selflessness is still required for Traditional Enlightenment.

Back then I thought that surrender like Charlie's was the ultimate in spiritual beauty. In addition, I had other friends who lived in that blessed state of surrender, witnessing their human lives with utter detachment.

- Unfortunately, a few years after the Shift, what happened to every one of those friends? (Charlie included.)
- Sadly, something similar happened to some of the world's most famous-and-trusted Enlightenment Teachers.

↬ What happened, in different ways, to these beautiful spiritual devotees who achieved Age of Faith-style surrender?

Powered by bliss, and caring far more about their consciousness than about human life — in the Age of Awakening that surrender became a problem.

Of course I don't know specifics about deeply personal choices made by world famous members of the Enlightenment Establishment. But I do know what happened to different friends of mine, some of whom were very close friends back in the day.

In general, these beautiful souls made one Energy Talk choice after another, choices that turned out to be unwise, choices based in belief that noticing energies was equivalent to noticing God.

Unbeknownst to them (or their teachers) their consciousness lifestyles shifted away from Traditional Enlightenment... and into Extreme Spiritual Addiction.

Unknowingly Surrendered to Discarnate Beings

Tragically, that's the common denominator. How could such a thing happen? Because these lovers of God didn't know better. Nor did their spiritual teachers, leaders of today's Enlightenment Establishment.

In these early years of the Age of Awakening, I'd estimate that millions of devoted spiritual seekers — and even spiritual *finders* — having reached Traditional Enlightenment, have wound up moving into the consciousness lifestyle of Extreme Spiritual Addiction.

Heartbreaking! I think of these beautiful lovers of God as **Casualties of the Shift.**

Leaders of today's Enlightenment Establishment never warned them:

"You're not really having sacred experiences of evolving within Enlightenment. Discarnate beings are playing with you."

Chapter 20. Learn More about a HIGH Astral Vibrational Frequency 199

Loyal to what they learned in the Age of Faith, neither these spiritual teachers nor their students have developed good skills of energetic literacy.

Consequently, these lovers of God couldn't protect themselves from today's new-and-unique consciousness challenges, such as astral beings turned opportunistic after the Psychic Barrier vanished.

For today's Smart Spiritual Seekers, energetic literacy matters. This Enlightenment Teacher has learned from decades of consciousness research, cocreating additional skills that have increased my discernment, allowing me to discover what has been going on; then cocreating effective strategies for countering this kind of mess.

Let's be clear. Smart Spiritual Seeker, am I now training you to gain energetic literacy skills?

Not here: You're seeking Enlightenment in the Age of Awakening. In particular, you're learning essentials to help you succeed at our Program for Spiritual Enlightenment. For now, that's our scope of work and, for now, that's plenty.

In that context, I encourage you to question the obsolete illusion that spiritual surrender to "higher beings" is always a good thing.

.....

Many of today's religious leaders, as well as meditators, yoga teachers, tai chi masters and more... they've been surrendering alright. Only that traditional kind of surrender hasn't brought them Enlightenment at all but, instead, a spiritual side trip.

.....

In this chapter, you'll read a typical example. Personally, I've researched hundreds of auras like these (out of many thousands of folks with much better consciousness lifestyles).

How about this, Smart Spiritual Seeker? When you read our next snapshot of consciousness, while reading it — or rereading it — consider how Reverend Carlton's once beautiful surrender to "spiritual" energy might have led his aura to turn so ugly. Okay, back to the usual sequence for our snapshots of consciousness.

This time, yes, you're learning about the typical *process* of long-term experience at a HIGH Astral Vibrational Frequency...

How Does It Feel?

First of all, this much isn't new: Thanks to his Consciousness Positioning Superpower, Carlton is experiencing himself and everyone else as if they're all "normal." Despite having his consciousness positioned at a HIGH Astral Vibrational Frequency, far as he knows, everybody he sees is miraculously connected to God.

Fair warning: As you read further details about Carlton's messed-up chakra databanks, you may be as shocked as I was at first — particularly since this man is such a successful religious leader. Nonetheless, most likely, what I'm about to describe seems to him like "business as usual." Indeed, he may believe that he's always "about the Lord's business."

Also, in case you find this fact interesting, for this particular snapshot of consciousness, I'm researching a screenshot from one of Carlton's highly successful YouTube videos. The pastor is in his glory, preaching to believers. Without further ado, let's explore an array of his chakra databanks, one at a time, our usual set for doing snapshots of consciousness. Plus, this time I'll be adding a highly relevant *extra* chakra databank. You'll see.

1. Carlton's Root Chakra Databank for Presence in the Room

Symbolic Size

Out to the moon. Over-functioning: Trillions of miles.

Quality

Carlton's human personality recedes far into the background. In the foreground what shows? Innumerable astral entities live within his aura, excitedly playing around, creating a great deal of astral flash

— as if throwing glitter to human observers. No question, this particular group of discarnate beings... exists at a HIGH Astral Vibrational Frequency.

2. Carlton's Root Chakra Databank for Connection to Objective Reality

Symbolic Size

Out to the moon. (Trillions of miles.)

Quality

Appreciating human reality on earth as quaint.

To Carlton, life seems like a truly enchanting playground that should be monitored by pastors like him.

You see, Smart Spiritual Seekers, by now his normal sense of self has given way to a different version, one more typical of the consciousness lifestyle of Extreme Spiritual Addiction. Basically, he now relates to people as if he were *a more advanced kind of being*. Inwardly, Carlton's view of people is dominated by the discarnates who run him now.

These beings are astral, neither human nor Divine. Research into Carlton's Root Chakra Databank for Connection to Objective Reality reveals what? His entities are having great fun, bringing their exotic allure to Carlton's role as an influencer. To the extent that Carlton has much subconscious (or conscious) clarity about his current way of life, he interprets this *process* as if, "I'm becoming more godly every day."

3. Carlton's Belly Chakra Databank for Sexual Self-Esteem

Symbolic Size

Out to the moon. (Trillions of miles.)

Quality

As if godlike, Carlton appears to be tremendously exciting and very, very special.

4. Carlton's Heart Chakra Databank for Emotional Receiving

Symbolic Size

Out to the moon. (Trillions of miles.)

Quality

Even though Carlton still has his original Heart Chakra Databank for Emotional Receiving, he no longer feels human emotions — quite typical for any human being with this consciousness lifestyle.

Currently, what Carlton receives at this chakra databank is about energy, not human emotions. At this time he feels all-powerful, as if able to move human beings around like pieces on a chessboard. Such an amazing thrill, a lordly kind of superiority!

5. Carlton's Third Eye Chakra Databank for Connection to Psychic Guidance

Symbolic Size

Out to the moon. (Trillions of miles.)

Quality

Carlton feels as though he deserves to receive all this guidance. As a spectacularly holy servant of God, he's being rewarded with a special kind of mastery over other believers. In general, the man is in perpetual high, as if his faithfulness to the Lord has made him "a miracle-bringer."

What more can I tell you about what I'm finding in this chakra databank? Very likely, Carlton believes that everything happening to him... comes straight from God. After all, he's a pastor.

But think about this, Smart Spiritual Seeker: What is the name of this chakra databank? Uh-oh, it's "Connection to *Psychic Guidance*," a name that's useful for all of us to keep in mind.

What's the purpose of this particular chakra databank? It's for receiving advice and help from *discarnate beings* — beings that now dominate all of Carlton's chakra databanks, to the extent of trillions of miles each.

No wonder, Carlton feels "godly," as if he's constantly blessing people; blessing them through his breath and words and energy.

Only this is astral energy, not Divine. As you know, there is a difference.

6. Carlton's Third Eye Chakra Databank for Connection to Spiritual Source

> Note: In this snapshot of consciousness, as well as our last one in this book (about experience at the Divine Vibrational Frequency), yes! I'm expanding the scope of our aura research to include this additional Third Eye Chakra Databank. "Connection to Spiritual Source" reveals the current quality of a person's relationship with God.

Smart Spiritual Seeker, what's going on there now, in this moment, for Carlton?

Since he's a professional minister, his connection to God might prove quite relevant, don't you think?

Symbolic Size

1/8 inch. In shutdown.

Quality

From Carlton's perspective, he's impressed by how much he helps his flock to "experience the Lord." The high he feels is a sign of his faithful service to God; fulfilling his Destiny to lead his flock. Yes, *he's totally satisfied* with his connection to the Divine.

How I Interpret this Snapshot of Consciousness

Ick, such a mess! Smart Spiritual Seeker, I hope you'll remember this example in general… long after the unpleasant details recede from your memory. Carlton's snapshot of consciousness may be the first you've seen yet where a consciousness lifestyle involves a man's sharing his aura with numerous discarnate entities.

Sadly, this kind of thing happens to every single person living the consciousness lifestyle of Extreme Spiritual Addiction. Of course, the person's beliefs may be different from Carlton's.

Likewise, he or she will always have unique experiences at the level of chakra databanks. However, let me give you the benefit of my research. What holds true for hundreds of people with this consciousness lifestyle, people whose chakra databanks I've researched in detail?

In Extreme Spiritual Addiction, all the following is quite standard:

- Regarding a person's Third Eye Chakra Databank for Connection to *Psychic Guidance*? It's over-functioning and jammed with discarnate spirits.
- Meanwhile, about that person's The Third Eye Chakra Databank for Connection to *Spiritual Source*? It's under-functioning to the point of being either puny or else completely shut down. How much interest remains in God? Zero.
- Please reread the final word at the last bullet: Interest in God is *zero*. Quite consistently, people in Extreme Spiritual Addiction have zero interest in God.

⌒ As a Smart Spiritual Seeker, does it seem to you that a teacher's total disinterest in God would be a plus?

Keep in mind, no consciousness lifestyle, including Extreme Spiritual Addiction, just happens to a person. In Chapter 28 you'll learn more about this. Meanwhile, please know this.

You Can Protect Yourself from this Kind of Mess

In fact, our Program for Spiritual Enlightenment is designed to protect you, while helping you to move full speed ahead toward self-actualization.

But what if you're reading out of curiosity, intending to study with a different spiritual teacher, highly skeptical as you browse through my book? I'm hardly the only spiritual teacher in this world. When choosing yours, aim for a *process* that authentically helps you, not merely sweet-sounding *content*.

Also, let's be crystal clear about this. Enlightenment in the Age of Awakening *never* means being anyone's puppet.

Divine Beings would never take over an incarnated soul in human embodiment.

By contrast, what happens when members of the Enlightenment Establishment lack discernment? They're easily seduced by the astral flash.

> As you'll recall, the higher the astral frequency of the discarnate being involved, the more that person's experience appears "*spiritual*." But in truth, what's happening is really *astral*.

Smart Spiritual Seeker, even if you've encountered Extreme Spiritual Addiction many times by now, it still can feel disgusting to read about it.

Why have I bothered to tell you about something so unpleasant? Simply put, I'm committed to helping you to move full-speed ahead toward Spiritual Enlightenment. Preferring to "stay positive" and avoid mentioning this kind of side trip? I wouldn't be doing my job, that simple.

In Conclusion

Why is Carlton's example worth noticing? Because his messed-up aura is hardly unique. Far from it.

Granted, positioning consciousness at a HIGH Vibrational Frequency doesn't always lead to such a mess. For instance, let's use the example of a different person — let's call him "Benny" — who gets high on cocaine. He does this just once, then stops forever.

If Benny really stops using that drug, it's possible for him to move forward and lead a normal life, in terms of his consciousness.

But what if he develops a cocaine addiction? Since he's living in the Age of Awakening, most likely, Benny will develop the consciousness lifestyle of Extreme Spiritual Addiction. Recovery will become starkly difficult, since it can feel excruciating to give up all that astral flash.

One more thought before our next couple of chapters, where we'll proceed to explore a far more inspiring topic.

Smart Spiritual Seeker, do you remember how, as a side project, we've been engaged in solving the Church-Wenters Mystery? In this chapter you've seen a snapshot of consciousness about a highly influential pastor. Sure, his super-exciting aura will subconsciously reach all churchgoers. Some will be greatly impressed by all that astral flash, but not others.

Even without consciously knowing what upsets them, some churchgoers may find various excuses to put off going to church. Would you blame them? I sure wouldn't.

No question, this particular group of opportunistic astral beings… exists at a HIGH Astral Vibrational Frequency. Seems to this Enlightenment Teacher, astral discarnates shouldn't be running the auras of church leaders, not if that religion aims to honor God.

CHAPTER 21.

Attention Spiritual Seekers: Astral Is NOT Divine

I hope you don't mind if I tell you this, but I consider that I am God.

Amelia, a One-Time Energy Spiritualty Client.
(Turned out, she was a fan of psychedelic "Magic Mushrooms.")

Drug experiences don't authorize people to call themselves "God."

Nor do other experiences of astral flash. Positioning your consciousness at the Divine Vibrational Frequency is an altogether different experience, bringing gratitude and humility, never arrogance.

Rose Rosetree

Phew! Finally we've completed our general survey of the main ways to position consciousness at an Astral Vibrational Frequency. By the end of Part II we'll devote a couple of chapters to exploring experiences at the Divine Vibrational Frequency. Yum!

Before then, this chapter adds some useful info for educating you further about astral experiences.

Expect knowledge that's directly relevant to seeking Enlightenment in the Age of Awakening; more knowledge than you've probably assumed was necessary; knowledge that may turn out to be more important than you're assuming right now; in fact, this last bit of astral education could prove very helpful for protecting you from spiritual side trips.

For example, this discernment chapter can prevent your going sideways, especially if you're still feeling a bit homesick for Heaven.

Already you know that I've gained a fair amount of experience over the past 50 years, having helped many students to move closer to Spiritual Enlightenment or even achieve it.

Along the way, I've encountered many a beautiful spiritual seeker who has taken a side trip, convinced that some astral experience or other... was Divine.

Smart Spiritual Seeker, to you, all this might sound theoretical. But I'll tell you this: Some of what I've witnessed has broken my heart. Afterward I would rededicate myself to learning more, serving clients more effectively; yet these failures still count as some of the greatest pain in my life.

As I remind folks from time to time at the Energy Spirituality™ Blog, I'm no mere theorist. Part II gives you the benefit of info that can protect you, increase your discernment, help you to succeed. Both of us would prefer that, right?

About being homesick for Heaven, in your sweet eagerness (or even, perhaps, desperation) many of you might be tempted to lower your standards a bit. At some time, you might feel temped to settle for astral flash... rather than holding out for real-deal Divine.

Therefore, this chapter is dedicated to giving you a discernment inoculation against today's mainstream religious-and-spiritual illusions. You can do better than these illusions and confusions. I'm here to help.

Astral Flash Alert

Astral is NOT Divine. Gain. That. Clarity. Now.

When seeking Enlightenment in the Age of Awakening, clarity about astral flash will serve you well. To begin, let's revisit what you've learned so far, given what you've read in snapshots of consciousness.

Given humanity's new Consciousness Positioning Superpower, it's no longer unusual for a person's awareness to move from one vibrational frequency to another; this process feeling so normal that we're clueless that it's happening at all.

Ignorance is bliss, they say. But I assure you, this kind of ignorance will never lead to sacred bliss, not for those of us who are seeking Enlightenment now. In order to make authentic progress, it can help to understand *why* astral is not Divine. In theory, positioning your consciousness at the Divine Vibrational Frequency might not seem unique, but it sure is.

Smart Spiritual Seeker, have you noticed a progression so far with our snapshots of consciousness about LOW, MEDIUM, and then HIGH Astral Vibrational Frequencies?

Each one feels more special than the last, leading many a spiritual seeker to mistake fake enlightenment for the real deal.

I don't get it. Why can an astral-type experience feel so very special, even connected to God? How can it feel that way when astral is supposedly so different from Divine?

Astral flash, that's why.

So let's explore what I call "**Astral Flash**."

Your Biggest Obstacle for Seeking Enlightenment Now

In my opinion, that obstacle is seeking astral flash. Why can this become such a big problem? Let's begin by summarizing what you know so far.

Smart Spiritual Seeker, remember how, back in Part I, you learned that astral flash means feeling an exciting kind of energy *which persuades you that something really important is happening?*

Nonetheless, that special feeling results from positioning consciousness at an Astral Vibrational Frequency, nowhere close to the Divine.

Related to that, what else have you learned?

> The higher your positioning of consciousness — within an Astral Vibrational Frequency — the more alluring it seems: extra-flashy (as in extra-astral-flashy).

Subconsciously charismatic, you could say. Taking this further, suppose that *your* consciousness is positioned at a HIGH Astral Vibrational Frequency.

For example, suppose that you're attending a spiritual retreat; just about everyone there has this same positioning of consciousness right now.

To you, most likely, everybody attending that retreat will seem beautiful and wise.

By contrast, what's it like to perceive those very same people when your consciousness is positioned at the Divine Vibrational Frequency?

Lovely, all of them, but so is everyone else in the world; so you would feel nothing especially enticing while these folks wear their big blissful smiles. Nothing spiritual significant is going on, so why all those Mona Lisa smiles?

Pretty Tricky, Actually

Most of us would expect experience at the Divine Vibrational Frequency to be the attention-getter, not some astral distraction.

But look, Smart Spiritual Seeker; already you've been warned in general about astral flash. Now I'm warning you in particular: When it comes to positioning consciousness at a HIGH Astral Vibrational Frequency, it is the ultimate in astral flash. Talk about illusions!

However compelling astral *anything* feels, it ain't Divine. This idea can take some getting used to. But beware flashy imitations of God, Smart Spiritual Seeker.

Don't believe for a moment that a teacher who makes you "feel something strong" is necessarily helping you.

> Suppose that you yearn for the spiritual equivalent of a long, happy marriage to God. How wise would it be to "prepare" by dating strippers?

Surprise? Almighty God Doesn't NEED to Do Flashy

Hey, Smart Spiritual Seeker, I don't know everything. Nonetheless, I've learned from thousands of sessions when I cocreated with Divine Beings like God, the Holy Spirit, Jesus, Buddha, Kwan Yin, St. Germain, Krishna, and other real-deal Divine Beings.

Sessions like these authentically helped my clients, as in the Age of Faith saying, "You will know them by their fruits."

Actually, since we happen to be living in the Age of Awakening, I'd like to update that traditional saying: "You will know them by their fruits, *not their flash*."

In order for you to receive good fruits as you seek to evolve spiritually, look! It won't hurt if you develop realistic expectations regarding Divine experience:

- How does it feel when your consciousness is positioned at the Divine Vibrational Frequency?
- Likewise, how does it feel once you cross the threshold into Spiritual Enlightenment?
- Either way, expect to feel whole; that is, whole but not dazzled. Compared with God, nothing else that you could experience... is simpler.

Consciousness at the Divine Vibrational Frequency

How might it feel, if not flashy? **Perfection Everywhere Now** is my favorite description. Credit for these words goes to Ann P. Meyer, founder of The Teaching of the Inner Christ. For a fuller description of what might happen, I'll add these examples:

Suppose that your eyes are *closed*. For a period of time (maybe seconds) your awareness feels big, expanded, and vibrating along with the presence of God.

1. Perhaps you will feel or see the so-familiar presence of Divine Light.
2. Or you might feel uplifted by Divine Love.
3. Alternatively, you might feel strengthened by Divine Power.
4. Either way, that formless form is filling you, surrounding you, soothing you.

Please give us more examples. This kind of experience is what I want.

Fair enough.

Another Example, at the Divine Vibrational Frequency

This time, imagine that your eyes are *open*. Although you might be alone, alternatively you might be in a room with plenty of other people.

Either way, for a few seconds, it might feel to you as though you have — in a way — disappeared. As if, at a big-and-magnificent distance, you're witnessing yourself there in that room. In which case, what matters more to you than any human thing whatsoever?

Yes, something might seem far more important than where your physical body happens to be right now. What matters is this: Where you are (mostly) instead.

That's because where-and-what-you-are has become very big; also, formless. Words couldn't do it justice. Actually, that's fine. You have no need for words, since you are simply being.

Alternatively

Smart Spiritual Seeker, another possibility is feeling the super-abstract, yet concentrated, **Creative Intelligence** of the Divine. Giving credit where it's due, that phrase comes from another teacher I've studied with, Maharishi Mahesh Yogi.

You see, Creative Intelligence is an excellent term for the impact of the Divine. To me, this means limitless creativity and also intelligence, dancing with all possibilities; allowing you to explore potential as pure as a vast landscape covered in fresh snow — only bigger than any human landscape could possibly be.

Once spiritual seekers move into Enlightenment, that creative intelligence is expressed our everyday lives. You could call that, "When Divine love, light, and power can strongly inform life at Human Vibrational Frequencies."

Although usually teachers like me simply talk about "Using your full potential in life."

Same thing, really.

All Experience at the Divine Vibrational Frequency...

What does it have in common? That Divine connection will welcome you, accept you, and gently transform you.

You'll find, Smart Spiritual Seeker, when your consciousness is positioned at the Divine Vibrational Frequency, being yourself takes no effort at all. Even the routine blinking of your eyes would take far more effort.

Thus far, as promised, this bridge chapter has brought you some well-deserved inspiration. Now it's my job to balance that by providing you with some practical warnings.

How WON'T Your Consciousness Get Positioned There?

First of all, please understand this principle: Wishing doesn't make it so.

For example, Kim might feel really-really homesick for Heaven, so she gives a heartfelt prayer to feel more connected to God. Absolutely, she really-really means it.

But does Kim's ardent prayer guarantee that she will receive what she's seeking?

Suppose that she has zero skills for positioning her consciousness at the Divine Vibrational Frequency. Will God make up the difference? You know, because God is nice?

This kind of wishey-hopey expectation was quite common during the Age of Faith, becoming especially rife during the New Age Years. Unfortunately, the answer is *nope*; at least, *highly unlikely*.

By now, Smart Spiritual Seeker, you know why. When it comes to positioning consciousness, emotional *content* doesn't guarantee *process*. Neither do stories from scripture nor other inspiring spiritual *content*.

- And speaking of wishing-hoping-thinking-and-praying, how likely are you to casually position consciousness at the Divine Vibrational Frequency?
- For example, suppose that you're hanging out with your friend Gwen. Maybe she's got a reputation for being "very highly evolved." Will that fix things for you?
- Again, nope. Sorry. Befriending somebody in Enlightenment isn't like palling around with some big shot in the mafia.

But, but, but...

Maybe That Doesn't Seem Fair

Especially if you grew up before the Shift, faith was supposed to fix everything, right?

Even if that didn't happen for you, personally? Okay, right, maybe you remember this part, how we spiritual seekers would often blame ourselves, feeling as though we'd been shamefully excluded, deprived of what all others received, due to their superior faith.

Regardless, Age of Faith obedience won't work well any more, even if you're good at it, not if you're seeking authentic spiritual awakening.

That doesn't seem fair. You say I'm living in the Age of Awakening. Shouldn't things come easier now, spiritually?

Good question. Let's return to the example where you're hanging out with your "highly evolved" friend Gwen. Couldn't something beautiful pass between Gwen and you, like a spiritual awakening in the form of a contact high?

Look, it's important to get this straight. Hanging out with that friend Gwen will NOT position *your* consciousness at the Divine Vibrational Frequency.

Why not? Because, Smart Spiritual Seeker, that experience involves a *process*, not a mood due to feel-good *content*.

Nor can you and your friend sense Divinity together... like some cosmic kind of shared sexual electricity.

Nor will you position consciousness at the Divine Vibrational Frequency just because you and Gwen are having a great conversation about religion.

Remember, *process* is different from *content*. Positioning consciousness at the Divine Vibrational Frequency happens only as a *process*.

Other Pretty Ideas that Don't Bring Divine Experience

But-but-but suppose that you meet a person who's supposed to be "There"? Like yoga teacher Amber, who seems to have such good vibes, and she's got this charming way of walking slowly with lips curved into a sweet, private smile. Oh, that Amber! She seems utterly at peace.

Suppose that Amber perfectly matches your ideal of being in Spiritual Enlightenment. Doesn't that mean you can **Catch a Vibe** from her? (That would be today's version of the Age of Faith ideal called "**Darshan**" — meaning that, supposedly, Spiritual Enlightenment is contagious.)

Let's live in reality, folks. Spiritual Enlightenment is given by God. Not caught like the measles, only prettier.

What can — and can't — we catch when it comes to consciousness?

Smart Spiritual Seeker, all of us humans share certain kinds of experience, due to having human bodies, our animal-type bodies.

You know, our physical bodies set off many connection experiences, such as "catching a yawn" while we're with others in a stuffy room.

By contrast, experiencing at the Divine Vibrational Frequency is possible only because *we humans are animals, but we're also much more than animals.*

Specifically, let's be clear: No other kind of animal living on earth can experience the process of transcendence, or positioning consciousness at the Divine Vibrational Frequency.

Also good to know: Generally, we humans have our clearest experience of the Divine during Technique Time, not some random digital time that you see if you're checking your phone to find the "sacred number" 11:11.

(Participation in the 11:11 fad being a tipoff that one is an astral enthusiast.)

What exactly is this so-important **Technique Time**? Simply this: Technique Time is dedicated time, when you do a wisely chosen activity; its purpose being emotional growth and/or spiritual awakening.

Note that "Technique Time" is a term of art in Energy Spirituality™. For sure, it's going to be very important as part of our Program for Spiritual Enlightenment, but why?

Experiences of the Divine Don't Happen ON DEMAND

Even your new Consciousness Positioning Superpower doesn't guarantee Divine-level experience. Think of Spiderman, practicing his ability to cling to walls. Does that also mean he can do magic tricks?

1. Unless you're doing a form of Technique Time that's designed expressly to help you position consciousness at the Divine Vibrational Frequency
2. AND you're doing that technique correctly
3. AND it happens to work for you at this particular time
4. What will happen?

Pretty unlikely that you'll win that particular prize! Speaking of which...

You Might Want to Ditch the Notion of Darshan

So Age of Faith! If darshan ever worked as advertised during the Age of Faith, that fabled *contagious high* sure doesn't happen now, in the Age of Awakening.

Instead, what's far more likely? Regarding most peoples you think are in Spiritual Enlightenment... sigh!

In the first place, their consciousness lifestyle isn't contagious. Second, those spiritually sexy people are probably not in Enlightenment.

So sorry, but this is hardly a statement I'm making lightly. **Discerning Who's in Enlightenment** requires some technical training. Along with good skills of energetic literacy, supplemented by specialized knowledge about aura-level characteristics of Spiritual Enlightenment — besides both these skills, what else is required?

Discerning Enlightenment necessitates doing responsible research, which takes time, human-type time, many minutes of time. Otherwise, it's so easy to guess right away... and guess completely wrong.

For instance, what will you find at my blog's "Spiritual Enlightenment List"? There you'll find thousands of comments where I've responded to requests for me to research the consciousness lifestyles of public figures, including spiritual teachers; most of whom turn out to be nowhere close to Spiritual Enlightenment.

Now let's turn to a related topic, a very important consideration for our Program for Spiritual Enlightenment.

How CAN You Position Consciousness at the Divine?

Very likely, you've done this sometimes; spontaneously you've positioned consciousness there, at the Divine Vibrational Frequency. Here come some examples:

1. As a nature lover, you're watching a lovely sunrise or sunset.
2. Or you've slowed down while hiking in a magnificent forest; and you're simply appreciating, when Aaah!
3. At a religious service, you have a private moment of grace. (More likely this comes at a random time, rather than some official "Let us pray" moment.)

Smart Spiritual Seeker, it's so important to understand that you're *un*likely to position consciousness at the Divine Vibrational Frequency during a religious ritual, no matter how sacred it's supposed to be. Although a good religious service can be highly effective for mood-making.

Remember, *process* is different from *content*.

4. At home, you're doing a form of meditation that has been expertly designed to produce transcendence.

In the Age of Awakening, sadly, it's rare to find any meditation practice that hasn't been corrupted (more on that is coming up in Part III).

But even if you do manage to learn an effective form of meditation, that doesn't guarantee positioning your consciousness at the Divine Vibrational Frequency; although this might hypothetically happen on occasion.

5. Quite spontaneously, for no special reason at all, your consciousness does a little click. Spontaneously, your

awareness expands. Suddenly there you are: bigger than all the night sky.

In Conclusion

Smart Spiritual Seeker, you might consider your relationship with God to be the big love story of your life — the really big one. Well, just like a human love story, it's not only beautiful but mysterious.

Now that you're clear about ways that astral is not Divine, you've done yourself a big favor, simply by freeing yourself up from this kind of illusion.

Smart Spiritual Seeker, why weigh yourself down by striving for fake enlightenment?

What a joy it can be, experiencing what the Divine Vibrational Frequency really can deliver. In our next two chapter, ah! You'll read about what it means to authentically position consciousness at the Divine Vibrational Frequency. Following that you'll explore this book's final snapshot of consciousness.

CHAPTER 22.

Uniquely Yours, The DIVINE Vibrational Frequency

A picture is worth a thousand words.

Anonymous

Only a thousand words? What would it be worth to you, having clear experience at the Divine Vibrational Frequency? Think that might be worth far more than all the thousands of photos currently stored on your phone?

Actually, all your direct experience at the Divine Vibrational Frequency goes into permanent memory, stored as process *rather than* content, *and kept sacred in your Storehouse of Impressions, retained now and also throughout your long future... as an eternal soul.*

Rose Rosetree

Experience at the Divine Vibrational Frequency is never guaranteed.

Right from the outset, let's be clear about that. Faith won't bring that to you, not as a *process*. Faith alone doesn't bring direct experience of Perfection Everywhere Now.

Being human, we can't demand such an experience. What can we do, though?

We can create conditions where such an experience is extra-likely to happen. Smart Spiritual Seeker, the best way I know to do that is to follow our Program for Spiritual Enlightenment.

Regarding alternative programs, please ask questions before believing whatever claims are made by any Enlightenment Teacher. Then use your good skills of energetic literacy to assess that teacher's chakra databanks, or else find an impartial expert to do that for you.

So Much Has Changed for Spiritual Seekers

Since you're living post-Shift, the process of seeking Enlightenment has changed considerably; you're in for some shockers soon, when we get to Part III, which we will in a couple of chapters.

Another big statement, one that I will *not* have the space to discuss at length in this book, concerns the nature of Spiritual Enlightenment itself. Here I'll add just this much:

- Two different forms of Enlightenment are available now. **Traditional Enlightenment** is the more famous kind, dating from the Age of Faith.
- Alternatively, **Age of Awakening Enlightenment** is available now; it's becoming more popular than the other version.
- Smart Spiritual Seeker, you can learn more about both versions at my Energy Spirituality™ Blog and online workshops.

For our purposes here, all that matters is that you *can* move toward Spiritual Enlightenment, and then *how* to make real progress.

Whichever version of Enlightenment your soul chooses, rest assured. Once in Enlightenment, your consciousness will be blended with the Divine. Our next chapter will provide specific details; you'll read a snapshot of consciousness for somebody in Enlightenment.

But are your real-life choices only *Enlightenment* or *nothing*? Meaning, no consistent experience at the Divine Vibrational Frequency unless you happen to upgrade your consciousness lifestyle for keeps?

Hardly!

Smart Spiritual Seeker, long before Enlightenment… you can have *momentary experience* at the Divine Vibrational Frequency.

What's that like? Keep reading this chapter. Learn how positioning consciousness there, even briefly, is quite a contrast to experiencing either Human or Astral Vibrational Frequencies.

How Does It Feel?

Most important, authentic experience at the Divine Vibrational Frequency doesn't feel spectacular. For instance, there's no astral flash. (Since that, by definition, is astral.)

Likewise, Smart Spiritual Seeker, experience at the Divine Vibrational Frequency does not feel humanly meaningful, not at the time. Why not? Because real-deal experience of the Divine is transcendent, beyond ordinary human emotions and personal sense of self.

In theory, you may be familiar with all this. After all, haven't you often felt homesick for Heaven? Only that is a longing, which can be quite different from a reality. By way of analogy, as a teenager you might have spent hours dreaming about being kissed by your crush. But real-life kissing would have felt somewhat different, right?

10 Qualities of Divine Experience

What follows is an honest list from this Enlightenment Teacher, who has actively helped spiritual seekers in the Age of Awakening. Below is a list of 10 qualities that you *might* notice when your consciousness is positioned at the Divine Vibrational Frequency.

1. The sense of *Perfection Everywhere Now.*
2. *Time* doesn't matter.
3. What you're doing as a human being doesn't matter either, not any more. You might *feel detached* from your "ordinary life," though not necessarily.
4. Emotions include spiritual joy, particularly the sacred emotion of *bliss.*
5. A sense of fulfillment soundlessly hums along in the background (or even in the foreground); bringing great

peace, reminiscent of the beautiful old saying, *"All is well and wisely put."*

6. Fulfillment seems to be *your natural state.*
7. *Being is what matters,* rather than doing.
8. Being yourself means the same thing as *being with God.*
9. You're supported by a sense of ease and flow, unlike any human striving, more *like Heaven*; the Heaven for which so many of us have felt homesick since the day we were born. Even if your last Heaven was an astral world, some direct connection to God was available to everyone there.
10. With consciousness positioned at the Divine Vibrational Frequency, *you don't care the least bit about future anything.* (See previous Point 2.)

How to Position Your Consciousness There

Any of the following, and more, can cause a person to position consciousness at the Divine Vibrational Frequency. Remember, though, there's only so much that we humans can visit as tourists, prior to taking up residence in Spiritual Enlightenment.

Afterward, what changes? It's as though, all your life you've been waiting on the doorstep of God's house, pressing the buzzer again and again, imploring God to please let you in. Yet God alone decides when to open that door. Not you.

At some time when you least expect it, through that door you'll go. And you'll *take up residence* there.

All that said, Smart Spiritual Seeker, here's a list of ways that you might succeed at *briefly* positioning your consciousness There, at the Divine Vibrational Frequency. You know, like *visiting.*

10 Possible Ways

Any of the following might temporarily position your consciousness at the Divine Vibrational Frequency.

1. A mystical experience, or *peak experience*, is simply given to you. For whatever reason, God briefly opens the door and lets you look in.
2. At bedtime, you *transition from being awake to falling asleep*. During that transition, for a brief-but-spiritually-powerful moment, effortlessly, your consciousness pauses at the Divine Vibrational Frequency.
3. Waking up, you *transition from dreaming into the waking state of consciousness*. Again, for another sweet-and-spiritually-powerful moment, your consciousness pauses at the Divine Vibrational Frequency.
4. *Soul-stirring beauty*, like a gorgeous sunrise, inspires you to go "Aaaaaah!" And there goes your consciousness, quite spontaneously, like an arrow released from a bow, flying straight to the Divine Vibrational Frequency.
5. *Falling in love*, when totally open to your beloved, for just a moment, you might position your consciousness at the Divine Vibrational Frequency.
6. Talking with someone you love, that person does or says something that's remarkable to you, and innocently you *look at that person with the eyes of love*. Then, for just an instant, your consciousness can become positioned at the Divine Vibrational Frequency.
7. *While making love,* sometimes it can feel as though a silent lightning strikes. All too soon your consciousness will return to a Human Vibrational Frequency, but before then your consciousness might briefly be positioned at the Divine Vibrational Frequency.
8. You're *doing a form of Technique Time* that is effective now, in the Age of Awakening. (See Chapters 26 and 27.)
9. When you're living in Spiritual Enlightenment, a strong Presence of the Divine is established *within your aura and consciousness*. More likelihood of quick positioning there!
10. In Enlightenment, what happens *whenever you blink?* (That is, I mean normal human blinking.) DURING: Your consciousness takes a split-second leap, positioning at the

Divine Vibrational Frequency. AFTER each blink: Your consciousness returns to a Human Vibrational Frequency.

Why Would these Brief Experiences Matter?

Smart Spiritual Seeker, most likely, you're familiar with the expression, "A picture is worth a thousand words." As noted at the start of this chapter, even one brief experience at the Divine Vibrational Frequency is worth far more than that, but why?

First, that's a preview of Spiritual Enlightenment.

Second, the soul-stirring joy is uniquely memorable — at least for people like you, Smart Spiritual Seeker.

Both of these are very human reasons why experience at the Divine Vibrational Frequency matters. In addition, that word "experience" really matters, signaling an authentic *process,* not merely some high-sounding *content.*

To progress on your Program for Spiritual Enlightenment, remember to apply something you've learned so far, only I'll now present it to you in terms of ... *content* and *process.*

....

Ever encounter people who rave about somebody being "really spiritual"? Then and there, privately ask yourself, "Which is this really about? *Content* or *process*?"

....

For example, remember our ongoing aim to solve the Church-Wenters Mystery? Of course, we expect religious leaders to speak eloquently in terms of religious *content,* such as persuasively quoting scripture. Back in the Age of Faith, this might have been enough to win our loyalty. But now?

Let's Add a Related Concept, Auric Modeling

If you're like most spiritual seekers today, you care about the "**Who You Be**" factor in people: Not only the message but *who* is the messenger; like a brilliant quote from Ralph Waldo Emerson, "Who you are speaks so loudly I can't hear what you're saying."

During the Age of Faith, spiritual seekers like Emerson were comparatively limited in terms of discernment. "Being a good judge of character" was the bigger deal, such as being able to spot a truth-teller versus a liar.

By contrast, what's different now? In the Age of Awakening, we're capable of far more perceptiveness, noticing subtle nuances without breaking a sweat. And yes, that means Perceptive You, Smart Spiritual Seeker.

Beyond all you know so far, here's one new reason why you're capable of that greater perceptiveness. In the Age of Awakening, every person with energy sensitivity has the wisdom resource that I'm going to call "**Auric Modeling.**"

That means, *subconsciously* you read every other person's aura, every detail about that person's 1,000+ chakra databanks.

Granted, you do this subconsciously, not consciously. It works as a *process*. And here's the beauty part. Even before gaining good skills of energetic literacy, deep down you can sense what's what.

Unfortunately, how you *consciously interpret* that info might not be totally reliable; this kind of sensing counts as just *Stage 1* Energetic Literacy.

Nonetheless, learning about auric modeling might impress you as pretty interesting news, especially since you're seeking Enlightenment, because…

Auric Modeling Can Help You to Reach Enlightenment

Given that you are actively seeking Enlightenment, let's consider 10 ways that auric modeling can contribute to your spiritual evolution.

1. Subtly, auric modeling is available to you from *every single human being* you meet in person, watch on TV, hear on the radio, etc.

2. Helpful to know, auric modeling is NOT available from emails, on social media or, sadly, from books; *energetically, none of these will inform you* about the writer's aura.
3. Whenever auric modeling is available to you, that download will be received *subconsciously* (only).
4. Consequently, any time you're in the presence of somebody in Spiritual Enlightenment *that Divine connection* will automatically become part of your subconscious download.
5. Even better, *all your experiences of auric modeling are automatically stored* subconsciously; helping you to recognize Enlightenment as a real-deal *process*, not merely *content* or some nice little theory.
6. Thus, in a way, you're constantly depositing more money into your subconscious **Bank Account for Auric Modeling of Folks in Enlightenment**, since you're likely to encounter quite a few people with that consciousness lifestyle, including actors, singers, and other public figures.
7. Next, *how about **your** auric modeling?* As you evolve spiritually, and even more so after attaining Enlightenment, your increasingly beautiful auric modeling... will benefit others. (Reread Points 1-3 to appreciate why, only this time proceed from the premise that your auric modeling can help other spiritual seekers.)
8. Such an inspiring idea! Due to auric modeling, your personal strivings-and-findings can subconsciously *inspire your fellow spiritual seekers.*
9. Never conflate auric modeling with *old-fashioned notions of darshan*, like a dramatic-and-obvious "Wham! Bam! Thank you for that instant Enlightenment takeover!" Beautiful auric modeling doesn't take people over.
10. Besides that, *subconscious* clarity about somebody else's auric modeling... *doesn't translate into conscious clarity.*

Altogether, though, this set of 10 points still looks pretty darned good, right? And it gets better.

To Enhance Auric Modeling, Add Conscious Clarity

Have I thanked you lately, Smart Spiritual Seeker? Please give yourself credit for persisting, chapter after chapter. By now you're nearly at the end of our Part II. All along you've been gaining many counter-culture spiritual concepts that add to your conscious clarity. How, exactly?

- Chapter by chapter, these concepts have likely passed your personal sniff test. Because you don't merely read. You think.
- Over time, very likely, these concepts will further prove their value (as my students can attest, students who are now in Enlightenment).

Of course, concepts like auric modeling and astral flash aren't yet common knowledge — nowhere close to mainstream. For this reason, you make it easier for those who follow you.

Sadly, spiritual seeking today is limited by society's ignorance of auric modeling and astral flash. The worst confusion happens when spiritual influencers live with consciousness positioned at a HIGH Astral Vibrational Frequency, nowhere close to the Divine.

For example, what if your friend Jesse, an Evangelical Christian, watches a YouTube video where Carlton is preaching? The pastor's auric modeling broadcasts the allure of astral flash, in keeping with his consciousness lifestyle of Extreme Spiritual Addiction. Confusingly, that flashy auric modeling might impress Jesse greatly.

- Because his conscious mind may think, "Wow, how GREAT!"
- Even while his subconscious mind says, "Uh-oh."

Guess what happens then? Deep down, most Carlton fans will become well and truly confused, mistaking astral flash for a Divine blessing.

And yes, Smart Spiritual Seeker, regarding our Church-Wenters Mystery, you've been putting together the clues. Quite likely, you've nearly solved it. Meanwhile, something lovely awaits you in our very next chapter.

CHAPTER 23.

Learn More about The DIVINE Vibrational Frequency

Surely the Presence of the Lord is in this place,
I can feel God's mighty Power and God's Grace.
There's a Holy Hush around us,
I see glory on each face,
Surely the Presence of the Lord is in this place.

Unity Church Hymnal

Perhaps this hymn was inspired by the author's split-second experience at the Divine Vibrational Frequency (process). But when a congregation sings these words, what's their experience? Most likely they're caught up in wishful thinking about Divine experience (content), their wishfulness enhanced by pretty music and group singing.

While singing, their consciousness is likely positioned at an Astral Vibrational Frequency, or else a human one. By contrast, experience at the Divine Vibrational Frequency is not a mood.

Rose Rosetree

Finally, here comes our sample of greatest interest to those of us who might still be feeling a bit homesick for Heaven.

Maybe you're wondering, how could Rose find a good sample photo for this snapshot of consciousness? From my perspective, that wasn't just an interesting question but a real sticking point. Do you think I just flipped through photos until I found one with "Glory on each face"? Of course not.

Smart Spiritual Seeker, by now you know that experience of the Divine Vibrational Frequency doesn't hit us over the head like a sledgehammer, nor do we "just sense It" as if flipping through photos on a dating app; with connection to God being obvious, like some hottie who's obviously "cool" since he poses seductively on a tiger skin.

"Surely the Presence of the Lord is in this place." Abstractly, when folks sing that hymn, what's true? Theologically, as *content*, the idea is correct; God really is everywhere.

In real life, though, *experience* of that presence is what we seek, and that *process* isn't contagious, not really, not caught like a yawn, as the automatic result of hearing a lovely hymn.

Finding a Photo Where Somebody Experiences the Divine?

Adding to the challenge of photo-hunting, I bumped up against this fact while seeking a picture for this book's last snapshot of consciousness:

How long will it typically last, an experience of consciousness at the Divine Vibrational Frequency?

Usually we're talking mere seconds — mere seconds of human time, anyway; although every Divine-level experience can quietly change your life for keeps. Given the fleeting nature of Divine positioning of consciousness, of course it can be hard to locate a research photo.

Adding to the difficulty, what *won't* help? Finding a photo of somebody who's high on recreational drugs. Perhaps you've heard that peyote, LSD, and similar drugs can help a spiritual seeker to "find God." Such a misunderstanding!

In our last chapter, when I listed different ways to position consciousness at the Divine, did you notice what *wasn't* included? Recreational drugs!

Sure, psychedelic drugs act on a person's mind-body-spirit system, altering how consciousness is positioned. Alcohol does this too, providing an external, chemical kind of transport, lifting a person's awareness away from Human Vibrational Frequencies, elevating consciousness to a *higher* vibrational frequency than normal. But which kind of "high"?

Let's Debunk Druggy Nonsense about "Finding God"

Look, Smart Spiritual Seeker, here's the deal about taking some kind of "spiritual medicine" that transports you to God. Usually:

- *Beer* positions consciousness at a LOW Astral Vibrational Frequency.
- Good quality *wine* positions consciousness at a MEDIUM Astral Vibrational Frequency.
- *Cocaine, peyote, or LSD* (during a good trip) all position consciousness at a HIGH Astral Vibrational Frequency.

Maybe you're curious, then. In order to find a research subject with consciousness at the Divine Vibrational Frequency, which drug or food would do the job?

For instance, could I google "Folks who love ice cream" and then find photo after photo of people hanging out with God?

Nope. And that's not merely the short answer, it's the only true answer.

How to find a photo of somebody with consciousness at the Divine Vibrational Frequency? That wasn't going to be so easy. For several days I was stumped. Then, Aha!

Problem Solved. But How?

In order to bring you this chapter's snapshot of consciousness, I found the photo of "Emma," somebody in Traditional Enlightenment; easy, since I have photos of many of my students who've crossed the threshold into Enlightenment. Before going into specific details about Emma's experience, let's answer this key question.

How Does It Feel?

Such a human question! As you know, positioning consciousness doesn't necessarily result in distinctive *content*; here we're trying to wrap our minds around the *process*.

Let's suppose that you're hanging out with your buddy Emma, and both of you are living in Traditional Enlightenment. How does it feel to regularly have your consciousness positioned at the Divine Vibrational Frequency?

Normal, that's the main thing. Living in Enlightenment feels normal, like both you and Emma are wearing feet on your ankles. Here come more details.

Emma's Snapshot of Consciousness

In general, human life usually involves seeing other people at a Human Vibrational Frequency. By the age of five, at the latest, most of us have stopped feeling as though that's a cosmic treat.

Subtly different is how Emma spontaneously views people when her consciousness is positioned at the Divine Vibrational Frequency; routinely she's encountering the sacredness of every unique human being.

Emma's not seeing through eyes of wonder, like a young child. Rather, she looks through the eyes of a grownup who happens to live in Enlightenment. There is a difference.

No fresh innocent baby smell, no liquid baby laugh: Emma looks and sounds and smells like a human adult who's graduated from puberty.

- *Spiritually*, gaining Enlightenment is a privilege.
- *Humanly*, it's just a normal, natural way of life... which happens to include using our full potential for wonder.

All that said, let's start exploring this new snapshot.

1. Emma's Root Chakra Databank for Presence in the Room

Symbolic Size

50 feet. Within normal range for Emma at this time.

Quality

Lit up from within, Emma radiates peace and also the potential for dynamic action; in this moment she feels an underlying joy.

Hummingbird-paced, that joy alternates with whatever human emotion is appropriate, given whatever is happens in objective reality.

At the time of this particular photo, she's posing for a friend; Emma feels happy to be hanging out with the person who's taking the picture. (Plus, as usual, she also happens to be hanging out with God.)

2. Emma's Root Chakra Databank for Connection to Objective Reality

Symbolic Size

50 feet. Within normal range.

Quality

Human life is filled with God's creativity and sweetness. People are fascinating.

Nature's amazing; that is, amazing in an everyday sort of way. Here on Earth, inanimate objects are real — brimming with distinctive qualities of life at Human Vibrational Frequencies.

Whatever happens in the moment with this objective reality, it's going to add more fun to Emma's game of life.

3. Emma's Belly Chakra Databank for Sexual Self-Esteem

Symbolic Size

50 feet. Within normal range.

Quality

Emma feels at peace regarding sex.

At the time of this photo, she's not actively paying attention to anybody's sexuality; but if she were to engage in a sexual encounter, she'd actively enjoy her role, feeling good about herself and her chosen partner.

Remember, living in Spiritual Enlightenment means using your full potential in life.

For most of us, interest in sex can be a vibrant part of life, whether or not we're in Spiritual Enlightenment, whether we have a human love partner or we service ourselves.

4. Emma's Heart Chakra Databank for Emotional Receiving

Symbolic Size

50 feet. Within normal range.

Quality

God wears so many human disguises, unfolding as a continual source of emotional delight.

Spiritual Bliss is the technical name for Emma's default for emotional receiving; this is supplemented by the ever-changing parade of her emotional reactions to life, here and now.

5. Emma's Third Eye Chakra Databank for Connection to Psychic Guidance

Symbolic Size

Shut down at this time, although structurally able to extend 50 feet.

Quality

Although Emma is capable of positioning consciousness to connect with astral beings, she has no desire to do so.

6. Emma's Third Eye Chakra Databank for Connection to Spiritual Source

As with researching Carlton, I'm going to include this second, different, Third Eye Chakra databank. Since Emma's in Spiritual Enlightenment, it will be interesting to learn about her relationship with God. What's happening now regarding her personal Divine connection?

Symbolic Size

50 feet. Within normal range.

Quality

To Emma, God is as real and present as her own elbows. Or thumbs. Or the air that is hers to breathe.

Also worth noting, Emma's sense of self lives in harmony with the Divine. Of course, no mere theory (*content*) can cause this to happen as a way of life. Instead, Emma spontaneously lives that way, given her own direct experience of Spiritual Source (a *process*).

How I Interpret Emma's Snapshot of Consciousness

Back to Emma's experience, ah! Beautiful, isn't it?

Actually, it's typical of other research I've done, chakra databank-level, regarding the quality of life for people in *Traditional Enlightenment*. Differently lovely are chakra databanks belonging to folks in *Age of Awakening Enlightenment*.

Either way, whichever version of Enlightenment a person attains, one's aura is glorious. More detail regarding specifics… will have to await another book, along with so much more knowledge that I would love to share with you in the future.

Meanwhile, What's Important for You to Know Right Now?

Personal experience of Enlightenment is never astral flashy, nor is it dramatic. Most notably, when awake, a person in Spiritual Enlightenment enjoys a sacred process, somewhat different compared with pre-Enlightenment; a process that's **Everyday Glorious.**

You see, for a person in Enlightenment, all your waking minutes develop a human kind of spiritual beauty; this happens in the background, and yes, this glorifies your personal relationship with God.

> Everyday glorious is worth aiming for; exactly *this* could be considered the main purpose of our Program for Spiritual Enlightenment.

And now, Smart Spiritual Seeker, thanks to your persistence, here is your second graduation while reading this book; this time you're graduating from Part II.

Well done! You've earned the standing to discover the specific DOs and DON'Ts in our program; these are essential for seeking Enlightenment in the Age of Awakening. Let our Part III begin.

PART III.

Your Personal Program For Spiritual Enlightenment

Smart Spiritual Seeker, you're now going to receive a *personal* Program for Spiritual Enlightenment, one that fits you like a custom-made glove.

In the Age of Awakening, it's not enough to "Follow what's supposed to work for everybody." You're an individual. And you know it! Therefore, your program for spiritual evolution must include plenty of *individual choice*.

Equally vital is *the effectiveness of what you choose for your path*. For instance, regarding which techniques you might choose for Technique Time, which ones have a high degree of effectiveness? These would be the ones to pursue.

As you'll soon see, wise choices are not necessarily in synch with what's most popular today in mainstream religious-and-spiritual circles.

Of course, in Part III I'm aiming to give you a complete program for spiritual awakening and more, a program that can bring you all the way to Spiritual Enlightenment and then help you to live happily ever after.

Seems to me, you deserve that much. After all, Smart Spiritual Seeker, you've persisted in mastering all the necessary background in Parts I and II. As a result, you'll be able to understand this practical Part III, where I'll lay out the specifics of our program.

Yes, you can start today. **Welcome to the first Program for Spiritual Enlightenment that's expressly designed to work now, during the Age of Awakening.**

Why I would make such a big claim? Seems to me, you have the right to know. So here goes.

Definitely an Age of Awakening Program

For several reasons that benefit you, hello! This is an Age of Awakening-Type Program for Spiritual Enlightenment.

First of all, this program was created after the Shift on 12-21-12; which isn't the case for most well-known spiritual teachings, such as meditation and yoga; likewise, not being true of mainstream religious traditions, either.

Second, just because something used to work pretty well before the Shift, does that mean it can be trusted now, during this new-and-different era on earth? No casual question there! Smart Spiritual Seeker, as a supplement to our Part III, you're invited to check out my blog, where you'll find energetic literacy research galore.

Simply search for articles about spiritual teachers with expertise in time-honored methods, methods that will have significant drawbacks until their beautiful teachers learn what to tweak and update. (See more in our *Afterword*.)

Third, it's important to know that I've spent many years researching this program, aiming to uncover secrets for living today's spiritual potential. For example, I've had the honor of publishing the first information anywhere about Age of Awakening Enlightenment, in workshops, blog posts, and even a prequel to this book, *The New Strong*.

For the past five years, I've been developing and teaching this program. At the start of this book, some of my students have graciously described their experiences in Enlightenment; plus, the final quote comes from a man who's well on his way, like most long-term Energy Spirituality™ clients.

Our Chapter 30 will give you longer descriptions from folks who describe their experience of living in Spiritual Enlightenment. Meanwhile, you've got a practical program to discover in our Part III.

Foundational for this Particular Program

Smart Spiritual Seeker, please know this about all the instructions you'll receive in Part III. They've been:

1. Cocreated with Divine help.
2. Meticulously researched.
3. Validated by skills of energetic literacy.
4. Successfully taught to students who have progressed remarkably in their spiritual evolution, including many who now live in Spiritual Enlightenment.
5. All these instructions come from an Enlightenment Teacher who is herself in Spiritual Enlightenment.

Isn't that True of All Spiritual Teachers Active Today?

Hardly! Do your own research; very likely you'll find that many of today's spiritual teachers have a consciousness lifestyle that is *not* Spiritual Enlightenment. Moreover, today's most popular teachings fall into one or more of the three following categories:

#1. Repeating Traditional Teachings from the Age of Faith

Commonly, spiritual teachers carry forward sacred traditions from an Age of Faith lineage.

As a consumer you may find that impressive: For instance, a teacher may quote extensively from scripture; reverently repeating time-hallowed truths from bygone masters; faithfully sharing religious teachings, meditation practices, yoga as a way of life, etc.

Sure, the *content* is all about God, but the *process*? Uh-oh, that brings us to the Church-Wenters Mystery — which I do intend to help you to officially solve during our Part III.

#2. Offering Energy-Enthusiastic Teachings

Many of today's spiritual teachers — and influencers — take a more contemporary approach. These teachers are **Energy Enthusiasts,** inspired by their energy sensitivity, impressing followers with their Energy Talk.

Smart Spiritual Seeker, how can you spot an energy enthusiast? The most obvious way is how they blur the distinction between spiritual awakening and Spiritual Enlightenment. According to my research, these folks are true to their inspiration — which is sweet. Except that the source of the teachings, although supposedly "spiritual" or Divine, is nearly always astral.

Who cares if a popular teacher gets away with vaguely calling people "awakened"? Well, you and I might care quite a lot, especially because we know that Astral and Divine Vibrational Frequencies are hardly interchangeable, except to the unsophisticated.

Again and again, research done with energetic literacy reveals another big problem with energy-enthusiastic teachings, a problem that you're in an excellent position to appreciate: So far, the majority of today's spiritual teachers don't know they have a new Consciousness Positioning Superpower. No wonder they misuse it, and encourage their followers to do the same.

All too often the source of the spiritual teaching is astral, not Divine. Despite impressive astral flash in that influencer's auric modeling (*process*), don't expect that kind of teaching to serve as a reliable guide to spiritual evolution (*content*).

#3. Megachurch-Worthy Religious Teachings

Strong religious traditions can help a churchgoer to feel spiritually safe-and-secure. Ever notice? Pre-Shift, Western religions often emphasized security, such as belonging to a large congregation or flock, guided by a knowledgeable shepherd.

Even today, most Evangelicals seldom yearn for Spiritual Enlightenment, and why would they bother?

Following traditional beliefs, they believe it's enough to be "Saved." Yet during the New Age Years, millions of churchgoers bravely deviated from the straight-and-narrow path they'd been told to obey; millions became church-wenters.

Surprisingly, during the years I've been editing this book, a shocking article was published in the Washington Post; appearing March 30, 2021; an article presenting new research that's extremely relevant to what we're calling the Church-Wenters Mystery. According to Gallup polling, for the first time since such polls have been taken, hello!

"Religious membership in U.S. falls below 50%." And only 48% of Americans "say organized faith is very important to them."

Previously unheard-of numbers, indeed! For sure, Smart Spiritual Seeker, we're already close to solving that Church-Wenters Mystery, and we'll get there soon.

In addition, I'll make sure that Part III includes precise definitions of consciousness lifestyles, because that topic is definitely relevant to our detective work... also being of personal interest to everyone who has ever felt homesick for Heaven.

> On the bright side, have you figured this out yet? In the Age of Awakening, Spiritual Enlightenment is one of the consciousness lifestyles available to us all, whether we're religious or not.

However, several other consciousness lifestyles are far more popular now. We can't simply demand Spiritual Enlightenment, stream the video, or purchase Enlightenment like a $120 Manduka Pro™ Yoga Mat.

Maybe you're wondering, *which consciousness lifestyle is best as you pursue Enlightenment?* That's a question we'll definitely answer in detail with Part III.

For now, know this. Smart Spiritual Seeker, our Program for Spiritual Enlightenment can help you to move into the best consciousness lifestyle available to you on demand; available if you make use of your relevant knowledge, your smarts and free will; a consciousness lifestyle bringing significant fulfillment to your everyday life, as well as propelling your spiritual evolution forward each day of your life.

And yes, this particular consciousness lifestyle will fast-track you toward Enlightenment.

What Exactly Will You Receive in Part III?

Smart Spiritual Seeker, this! You'll receive:
1. Specific DOs and DON'Ts that make this program effective.
2. Six Sweet Golden Rules for gracing your path.
3. Altogether, you'll learn what's essential for seeking Enlightenment in the Age of Awakening.

And rest assured, this Program for Spiritual Enlightenment is *manageable*. Simple, really. Receiving these simple-and-specific instructions may, actually, come as a relief.

Look, I know that many spiritual seekers would do just about anything to stop feeling so homesick for Heaven; no wonder, some of you have been working way harder than is needed, or productive.

Imagine that! Trying too hard, in ways that don't even work well any more, not in this Age of Awakening; hey, I'd love to help you do better.

Here we go, Smart Spiritual Seeker. Here's to an easy, straightforward path for your spiritual fulfillment!

CHAPTER 24.

Today's New Consciousness Smarts for Seeking Enlightenment

Tell me to what you pay attention and I will tell you who you are.
Jose Ortega y Gasset, Philosopher

....

To progress toward Spiritual Enlightenment, encourage yourself to be interested in Human Vibrational Frequencies. Sure, you could do fancier tricks when positioning your consciousness, but that's for Technique Time, not most of your waking hours.
Rose Rosetree

....

As befits a chapter on SMARTS, let's begin by reviewing some knowledge you've already gained, then add to it. Let me warn you about one thing: Smart Spiritual Seeker, the conversation we're about to have... is going to turn distinctly counter-culture.

For context, what happened to you, and all the rest of us humans, in terms of our consciousness; what happened to us all during the decades right before the Shift on 12-21-12?

In terms of consciousness, something momentous occurred. Remember, the Psychic Barrier had been thinning for millennia, a process that accelerated greatly during the last 100 years of the Age of Faith; then that thinning achieved a dizzying pace during the New Age Years, from 1980 until the Shift.

People started to notice they were energy sensitive, feeling energies in themselves and others. As a result, folks began speaking

Energy Talk, substituting random astral perceptions for more ordinary conversation about human reality.

Energy healing practices, psychic work and channeling, meditation and more: So many energy-related practices became fads during the New Age Years; seeming like cosmic discoveries to millions — at least, seeming "Cosmic, man" at the time.

Who among us understood clearly what was happening? The heady thrill of a rapidly-thinning Psychic Barrier was akin to humanity's collective puberty, required for humanity's spiritual coming of age, a transition resulting in a wild array of new values and practices. Idealistic mind-body-spirit ideas went mainstream, as if Energy Talk (*content*) were sacred and could transform the world.

In retrospect, the *process* of opening up to energy was happening too, although not automatically bringing healing and transformation, as millions believed.

Instead, humanity's energy sensitivity brought many new inner experiences; for many of us, experiences began changing so fast that we were grateful for any teachers who claimed to make sense out of things.

In retrospect, though, popular thought leaders like Oprah Winfrey didn't add much responsible *content* for understanding our experiences; in retrospect, they might have confused us far more than they helped us.

After the Shift, after the Psychic Barrier disappeared for good, all of us gained access to something magnificent, our new Consciousness Positioning Superpower. Only who knew we had it, let alone understood how to use it?

Ever since these subtle changes became universal, sad to say, many an Enlightenment seeker has been snacking on New Age Leftovers.

So Many People Are Snacking on New Age Leftovers!

Remember that expression? Back in Part I you were introduced to "New Age Leftovers": an outdated alternative to today's new consciousness smarts.

Chapter 24. Today's New Consciousness Smarts for Seeking Enlightenment

> Countless spiritual seekers, coming from all walks of life, are still partying as if it's 1980... or other New Age Years. They're partying and snacking on leftover beliefs and techniques; transitional leftovers that could be pretty stale by now.

Maybe, without meaning to, you have also indulged in this kind of fun.

What if no specific instances come to mind? Here's an easy way to find plenty: Just hop onto Facebook or Twitter; today and every day, you'll find examples galore. Commonly you'll find people who do any or all of the following:

1. Expect *special treatment* due to their energy sensitivity.
2. Prefer to *notice energy* whenever possible, routinely positioning their consciousness at an Astral Vibrational Frequency.
3. Affect *a more spiritual-than-thou* way of talking; such as refusing to give direct answers to your questions about objective reality. (You know, life that is "merely" at Human Vibrational Frequencies.) Instead, they respond to your questions with their fluent Energy Talk.
4. Choose to describe — or define — people in terms of their *aura colors;* from this teacher's perspective, these energy enthusiasts are playing at Stage 1 Energetic Literacy, rather than developing productive skills.
5. Avidly pursue chakra "healing" or other forms of *energy healing as a cool hobby*. Producing results doesn't matter, so great is the thrill of playing with the energies.

So ironic! Every minute that a person squanders on fooling around with energy, what else happens that's really valuable for spiritual evolution?

Nothing — at least if that person wishes to gain authentic emotional growth or spiritual awakening.

How Can You Avoid Snacking on New Age Leftovers?

For starters, our Program for Spiritual Enlightenment requires using Human-Type Language, rather than Energy Talk. Dare to take an interest in ordinary human things. It's not "unevolved" to spend your waking hours doing normal human things in a normal human way. Normal compared to what?

Please don't be taken in by **Energy Pride,** which means taking personal credit for having energy sensitivity or doing Energy Talk. Purposely or not, Energy Talk is a form of bragging; folks are showing off how "evolved" they are — an understandable, yet unhelpful, expression of energy pride.

Not quite knowing what they're doing, many truth-seekers today have fallen into undesirable habits of positioning consciousness; as if noticing energies were a kind of awakened-person's triumph, far superior to "unevolved" and ordinary human reality.

Let's be clear. Any displays of energy pride amount to playing around, randomly, with our new Consciousness Positioning Superpower.

- Once you understand how unhelpful it is, doing Energy Talk, you can easily stop doing it. Make a habit of using Human-Type Language when you speak to others.
- Also helpful is to start (privately) flagging when other people are doing Energy Talk.

How can you tell? Simply listen to the words being used. When people substitute Energy Talk for Human-Type Language, what's your clue? You'll hear words like *energies* and *vibes*, also plenty of *"It feels like."*

Seriously, What's the Appeal of Energy Pride?

Smart Spiritual Seeker, let me give you the benefit of what I've learned about energy pride over the years, what I've aura-researched for years and, most important, what I've helped many of my students over the years… to overcome.

1. Energy Talk helps people to *feel proud* because they're creating a new way of seeing life, not like "ordinary" people.
2. Because they discovered energy sensitivity on their own (no teacher needed), guess what? Many folks with energy pride consider their newfound ability to be *"genius."*
3. Spontaneously positioning consciousness at an Astral Vibrational Frequency, folks will share *insights that feel really important* — that is, important mainly due to being astral.
4. This Energy Talk has a lot in common with the *"fabulous insights"* pot-smokers discover while high.
5. Sure, energy experiences can seem exotically wonderful. But keep in mind, this *process* involves something astral, not Divine; meanwhile the *content* may not make much sense to others (unless they're also feeling that particular kind of high).
6. A bit like code-switching, religiously-minded believers often uplift each other with **Bible Study in Everyday Life**; jumping from human reality to God-flavored interpretations of life. Call that **Christian Energy Talk!**
7. Sure, discussing religious *content* feels important. But, hello! Due to our shared superpower, the *process* usually involves positioning consciousness at a LOW or MEDIUM Astral Vibrational Frequency. This may feel "godly." But isn't.
8. Seekers of psychological wholeness have their own popular way of escaping reality, **Taking the Psychological Bypass**. This means intermittently probing themselves and others for subconscious issues, as though that would really fix anything.
9. Ironically, this supposedly vital psychological *content* gains allure from the *process* of positioning consciousness at a LOW or MEDIUM Astral Vibrational Frequency. (Already you've learned that "subconscious" is synonymous with "astral," remember?)
10. So much self-help that helps nothing! What may be the wackiest part of all? To position their consciousness at an astral frequency, *folks no longer need beer or wine or weed*. Therefore, it's incredibly easy to do astral self-help for countless hours each day.

For sure, energy pride hobbies are not the least bit helpful for seeking Enlightenment.

If you didn't used to know better, Smart Spiritual Seeker, now you do. You've got the relevant consciousness smarts. So stop participating in these space-out conversations. Although the *content* may seem enticing, the *process* will encourage positioning your consciousness at an Astral Vibrational Frequency.

In that context, here comes the first golden rule in our Program for Spiritual Enlightenment, a rule that allows you to *subtract* consciousness-complications from your life.

Simple and Elegant

Smart Spiritual Seeker, just because you've got that exciting Consciousness Positioning Superpower, don't overuse it. Instead, during most of your waking hours… don't use it at all.

> **Golden Rule 1. VALUE Your Experience at Human Vibrational Frequencies**

As you know, Human Vibrational Frequencies are the appropriate default for your consciousness: not Astral or Divine Vibrational Frequencies.

Central to our Program for Spiritual Enlightenment, you'll benefit from valuing this human life of yours; taking an interest in your fellow humans, actively doing your reasonable best to succeed at work, giving to others as appropriate.

Human is neither astral or Divine, nor should it be. With practice, telling the difference is simple. For instance, whenever you notice things in objective reality, or say things out loud, or do things… that's your ticket to positioning your consciousness at a Human Vibrational Frequency.

Maybe you've already been living with Golden Rule 1. If not, you can begin today, upgrading unproductive habits, like trying to "manifest" success by daydreaming or doing Energy Talk.

In the following chapters you'll learn more golden rules, of course, including ones that directly concern official **Technique Time**. For now, let's define that as what happens when you actively use your Consciousness Positioning Superpower, and use it productively.

Meanwhile, here's a wise way to use your new consciousness smarts when you're not in Technique Time.

Starting today, during your waking hours, take an interest in this human life of yours. Human Vibrational Frequencies are the natural default for people like you and me; besides, "human" can be pretty darned fascinating.

No need to seek more exotic experiences; even fictional Spiderman doesn't spin webs and climb walls *all day long.*

But what if I'm used to exploring energies all day long? How can I stop?

This can help: Simply Reinsert Yourself into Objective Reality

Whenever you realize you've been daydreaming, etc., you can easily **Reinsert Yourself into Objective Reality.** More details will follow in this chapter. Right from the outset, know this.

What you do will be both specific and simple, very simple. Immediately afterward you'll be supported by your Consciousness Positioning Superpower, which gives you the chance to start over, with awareness now positioned at a Human Vibrational Frequency.

Smart Spiritual Seeker, I think you'll find this reinserting business is surprisingly easy to do. Consider it kind of a knack, related to taking an interest in your human life; a knack that will also help you to accomplish more in life (and maybe even make more money).

- Never monitor your consciousness. But if you happen to notice that you're spacing out, simply reinsert yourself into objective reality.

⌒ In general, trust that your consciousness is naturally positioned where it belongs, simply because it's natural to participate in your human life... as if you were human.

Of course, living this way — and, as needed, actively reinserting yourself into objective reality, until this becomes the default for your waking hours — living this way will help you greatly to succeed at our Program for Spiritual Enlightenment.

Reinserting Yourself into Objective Reality Can Be Simple

As you'll recall, **Objective Reality** means what people say and do, as well as touching physical objects, etc. To position your consciousness there, either *talk out loud* or *move one small part of your physical body,* like your right wrist (not your entire right arm).

Choose one of these alternatives, then continue for about 10 seconds.

⌒ Boing! You've refreshed the screen of your consciousness, akin to refreshing the screen on your computer.

⌒ Consciousness-wise, you'll have a fresh new chance to follow Golden Rule 1.

Following that, get busy with actually doing something, such as talking to other people as an active member of the conversation. No big drama! No complicated or flashy content!

Simply let the process of ordinary living as a human being... become the default for your waking hours.

Would you please give some specific examples? I'm afraid of doing this wrong.

No worries! And sure, examples can help you to see how simple it can be for you to use this everyday skill.

What If You're with Other People at the Time?

For instance, suppose that you're hanging out with friends and they're all doing Energy Talk. What can you do to avoid getting all vague and woo-woo, with astral positioning of your consciousness?

Reinserting yourself into objective reality can be easy: Change the subject. Say words that shift the topic of conversation back to something human.

1. Either *talk about something* in objective reality
2. Or else *ask other people questions* concerning something in objective reality.

For example, "What did your friend Christopher do? You've told us *why* you think he did it, and *what* you think his energies are like, but please... Tell us what Christopher actually did. And what kind of thing did he say?"

What If You're Alone?

Reinserting yourself into objective reality can be totally easy when you're by yourself.

1. Simply move one small part of your physical body for about 10 seconds. On different occasions, mix it up; like moving your left elbow the first time; a second time, move the big toe on your right foot.
2. Alternatively, talk or hum for 10 seconds.

Either choice will position your consciousness at a Human Vibrational Frequency.

After 10 seconds, you're done. Automatically you've reinserted your consciousness into reality, human reality. Next, either go back to whatever you were doing before, or else start doing something else.

Another Helpful Skill: Shallow Up

Suppose that in the past you've been doing a lot of invisible astral travel. As a result...

You've been positioning your consciousness at Human Vibrational Frequencies, sure. But you've been doing that grudgingly. Because doing this seems so basic, so uninteresting, like how you used to be so easily satisfied before becoming energy sensitive.

You know, Human Vibrational Frequencies can definitely seem "basic" if you're used to doing a lot of Energy Talk, etc.

Actually, this isn't too different from recovering from a lifestyle where you used to smoke a joint every day, or have a glass of wine. (Neither of which will work when you're on this Program for Spiritual Enlightenment.) Getting used to "plain vanilla" living can seem annoying for a few days (or even weeks) but keep at it. Do you want Enlightenment or not?

Give our program a chance. It can benefit you in so many ways, in addition to helping you to evolve spiritually.

One of my Energy Spirituality students, now in Enlightenment, was struggling for a while with the seemingly "boring" quality of Human Vibrational Frequencies. That's when this student, Leo Gabrielsen, came up with the term **Shallow Up!** I love that.

By definition, compared to Astral or Divine Vibrational Frequencies, Human Vibrational Frequencies are slower, shallower, heavier. As a baby you gave them a chance. Give them a new chance now.

> *How can shallow be good? I don't get it. How can acting like a shallow person help me to gain Enlightenment?*
>
> *After a while, it's fun. Sometimes you'll notice some shallow-and-obvious things about subjective reality. Or you'll even talk about them. Resist any habits to fancy this up: No probing for deeper feelings or what causes them, because that would become your ticket to ride... on an Astral Vibrational Frequency.*

Reinsert Yourself into Objective Reality = Shallow up

They mean the same thing, really. Get it?

Whichever term you prefer, doing this can be easy. It's simply a knack; 10 seconds of innocently using your voice, or moving your body, will suffice. Automatically that will refresh the screen of your consciousness, positioning your awareness at a Human Vibrational Frequency. Then start doing a normal, everyday, human whatever.

Soon you'll grow used to a down-to-earth life. Before then, if you find yourself spacing out, Reinsert Yourself into Objective Reality. Shallow up!

Automatic Do-Over

Every time you refresh the screen of your consciousness, indirectly you'll strengthen the habit of having Human Vibrational Frequencies become your default for living.

Golden Rule 1 is essential for moving forward toward Enlightenment. Simply live like a human, being interested in friends and other (human) people of your choice, accomplishing human things. Since you're seeking Enlightenment in the Age of Awakening, let me break it to you:

> **Taking out the garbage may not be glamorous, but this can do far more for your spiritual evolution than indulging in Energy Talk.**

Definitely, You're Learning Specifics Now. Hooray!

Smart Spiritual Seeker, more Golden Rules will follow in our Part III. Just for fun, before moving forward, maybe give yourself this little assignment: Can you guess what our other five Golden Rules might be? Make yourself a list.

Whether or not you guess correctly, congrats! Just like the rest of saying things and doing things in human reality... whatever happens afterward can become informative. How appropriate, since we spiritual seekers are evolving here at Earth School, the Learning Planet!

CHAPTER 25.

Technique Time: Why It Matters for Gaining Enlightenment

Time is the coin of your life. It is the only coin you have, and only you can determine how it will be spent. Be careful lest you let other people spend it for you.

Carl Sandburg, Poet

....

Wise people have always taken a passionate interest in how they spend their time. What's an essential skill now, for Seeking Enlightenment in the Age of Awakening? Do 20 Daily Minutes of Technique Time, neither more nor less.

Rose Rosetree

....

Most people don't know this yet. Why does it matter, doing a full 20 minutes' worth of daily Technique Time?

But then again, most people don't know much about how to live well in the Age of Awakening, let alone how to pursue an effective Program for Spiritual Enlightenment.

Smart Spiritual Seeker, do you know why Technique Time matters so much? When you make it your business to pursue Enlightenment, during your waking hours, only two different kinds of time can help you.

⤳ Technique Time, to *enliven* spiritual awakening.

⤳ And regular human living, to *integrate* spiritual awakening.

Exactly what is meant here by spiritual awakening? Already you know some important things about that; particularly, how spiritual awakening is not the same thing as Enlightenment. Now let's take your understanding further.

Authentic Spiritual Awakening

The meaning is simple: Whenever you expand your personal experience in a spiritually productive direction, that counts as authentic spiritual awakening.

So, how to accomplish this? Do an effective form of Technique Time. This will position your consciousness, in an uplifting way, at an Astral or Divine Vibrational Frequency.

As a result, your official Technique Time will count for spiritual awakening, allowing you to progress further in your spiritual evolution. Every one of your 20 daily minutes can help you do this.

Equally important, since you're a Smart Spiritual Seeker, don't *seek out spiritual experiences* outside of your Technique Time, such as looking for signs from God, or chatting up angels; don't break up your day with random forms of seeking. Any of this will count as Technique Time, likely positioning your consciousness in an Astral Vibrational Frequency.

Nor will it help you to *avoid* Technique Time. Did you know? Countless people today do nothing. Maybe they'll take a nap every afternoon and call it "mindfulness." Others wait fatalistically to be *given* more spiritual awakening. Instead, you can make it your business to pursue Enlightenment actively, intelligently, and as a person living at this time on Earth.

Purposely select a well-designed form of Technique Time, then do it. That simple. (More on specific techniques in our next two chapters.)

Altogether you're about to learn how essential it is, balancing-and-integrating that special time wisely — which is precisely where regular human living comes in. (More on that's coming in *this* chapter.) Because, great as Technique Time is…

Never Underestimate the Spiritual Power of Regular Human Living

First of all, what exactly do I mean by Regular Human Living? That's when you say things and do things, human things, with your consciousness positioned at a Human Vibrational Frequency — merely saying and/or doing "ordinary" human things, nothing fancy added.

That's right. If you seek Enlightenment, never take for granted the value of good old regular human living. And please know, this doesn't have to mean, "Chop wood. Carry water."

After all, this famous saying originated thousands of years ago, deep into the Age of Faith, long before modern conveniences. Living now, what kind of activity counts as regular human living?

- Talking on your mobile phone with a friend.
- Doing your honorable best to earn a living.
- Hey, you might even be having fun on a "weekend."

Maybe you know? Weekends were unknown to the religious masters of yesteryear… nor to anyone else; the custom didn't become popular until the 1930s… less than 100 years before the Shift.

Regular Human Living Allows You to Balance-and-Integrate WHAT?

Simply put, you'll balance the gains from that day's precious Technique Time.

Please know that most of your waking hours, every unfancy minute can count as spiritually valuable for our program. Yes, you just read that right, *spiritually valuable*. Regular human living means spending most of your waking hours with your consciousness comfortably positioned at everyday human life.

Contrary to what you may have been told, that's not "merely" living, no-no! Instead, you're integrating that day's spiritual awakening.

Initially the spiritual awakening part might appear far more important, as if the Technique Time is cosmically tasty, like a hot pizza delivered to your home, whereas "ordinary human living" has all the charm of snacking on the delivery box.

That perspective will change, however, as you lose obsolete Age of Faith values, like "The more hours I can meditate each day, the faster I will evolve."

Does limiting the amount of "Technique Time" really matter, so long as your heart is pure?

Only totally! Our next golden rule will give you a very specific goal for this.

Yes, This Goal Matters

Happy news, Smart Spiritual Seeker! Compared to when you first learned how to tell time, long ago, how easy it can be for you to follow our next golden rule.

Golden Rule 2. Do 20 Daily Minutes of Technique Time, Tops

This specific amount of Technique Time is essential for succeeding at our Program for Spiritual Enlightenment.

Earlier I defined Technique Time as "Dedicated time, when you do a specific activity of your choice; and the purpose is emotional growth and/or spiritual awakening." Now let's advance your understanding, Smart Spiritual Seeker.

1. *Humanly*, what is Technique Time? You're using the specific technique of your choice in order to improve your inner quality of life.
2. *For positioning consciousness*, the distinction is clear: The activity you're doing only counts as Technique Time when you explore an activity expressly designed to position your awareness at an Astral or Divine Vibrational Frequency.

> *This is when I start to doubt that you're really a spiritual teacher. Rose, even I know this. To the truly enlightened, everything counts as spiritual. Aren't human activities only valuable if we can see them all as spiritual?*
>
> *Maybe so, back in the Age of Faith; living now, I'd call this a form of mood-making that won't really help you at all. Look, only you can choose whether you want real Spiritual Enlightenment… or you'd prefer to sweet-talk yourself into pretend-Enlightenment.*

Important point here: No matter how homesick for Heaven you may feel, never try to "make things spiritual." For example, don't guess how "Spiritual" different activities might be. Just use plain vanilla common sense about what counts as Technique Time. Glad to say, our next two chapters can help bring you that kind of discernment.

> *All this is starting to make sense to me. Except what's so special about 20 minutes? Why make a rule about that?*
>
> Good question!

The 20-Minute Rule Prevents Over-Using Your Superpower

Trust me on this, Smart Spiritual Seeker. This 20-minute figure comes to you very well researched. So don't fudge the timing.

Underlying Golden Rule 2 is a concept that's essential for seeking Enlightenment in the Age of Awakening. Did you know this?

> *Integrating* Spiritual Expansion matters at least as much as *gaining* that Spiritual Expansion in the first place.

After you've mastered Golden Rule 6, you'll understand better why this is so. Meanwhile, since you and I are both human, let's proceed systematically and continue with practical Golden Rule 2.

Smart Spiritual Seeker, it's vital for you to recognize the spiritual power of regular human living.

Our Program for Spiritual Enlightenment is simple: For most of your waking hours, you'll live in the here and now, saying and doing "ordinary" human things. (And, remember, not seeking out astral flash. Soon you'll lose your taste for that kid stuff anyway.)

Also included in regular human living are: Talking to other people, listening to them; having fun; dancing; learning more about life every day. Human life can bring infinite variety, right?

Sadly though, far too many seekers today believe that human life is stupid and "unevolved." What's the point of talking to people, earning a living, eating ordinary meals, and so forth? Confused spiritual seekers may well consider activities like these to be necessary evils, while (supposedly) the beauty part of a day involves spending as long as possible on a yoga mat.

Starting now, if necessary, actively question this kind of belief. In effect, that's disrespecting what God has generously given us humans for our evolution here at Earth School.

Contempt for life comes in many forms. For instance, I used to disdain regular human living, sneering at it like garbage… until I was way past 40 years old. Eventually I lost that attitude. Hey, if you've developed that kind of contempt, you can lose it too.

Ever since the Shift on Dec. 21, 2012, we have no need to try meditating for 15 hours a day (as I did in 1972, on one of my courses with Maharishi Mahesh Yogi). Truth is, we'll evolve way faster spiritually when we accept-and-enjoy our humanity.

Human Life Is Amazing. No Need to Overcomplicate!

Smart Spiritual Seeker, might I suggest? If you're aiming for Spiritual Enlightenment, your human life can definitely count as interesting.

Pursue that human interest while doing ordinary human things, rather than trying to raise yourself upward, seeking some wishy-hopey alternative reality.

For example, if you make a cup of coffee, simply make the cup of coffee. If you drink it, drink it. (Also chop wood and carry water... if that is literally needed for your subsistence farmer lifestyle, which I doubt.)

By definition, living as a human today does NOT mean fancy-dancing in consciousness, although that sure comes easy now, due to our new Consciousness Positioning Superpower. While brewing that cup of coffee, please don't:

1. Analyze yourself.
2. Visualize that you're brewing the coffee.
3. Start tapping on yourself, or doing other energy healing.

In short, avoid doing consciousness extras in order to escape from reality here on Earth. Instead:

1. Say things spontaneously.
2. Do things without the forced intensity of a bad amateur actor.
3. Feel things without seeking drama... or grand answers to "the meaning of life."

Say things? Do things? Feel things? All this comes naturally for us mortals, unlike what we might wind up doing with some unfortunate, over-complicated, versions of Technique Time (which you'll read about in Chapter 27). For now, just keep it simple.

Let's Get Practical About Golden Rule 2

How on earth can you manage doing just 20 Daily Minutes of Technique Time, and not more? Make three simple choices. I'll coach you through them right now.

Choice 1. Timing the When

Decide whether you'd like to do one chunk of 20 minutes or you'd prefer 2 periods of Technique Time that add up to 20, such as 10 + 10.

Incidentally, any time of day for your Technique Time is fine, except please not within one hour of your bedtime. Otherwise, you won't have enough regular human living to sufficiently integrate that Technique Time.

Actually, earlier in your day is better than later in the day, when you have a choice. (Which you probably do.)

Whenever you choose to schedule your Technique Time, it's best to follow that routine pretty regularly. If you must deviate on a particular day, I recommend that you follow your new schedule for a few days in a row. Afterward, if you prefer, switch back to what you had before.

Avoid doing a daily improv. Instead build Technique Time into your daily routine, like how you might brush your teeth at approximately the same times, morning and night. Isn't it better to give yourself a routine rather than agonizing, "Will I manage to brush my teeth today? Ooh, when can I find the time!"

Developing steady habits can simplify your life in many ways. Who among us really-truly needs more complications?

Choice 2. How to Time Your Timing

Suppose that you're doing your morning Technique Time, aiming for 10 minutes. Which form of timing would be preferable?

1. Ten minutes by the clock.
2. Or "Until I feel satisfied."

Definitely choose that first option. And please, avoid setting an alarm. Instead, use a standalone timepiece; whether it's a watch, a clock, or some other electronic device that automatically displays the time.

Then, how can you check the time? When you think you might be close to the end of your allotted number of minutes, take one quick glance at your timepiece. What if you've more time is left? Close your eyes and continue.

Not that all forms of Technique Time require that you close your eyes, but many do.

By contrast, no valuable form of Technique Time is compatible with staring at a clock, keeping track of the time.

Choice 3. Technique Time Outside Your Official Time

Before beginning our program, many of my clients have squandered hours daily on **Unofficial Technique Time.** Those casual minutes add up.

Unofficial Technique Time means doing little bits on the fly. Like you see a stranger on the street and decide to vibe out that person's energies. Or else pray for God to bless that person.

Hello! Unofficial or not, all Technique Time counts. Of course, it's way easy for those little improvs to add up to far more than 20 minutes daily. Using your Consciousness Positioning Superpower is already ridiculously easy to overdo. Do you want to progress on your Program for Spiritual Enlightenment or not?

Here's my advice. Whenever you feel the urge to do Technique Time, write a note to yourself or send yourself a text. Summarize what you'd like to do, like "Pray for that sad-looking guy on the street who seemed drunk."

Then, before your next official Technique Time, review your relevant notes or texts. Decide what you're going to do, and stick with that.

Maybe you're wondering, which form of Technique Time is best? For instance, should you meditate?

Very likely my answer to questions like these will surprise you. Feeling brave? Determined to live like a SMART Spiritual Seeker? Then keep reading.

CHAPTER 26.

10 EXCELLENT Choices for Your Technique Time

After I learned from you about Technique Time, my main attention was on NOT doing more than the max 20 daily minutes, tops. Only recently have I started to appreciate the importance of also actually DOING the full 20 minutes of Technique Time, EVERY DAY!

Alexandra, IT Consultant, in Spiritual Enlightenment

....

Choosing Technique Time wisely, and then doing it daily, is important for a Smart Spiritual Seeker.

Rose Rosetree

....

Since our topic in this chapter is helping you to make excellent choices for your Technique Time, let's begin with your experience of telephones. Smart Spiritual Seeker, are you old enough to remember life before mobile phones? How about landlines only, and always black ones at that?

Since the Age of Faith gave way to the Age of Awakening, telephone technology has developed considerably. What if, today, a friend were to tell you this? "Any kind of phone's fine with me. They're all the same." No doubt, you'd wonder what the heck was wrong with your friend.

Well, how about technology for emotional growth and/or spiritual awakening? In your lifetime that has changed at least as much as new-fangled telephones, which first became popular around 1900, starting with landlines and eventually bringing us far more choices.

What if you're still tempted to think, "All forms of Technique Time are equally good"? Then I've got a really important Golden Rule for you.

Golden Rule 3. Choose Your Technique Time WISELY

Does "WISELY" Mean Following Whatever Is Popular?

Of course not; for instance, countless beautiful spiritual seekers — as well as their teachers — are now blissfully snacking on popular New Age Leftovers, remember?

Sadly, many of these blissful teachers lack energetic literacy. When will they stop embodying "O Come, All Ye Faithful"? When will they start reading chakra databanks?

Perhaps, in the future, many spiritual teachers will develop sophisticated versions of Stage 3 Energetic Literacy. They'll insist on researching whether the techniques they advocate are actually effective.

In this chapter and the next, you'll benefit from state-of-the art recommendations for choosing Technique Time WISELY. Good news first — and it comes in *this* chapter: Which choices are especially effective?

By contrast, our next chapter will warn you about Technique Time choices that aren't so hot.

Following our Program for Spiritual Enlightenment, the choices in this chapter aren't your only good options. However, these 10 are definitely good, which gives you plenty of options for evolving at top speed. Only use forms of Technique Time that appeal to you. Since you're not just anybody, right? You're you.

Are These 10 Techniques the Flashiest Ones I Know?

Definitely not. Many of us have been influenced by mainstream culture, with its emphasis on astral flash; as a result, you may be in the habit of preferring Technique Time choices that seem thrilling.

Remember, though: Astral flash won't help you to evolve spiritually, no more than smoking weed would count as a constructive spiritual experience. If you're seeking Enlightenment, always avoid astral flash.

Instead, choose honest forms of Technique Time that will work for the purpose intended, which is cumulative spiritual awakening. Altogether different from energy-flashy entertainment!

My Top Two Tips for Success, Regarding Technique Time

First, whichever form of Technique Time you choose, do all the steps required, neither adding nor subtracting anything.

Second, where should you look for results? Feeling refreshed afterward, that's where — rather than jonesing for thrills during the practice itself.

If that's true, how boring! What if I have friends where the main thing we talk about is our spiritual experiences?

Avoid such topics, Smart Spiritual Seeker. Otherwise, you could feel like a loser, even when really you are the one who's evolving fastest. During those conversations, start changing the subject.

You're now on a Program for Spiritual Enlightenment, not some kind of reality show for keeping up with the Trippy Joneses... or any big talkers you know, who love to brag about their inner lives.

You live in a society, right? Do you think that society needs more braggarts? Seems to me, we need more folks who are using their full potential in life, folks who are active and engaged; in short, people living in Spiritual Enlightenment. That can be you.

So Vital to Understand

Effective Technique Time doesn't need to feel *inspirational*, no more than it needs to impress you as *flashy*. Often you'll enjoy it, but sometimes you may feel as though nothing special is happening. Of course, short of hiring an expert with skills for delivering something akin to a snapshot of consciousness, you have no way of knowing precisely how well you're doing.

The closest I can come here, in book form, is to provide a simple, straightforward List of Excellent Techniques, coming up in this chapter.

What else is important to know at the outset? Never, ever, multi-task during your Technique Time by *trying to evaluate how it's going*. That's like driving with the brakes on.

> **Spiritual evolution is my passion project. What can help me commit to one practice rather than a gazillion alternatives? And what can help me trust that my choice is worthwhile?**
>
> *Just choose one, already. Preferably choose one of the 10 practices summarized soon in this chapter. Give that technique a chance. After a few weeks, evaluate. Is your life improving in any way? If the answer is yes, keep at it.*

Improving your human life is the purpose of Technique Time, in addition to emotional growth and spiritual evolution.

What IS Technique Time, Anyway?

A well-chosen technique will allow you to use your new Consciousness Positioning Superpower *productively*. Your consciousness will move to an Astral or Divine Vibrational frequency. Also important: No struggle will be required to position your consciousness there. Yet that effortless shift to your consciousness will be good enough to help you evolve spiritually.

What else is important to know from the outset? A good choice of Technique Time is clean; not producing icky side effects.

As for trusting your chosen form of Technique Time, even if you've stopped expecting astral flash, sometimes you may feel like, "Nothing special is happening." What's the most common reason for that?

Blame your amazing Consciousness Positioning Superpower, which makes it ridiculously easy to position your consciousness at a higher vibrational frequency. Imagine: There you are, in Technique Time, yet you're *not* inwardly groaning and grunting, as if bench-pressing 300 pounds.

Not really a problem! Trust your well-chosen, effortless time each day for spiritual evolution.

Reminds Me of this Joke

Smart Spiritual Seeker, for any of you who are still skeptical that good techniques since the Shift can be effortless? I offer you this joke about Doug, who went to a dentist in order to remove a painful tooth. When the bill came, Doug grew irate. He called up the dentist to complain.

"You charged me all that money when it only took you 10 minutes to pull out my tooth!"

The dentist's reply was simple. "Look, I could have taken four hours, four extremely painful hours. Would you have preferred that?"

Expect Success

Exploring this Program for Spiritual Enlightenment, simply do your part. Then you'll evolve spiritually at maximum speed. In particular, Smart Spiritual Seeker, the process of doing Technique Time should never become an excuse to get all self-conscious about how fast you're growing, or even which vibrational frequency you're experiencing. Instead, simply follow these steps:

1. Choose your Technique Time wisely.
2. Follow the rules of the technique.
3. Put in your time.
4. Get the results.

Now Let's Get Practical About Golden Rule 3

In no particular order, here are 10 excellent choices for Technique Time. Each one will position your consciousness at an Astral Vibrational Frequency, with possible quick moments at the Divine Vibrational Frequency.

---

1. Creative Imagination

If you don't already know how to do this this kind of technique, I'd recommend Shakti Gawain's excellent how-to on *Creative Visualization*. Only skip the magical thinking part about how you're supposedly "manifesting" results.

It's enough to close your eyes and pretend (or visualize) something that you desire, since you'll gain the benefit of doing some good Technique Time.

2. Pranayama

Even a simple breathing exercise can work fine, eyes open or closed as you prefer. Naturally, you'll avoid any forcing, right?

Choose from innumerable pranayamas. For instance, you might enjoy Alternate Nostril Breathing. (For instructions, search on "Alternate Nostril Breathing + WebMD".) Also, you'll find a wide array of breathing exercises in my Technique Time how-to, *Let Today Be a Holiday*.

Whichever breathing exercise you do, make that a no-frills version.

3. Real-Deal Yoga

Traditional yoga asanas are brilliant, and also extensively researched. Do every position slowly, stretching and then holding that stretch for a while.

Alternate that with laying down on your back (or similar); closing your eyes; and noticing the ripple effect on your body... thanks to doing the previous asana.

Never strain. Don't break a sweat. And please, never bother with showing off.

4. Energy Healing Where You Cocreate with the Divine

In the Age of Awakening, we can learn techniques expressly designed for cocreating energy healing with God.

By contrast, avoid instructions from psychics that supposedly hook you up with "God's messengers." Sadly, these methods conflate *dependence on discarnate beings* with authentic *cocreating with God.*

Learn honest skills from a teacher with expertise at cocreating in the Age of Awakening, rather than "healers" who use outdated methods from the Age of Faith. One example of cocreating is to learn Spiritually Sparkling® skills. (Find details at www.rose-rosetree.com/workshops/.)

5. Talk to God or Another Divine Being

Build that Divine relationship. Build it your way.

Talk to God about any topic you like; your eyes open or closed, using your voice or simply thinking. Important: Don't consider this to be prayer. Nor would it be wise to expect magic; don't ever sit and wait for an answer. "Talk" means that *you talk.*

6. Sacred Reading

Choose something uplifting, like a hymn or a prayer. Alternate reading slowly with eyes open; then close your eyes and contemplate the meaning of what you've read.

Please, never don't try to "get somewhere" or have a flashy experience. But hey, you knew that.

7. Praise Dancing

Improvise a dance that expresses your love of God. Up to you whether or not you dance along to recorded music: Because you have every right to improvise a praise dance as you see fit.

8. Devotional Music

Invite any Divine Being you like to be your audience. (If you like, imagine Him or Her standing in a particular location in the room where you're doing the Technique Time.)

Slowly sing a hymn or chant, or improvise other sacred music.

9. Read Auras

Of course, reading auras since the Shift doesn't have to involve "seeing the colours." Warning: Directly or indirectly, these old-fashioned methods involve being influenced by discarnate spirits. Avoid that, since you're seeking Enlightenment.

That said, aura reading can be a magnificent form of Technique Time. Make it your business to find a skilled teacher who knows how to read chakra databanks, somebody who can read auras from regular photos. Demand nothing less than Stage 3 Energetic Literacy — since this is what you can learn. Automatically you'll cocreate with the Divine. As a side benefit, you'll also learn a ton about people.

10. Open Your Heart of Compassion

Spend a bit of time building compassion toward yourself. This technique has two parts, as I'll summarize next.

More about How to Open Your Heart of Compassion
First, talk aloud, describing something that has happened in your life, something bothersome; make that one specific incident — preferably fairly recent.

For this technique, what's important? Describe that incident in the language of objective reality, rather than analyzing what happened energetically or psychologically.

> **Second,** repeat your objective-reality version of the incident; only this time, describe what happened from the premise that *you were wise, good, in the process of learning something valuable*, etc.
>
> That simple: Be sure to do both parts, scaling how long you talk so as to fit the amount of time you've budgeted for this activity.

To Benefit Most from Each Day's Technique Time

With any of these 10 forms of Technique Time, how can we make them good? If the answer isn't effort or faith, what else can help us to succeed? Practical information that follows can do the trick.

Avoid Most Group Activities for Technique Time

Such fun, those classes! Socially, they're great. In terms of consciousness, though, taking a spiritual class can lead us to position consciousness at a Human Vibrational Frequency; you know, a social experience. Alternatively, what's the purpose of Technique Time? Something different: This is for your personal evolution, not shallow-up time.

Presumably you're pursuing a form of Technique Time that can help you toward experience at a lovely Astral or Divine Vibrational Frequency. But did you know this? Hanging out with other people can be a fine choice for regular human life, but this seldom works for Technique Time. Remember, Technique Time is your unique opportunity during each 24-hour cycle. It's your big chance to go deep.

During the New Age Years, it seemed as though *the energy of the group* was the most important thing for bringing you great results, like the more the merrier.

Alternatively, haven't you heard some friends doing a lot of Energy Talk about loving a particular Bible Study or yoga class, because *the teacher is so special?*

Only, by now, guess what? Energy Talk is notoriously inaccurate, just like any other form of Stage 1 Energetic Literacy. Besides, the main appeal of that pastor or yoga teacher might well be astral flash.

Smart Spiritual Seeker, some group events can prove beneficial. For now, though, let's keep things simple: Do Technique Time on your own. Afterward hang out with friends.

Also Good to Know

Since you're seeking Enlightenment in the Age of Awakening, now hear this: Spiritual evolution doesn't happen because we join a club.

Smart Spiritual Seeker, you won't attain Enlightenment because you regularly study with a nice group of people. Such an Age of Faith notion! Now that we're in the Age of Awakening, what *is* true? Enlightenment involves your relationship with God. Not buddying up with other humans.

Granted, a skilled teacher might be able to structure a workshop or class in a way that includes effective Technique Time, but finding a teacher like that is rare. Don't depend on it.

Practical DOs and DON'Ts for Quality Technique Time

For sure, your choice for Technique Time matters enormously. In addition, you'll benefit most by following these simple DOs and DON'Ts, which apply to all EXCELLENT Choices for Your Technique Time:

1. DON'T play music to put you in "the mood."
2. DON'T try to manipulate your emotions, like "Turn that frown upside down."
3. DON'T analyze anything psychologically. Spare yourself!
4. DON'T concentrate. Your natural flow of thoughts is preferable.
5. DON'T aim for an experience of astral flash or — for that matter — spiritual awakening. Just do the technique already!

6. DON'T keep your phone on. Before starting any Technique Time, turn off all electronic devices.
7. DO ask any roommates to leave you alone until further notice. Likewise, pets belong outside your room, separated from you by a physical door.
8. Except for Choices 3 and 7 on our list of 10 practices, DO sit down during your Technique Time, preferably with your back not supported. Avoid crossing your arms or legs. Definitely, DON'T lie down or otherwise "Try to relax."
9. DON'T snack during this sacred time, although it's fine to drink water.
10. DON'T ever put together your own special mashup of different techniques. Choose one, designed by an expert; then do that excellent technique as taught.

Smart Spiritual Seeker, you know what else is vital for productive Technique Time? *Learn which choices will waste your time... or worse.*

Can you guess which 10 TERRIBLE choices we'll be discussing in our next chapter?

CHAPTER 27

10 TERRIBLE Choices for Technique Time

Some people are afraid of what they might find if they try to analyze themselves too much, but you have to crawl into your wounds to discover where your fears are. Once the bleeding starts, the cleansing can begin.

-*Tori Amos, Singer-Songwriter*

What's one of the biggest surprises I've encountered as the founder of Energy Spirituality™? When folks analyze what's happening to them **subconsciously,** they're positioning consciousness at an **Astral Vibrational Frequency.**

Whether the language you prefer is psychological or metaphysical, hello! Either approach counts as Technique Time.

Rose Rosetree

Just because the promise of "cleansing" sounds appealing, does that mean a technique will necessarily be good for you? For example, do you recognize that popular approach advocated in our quote by Tori Amos? Reputedly this sort of psychological self-analysis will bring "cleansing."

Only maybe it won't. Research that I've done for clients suggests not. Even the best psychotherapists know better than to "Be my own therapist."

Would Papa Freud have recommended this? Hardly — yet ever since the New Age Years, this irresponsible advice has gone mainstream. Here and now, I'll be giving you a different kind of recommendation.

Controversy alert: In this chapter, I'll be calling out some psychological self-analysis and other self-help techniques, spiritual techniques, and religious techniques — which are reputed to be great for you. Except that energetic literacy research on real-live clients suggests otherwise. (Sorry! I assume everybody means well, but that's not always enough.)

> *What if I strongly believe in a technique, or it's popular with millions of people? Won't that technique automatically be good for me?*
>
> *No, since you're no longer living in the Age of Faith.*

Actually, this chapter may shock you more than anything else in our entire Program for Spiritual Enlightenment: shock you but maybe also help you.

Please, Don't Call Our Next Golden Rule "Negative"

You see, our next golden rule involves discernment for selecting your Technique Time; discernment that isn't casually negative but rather aims to protect you; discernment that I'm offering you as a matter of caring on my part, since you're seeking something as important as Enlightenment.

Golden Rule 4. Avoid Social Pressures that Could Lead You Astray

Social pressures: Of course, social pressures can distract a person who's homesick for Heaven, and willing to try almost anything… on the chance *that particular thing* might bring on Enlightenment.

Smart Spiritual Seeker, since you're a grownup, can't you figure out pretty fast if other people are pressuring you? One tricky exception is when friends and/or celebrities start raving about a trendy technique. Supposedly it's *amazing*. Even worse, it seems like everybody who's anybody is into *this very best-ever, totally super-duper, amazing-amazing practice.* Supposedly this will make you an ultimate human, bringing instant Spiritual Enlightenment.

Smart Spiritual Seeker, question social pressures like these. Frankly, they're the spiritual equivalent of life's perennial *get rich quick schemes*. Don't fall for them. Already you know about better forms of Technique Time, choices that are downright EXCELLENT.

Now let's refine your knowledge further. Before naming the 10 specific TERRIBLE Choices for Technique Time, let's take up the topic of respecting your personal spiritual path.

RESPECTING Your Personal Path

Smart Spiritual Seeker, enthusiasm comes easy. But respect? Choosing options that are respect-worthy — that depends on you. So let's add to your *spiritual* understanding of the significance of Technique Time.

In our Program for Spiritual Enlightenment, **Technique Time** is a term of art, referring to a sacred part of your personal path toward Enlightenment, 20 minutes per day that you choose wisely and pursue responsibly. Another term of art from Energy Spirituality is simply **Technique**: a well-designed skill, a skill that's both tested and reliable, a skill that can help you advance toward Enlightenment.

The techniques recommended in our *last* chapter have been selected for you by a consciousness engineer and Enlightenment Teacher. In this chapter, you'll benefit from that same expertise... Only now I'm bringing you help in the form of specific warnings.

I still don't get it. What is "RESPECTFUL" Use of Technique Time?

Maybe in the past you've felt tempted to mix-and-match different techniques. Perhaps you're planning to "put your own stamp" on something provided in this program, adding something in order to create your own combo, which you're sure would be fun.

Sadly, that "contribution" could cause you to waste that day's Technique Time... or worse, might cause you to take a side trip away from your spiritual path.

With all respect, *unless you have the standing to develop techniques that involve consciousness,* how would you be able to tell what is (or isn't) much good?

As a consciousness engineer, I can protect you from unknown-but-still-negative consequences, results of misguided experiments that could show up in a month, a year, or a decade.

This isn't like adapting somebody else's recipe: Your spiced-up Technique Time isn't like some aggressively-seasoned casserole, which could announce its icky taste to your mouth... immediately.

On a regular basis, my Energy Spirituality sessions include helping some clients who followed a teacher of dubious skill; or else those clients made something up on their own, loved doing it, even believed it to be Divinely inspired, and only later did they discover some pretty awful unintended consequences.

For this reason, I urge you. Please don't succumb to popular-but-misguided **New Age Technique-Time Pressure.** No doubt you've encountered this, how you've just got to pursue the latest in healing, psychology, religion, or spirituality. (Supposedly.)

You and your friends may have thought, "I'm special, so why not prove it? I'll make up my own very special technique. Why not me?" Here's another example of popular mind-body-spirit thinking, magical thinking, wrapped up in sugar:

"All of us are God's children. Of course, you're qualified to design your own techniques. You know best."

Sure, if you don't care about ever attaining Enlightenment!

Otherwise, Smart Spiritual Seeker, avoid making naïve choices about your Technique Time. Find a teacher you trust; then give that teacher's instructions a chance.

Now Let's Get Practical About Golden Rule 4

For example, why avoid social pressures that promote random forms of Technique Time? Here come 10 examples. Yes, every single 1 of the 10 practices summarized next — currently it's crazy-popular. If you were to believe in mere trends as the ultimate wisdom, uh-oh! You'd be tempted to follow right along, inadvertently *preventing* yourself from reaching Enlightenment.

Seriously! The stakes could be that high. Each of the following 10 Terrible Types of Technique Time won't merely waste your precious time. Very likely, regularly doing any one of them can move you into an unproductive consciousness lifestyle, disallowing authentic emotional growth, preventing further spiritual awakening; at least, limiting your evolution until you make some big changes.

Make no mistake. If you're seriously seeking Enlightenment, you'll avoid every one of the following forms of Technique Time.

1. Be Your Own Therapist

Psychological healing, and especially Pop Psych, have gone totally mainstream.

For instance, you'll find diagnostic words like "obsessed" used casually in everything from newspaper articles to Instagram pix for *DIY-obsessed rainbow-colored food*.

Look, if you need psychotherapy, hire a professional.

2. Meditation and Spiritual Initiations

Within the first decade of the Age of Awakening, mainstream meditation techniques have been corrupted.

Many sweet-and-well-meaning teachers have auras as messed-up as Preacher Carlton's. Sorry to report this, but consider yourself warned.

3. Religious Prayers

Repeating set prayers from your family's religious tradition can seem beautiful; quite likely, you've been taught to view these time-hallowed prayers as the ultimate in sacredness.

Yet they're not — not unless you aim to connect to God like an obedient, begging child, and thus not progress significantly toward Enlightenment in the Age of Awakening.

Look, you can choose better.

4. Asking Your Angels for Guidance

By now you know the difference between Divine and astral, right? If you're seeking spiritual guidance... talk to God.

Otherwise, chatting up spirits will encourage opportunistic astral beings to start playing with you. Hey, I know that's very different from what you've been taught. Grieve, if you need to.

As with all these TERRIBLE Choices for Technique Time, you've been misled — probably not on purpose, but misled nonetheless.

5. Psychic Development

Back in the Age of Faith, this was okay to do.

But now? Intuitive work, channeling, and mediumship have all become ways to move into a dead-end consciousness lifestyle.

6. Healing with Reiki or other New Age Healing Modalities

Sorry, but the truth is that opportunistic astral spirits have entered the arena.

Especially problematic for your aura are **Initiations, Attunements,** and **Transmissions** — where you let go and allow the "energies" to improve you.

Please, keep your good memories. Now it's time to move on.

7. Faith-Based Spiritual Cleansing

Being **"Slain in the Spirit"** is supposed to bring you a wonderful blessing. Doesn't it come from a respected Evangelical?

Alternatively, a group of healers from your church might offer you a free healing through **Laying on of Hands**. Oooh!

Sadly, neither type of healing is free… free from the impact of astral-type-garbage entering your aura.

And now that you're no longer living in the Age of Faith, don't believe for a minute that your sweet believing-ness will protect you.

Once again, whatever you've been taught in the past… won't protect you now. Don't give up God, but please do give up on these dangerous forms of Technique Time. Smart Spiritual Seeker, you'll emerge stronger than ever.

8. Visualizing a Golden Bubble

Although touted as a way to protect your aura, this kind of practice doesn't work as intended.

Actually, it backfires, aura-wise. Regardless of how masterfully intricate your visualizations may be!

9. Practice Seeing Aura Colors

Smart Spiritual Seeker, you'll never get to Stage 3 Energetic Literacy that way.

Even worse, old-fashioned practices that involve clairvoyance are now gateway practices to being influenced by astral spirits.

And the irony is, trying to see auras doesn't even lead to good quality energetic literacy.

10. Ground and Shield Your Aura

So much busywork, so little by way of results!

> Meanwhile what, exactly, does one receive in exchange for all that fussing-and-fixing? Usually the result is a messed-up consciousness lifestyle that over-emphasizes energies.
>
> Consider yourself warned, Smart Spiritual Seeker. Not a single 1 of these 10 techniques is compatible with our Program for Spiritual Enlightenment. For that reason...

As You Pursue this Program, Use Discernment

TERRIBLE Choices for Technique Time? Just so you know, "terrible" isn't a word I would ever use lightly.

So far, I've dedicated 50 years of my adult life to helping people with spiritual evolution. How jubilant does it make me feel, regarding folks who have been (or could be) my colleagues... when they start devoting their lives to something that robs them of good results?

How jubilant? Not one bit. Many a New Ager friend of mine used to have a glorious aura, but no longer.

Quite possibly you too know folks in the same boat: such beautiful, caring people, and with so much faith. Yet that hasn't protected them.

Hello, we're in the Age of Awakening now. Old-fashioned faith isn't enough any longer.

Smart Spiritual Seeker, it matters that you're learning how to safely seek Enlightenment now, in the Age of Awakening. Do you think that kind of knowledge grows on trees? Then you must live in a much fancier neighborhood than most of us.

In Case You're Wondering

How do I move past the tragedy of so many beautiful people I've known, people now doing so badly in their consciousness lifestyles? I continue to love them as *good people*, but I also recognize them to be casualties of the Shift into the Age of Awakening.

Unknowingly they've misused their Consciousness Positioning Superpower; despite indications that they were in trouble, these trusting souls kept on believing whatever they'd been promised, obeying whatever they'd been taught during the Age of Faith, expecting that obedience and surrender would protect them for life.

In addition, for many of these seekers who now have messed-up auras, there's one extra reason why they couldn't what was happening to them. They'd learned to **Be Positive**, currently a popular belief among many spiritual idealists.

But Isn't the Sign of Spiritual Attainment Being "Positive"?

Heck no! And that's not a "negative" no. See what I did just there, Smart Spiritual Seeker? I gave you the benefit of some discernment.

Following our Golden Rule 4 can protect you from wasting your Technique Time, or worse. Let's not kid ourselves about the prevalence of social pressures regarding mind-body-spirit and "being positive."

If you spend much time on social media, haven't you noticed? Look at the big celebrities in mind-body-spirit and religion. Hardly difficult, is it, to *find* these famous folks, with their fabulous Search Engine Optimization (SEO)? In public, at least, they tend to be so very, very positive. One current example is Gwyneth Paltrow's crazy-successful business called "Goop."

This website appeals to people in search of mind-body-spirit success. Mostly, Paltrow sells products, including her popular candle called "This Smells Like My Vagina."

Such a shameless commodification of spirituality! But is the former actress excoriated for that? Quite the opposite. Gwyneth's so positive, such a success story! However, I'd draw the line at calling her a person to trust.

Likewise, to a greater degree than you might yet realize, thoughtful people like us are under enormous social pressure to try on whatever's in vogue about what it means to be "spiritual."

Good to know: This unproductive kind of obedience is totally optional. Let's keep things simple, not simplistic but simple, okay?

Let Spiritual Self-Authority, Not Fads, Light Your Way

Smart Spiritual Seeker, our Program for Spiritual Enlightenment comes with standards: Do 20 daily minutes of Technique Time, and use skills that don't lead to unproductive consciousness lifestyles, rather than Enlightenment.

Remember, better techniques are available than the TERRIBLE Ten that I've warned you about in this chapter.

What can help you let go of them? Employ a strength that we all possess, if only we dare to use it: **Spiritual Self-Authority.** This can help you enormously, unless you apply it where you have no business doing so.

What exactly is Spiritual Self-Authority? We touched on that a bit in Part II. Now let's learn more. In order to use your spiritual self-authority:

- Pay attention to what you strongly like.
- Or strongly dislike.
- Value your opinion over religious authorities, famous celebrities, and even (if you're an adult) your mother.

Regarding TERRIBLE Choices for Technique Time, self-authority can supplement what you've learned about Golden Rule 4.

Sometimes a perfectly good technique is simply not for you. Self-authority can deliver that message in the form of personal knowledge, such as how you physically feel, your emotions, your thoughts.

In your sweet idealism, while pursuing your spiritual path, don't ignore your own self.

Despite the Value of Self-Authority, Also Know Its Limits

You see, Smart Spiritual Seeker, self-authority does have limits. For instance, how about choosing which forms of Technique Time would be good for you?

Quite often I encounter confusions about this when I help clients with Soul Thrill® Aura Research, a research specialty that can be done for you by any Energy Spirituality™ expert.

This protocol provides detailed insights, drawn from your own chakra databanks; insights for discerning whether a particular technique is either *good* for you, *ho-hum-ish,* or *downright terrible.*

In general, it's helpful to know whether your Technique Time choices can set in motion subtle problems; moreover, many such problems may not show up for months or years.

Another pointer for you, Smart Spiritual Seeker: When choosing Technique Time, don't be influenced by feeling homesick for Heaven. When selecting techniques for emotional growth or spiritual evolution, do the best research you can.

Ordinarily intelligent consumers can turn extremely gullible when it comes to choosing techniques for emotional growth and spiritual awakening. In this regard, although I haven't seen it all, I've sure seen more than enough of that, over the past 50 years.

Upsetting stories come to mind, but I'll spare you them. Instead, here's a Teaching Tale that might bring you a chuckle.

How Much Does a Five-Year Old Know about Snow?

Little Bobby lived in a suburb where snow was a rare event, which is why his dad was able to tell this story.

One January evening, a sprinkling of snow transformed the grass in front of Bobby's house. Looking out the window, this five-year-old saw the thrilling sprinkling of snow.

Like a shot, out he ran outside in his pyjamas and started jumping all over the yard.

"There's so much snow," Bobby screamed in delight. Super-excited, this adorable little guy... proceeded to build... *a snowball.*

You Know More than Bobby About Nearly EVERYTHING

But unless you've devoted your life to discernment about spiritual growth, please don't consider yourself an expert on forms of Technique Time. For that reason, among others, you're wise to study with an up-to-date spiritual teacher.

Our Program for Spiritual Enlightenment is designed to protect you. In that vein, what will I share with you next? A truly nourishing feast of knowledge — because, given all you've learned thus far, you're finally ready for inside info on consciousness lifestyles.

Among other benefits, this knowledge can help you to finally solve the Church-Wenters Mystery.

CHAPTER 28

Consciousness Lifestyles, The Test of Enlightenment

*Our Father who is in Heaven.... **Give** us this day our daily bread.*

Jesus of Nazareth, Quoted in the New Testament

*In the Age of Awakening, let's not passively wait for spiritual nourishment. Each day we can actively move toward Enlightenment by making choices that bring a good consciousness lifestyle — empowering each of us to **find** our daily bread, which can help us to evolve faster spiritually.*

Rose Rosetree

Smart Spiritual Seeker, let's continue to refine our Program for Spiritual Enlightenment. This time we'll discuss something never taught by Jesus, Buddha, nor any other spiritual master from the Age of Faith — at least none that I've encountered.

Let's explore **Consciousness Lifestyles**, patterns that develop due to everyday habits with positioning consciousness. Although these habits can pose a terrible problem for many in these early years of the Age of Awakening, not to worry.

At least as important, *your* habits can improve by following our Program for Spiritual Enlightenment; in turn, this can help you to evolve significantly every single day.

> *Then why care about other consciousness lifestyles? With all respect, Rose, why waste time discussing any consciousness lifestyle apart from the one all of us want, Enlightenment?*

By the time you've finished this chapter, answers to these questions will be crystal clear.

Meanwhile here's a short answer: Seeking Enlightenment in the Age of Awakening, it's essential to know about consciousness lifestyles because... no longer do we have the luxury of ignoring them.

Really, Today's Spiritual Seekers Don't Have that Luxury

Admittedly, it's not traditional to give a moment's thought to consciousness lifestyles. Before the New Age Years, even the world's most famous spiritual teachers didn't have so much as a *concept* for this. Why not?

During the Age of Faith, there was precious little variety to consciousness lifestyles. Human beings had only two options: either Spiritual Enlightenment or Nothing Worth Mentioning. Mostly, the latter.

Remember, Smart Spiritual Seeker, back then a Psychic Barrier simultaneously *protected* humanity... and *held people back*. Almost always, consciousness was stuck at Human Vibrational Frequencies; when nobody had more freedom than that, neither Einstein nor Mozart, nor anyone else alive pre-Shift.

Very rarely, geniuses like Einstein or Mozart would receive a powerful download of knowledge, supplementing their talent, but even that wasn't an everyday experience like humanity's new superpower. Not coincidentally, during the Age of Faith it was exceedingly rare for anybody to attain Enlightenment.

By contrast, what's true now for every human being with normal mental health — every single clergy member and churchgoer, every energy healer, renunciate, or other spiritual seeker?

Simply due to living now, each one of us has the new Consciousness Positioning Superpower. Inescapably, how we make use of that... will result in a consciousness lifestyle. In this chapter I'll summarize the main options, helping you to understand (*content*) which consciousness lifestyles (*process*) are possible for you and others.

Along the way I'm going to share some radically counter-culture insights into **why** every single consciousness lifestyle might seem impressive to some folks, even seeming like Enlightenment.

> Every consciousness lifestyle can seem impressive, despite the fact that 6 out of 7 are nowhere close to Spiritual Enlightenment.

In the process of learning all this, guess what? A certain mystery will finally be solved.

Will Our Next Golden Rule Shock You?

You might assume that every seeker of Enlightenment has clear standards for what matters. Quite the opposite is true, at least in these early years of the Age of Awakening. Understanding the nature of Enlightenment is hardly simple and universal, like 2+2 = 4.

In daily life you may encounter varied references to spiritual teachings, whether through social media, websites, overhearing conversations, or reading books by famous "experts," including many who have become household names, A-listers in the Enlightenment Establishment.

Actually, the majority of these folks, by now, are leading quite a different consciousness lifestyle. Sadly, most of those household names — however famous — are no longer reliable guides, not unless you long to attain what they have, Consciousness Lifestyle #7 (which you'll definitely read about in this chapter).

No wonder it's vital to add more discernment to what you already know about Enlightenment, a discernment that can protect you on this Program for Spiritual Enlightenment.

> **Golden Rule 5. Understand What Enlightenment IS and ISN'T.**

Countless spiritual seekers faithfully do their daily practice, trusting that meditation or yoga or eating raw (or whatever) is moving them toward "the goal." Yet many sweet believers are extremely vague about that goal... if not completely misinformed.

Of course, when seeking Enlightenment, you'll do far better if you know where you're headed. Knowledge in this chapter can protect you from equating Spiritual Enlightenment with some pretty dismal alternatives.

So long as I'm making controversial statements, here's one more. Because, as an honest Enlightenment Teacher, I need to clarify this:

Traditionally, Age of Faith leaders taught that Enlightenment, once attained, is permanent. No longer true!

Why would I make such a statement? Becoming sadder but wiser, through extensive research using expert skills of energetic literacy; since I've done a great deal of research on this, ever since the start of the Age of Awakening; research of this kind has convinced me that most of today's consciousness lifestyles are really quite fluid.

You see, folks today can move from Enlightenment to an altogether different consciousness lifestyle, just as we can move from any other consciousness lifestyle to a different one; the only exception being the one truly dead-end consciousness lifestyle. You'll find a description of that end of our list that follows in this chapter.

Nothing I'm showing you here, regarding this topic, is presented for shock value. Rather, it's my responsibility as an Enlightenment Teacher to share what I've learned through research that, initially, shocked me too.

One example is how I've used energetic literacy research to help thousands of my clients to finally learn what's going on with *their* current consciousness lifestyles. Only then could they progress toward Spiritual Enlightenment, rather than some spiritual side trip of aura-level imbalance.

Smart Spiritual Seeker, I'm committed to *protecting* you from today's common problems with consciousness lifestyles. Equally strongly, I do look forward to *inspiring* you.

What Enlightenment ISN'T? That's Vital to Understand

Surely you've noticed. Today's Enlightenment Establishment boasts experts at nonduality, religion, meditation, yoga, energy healing, and more. Often these experts seem very relaxed, very chill — and to some, these "virtues" represent sufficient "proof" of being spiritually evolved.

Smart Spiritual Seeker, don't assume that any of these experts is trustworthy. As a consumer, you always have the right to ask questions, beginning with this one: "Does this person have the standing to help me as a spiritual teacher?"

Enlightenment Teachers had better be in Enlightenment themselves, namely, *process*-type experience, rather than smoothly talking the talk (*content*).

Beyond that, at a time when so many different consciousness lifestyles exist, wouldn't it be helpful to be able to tell those options apart? Discernment is of the essence, especially since, as you'll soon see in detail, all side trip consciousness lifestyles can masquerade as Enlightenment.

Disclaimer: In this chapter you'll be reading practical concepts that are rare in the world today, down-to-earth knowledge that can bring you discernment. However, let's be clear that I'm *not training you* to discern anybody's consciousness lifestyle. (Not here, anyway. After all, you're learning a Program for Spiritual Enlightenment, which ought to be plenty for one book, don't you think?)

What Else Enlightenment ISN'T. Hello!

It's not obvious. Maybe it seems to you that understanding who's in Enlightenment should be obvious, and any truly spiritual person ought to be able to tell. Far from it, actually. For example, a popular post at my blog is called, "What Enlightenment Looks Like."

This is an ongoing "Discernment Jamboree," an informal way to develop discernment and consumer smarts, a blog resource that's free to all comers.

> *Honestly, why would I spend time on that kind of discernment? What's in it for me?*
>
> *Well, if you care about gaining Enlightenment, this discernment is vital. Among other things, if you read that article just cited, hey! Very likely you'll quickly discover how much you don't know yet about the goal of your spiritual quest.*

Reading comments at that recommended blogpost, you may be shocked (even horrified) at how vague many Enlightenment Teachings are regarding their goal.

Imagine if your friend Maya was centering her life on becoming a multi-millionaire, yet she barely knew much money was in a $100 bill. Not only are many spiritual seekers walking around with vague or misleading ideas about Enlightenment; they're equally clueless about any of the other consciousness lifestyles described in this chapter.

Yet every Smart Spiritual Seeker needs to be aware of all current consciousness lifestyles. No ivory tower knowledge, this! Call it *protecting yourself.* And now...

How I'll Educate You Here about Consciousness Lifestyles

Smart Spiritual Seeker, for each of the seven options that follow, you'll find this same sequence of information:

1. First, I'll *name* that particular consciousness lifestyle.
2. Following that, you'll find a *description* of having that consciousness lifestyle.
3. Next comes "The Typical Range for Positioning Consciousness." Regarding folks with each consciousness lifestyle, while awake, *where do they typically position their consciousness*?

4. Finally, you'll learn why that consciousness lifestyle may *seem like* Enlightenment.

Does that last idea seem shocking to you? As you read about each of the seven following options, maybe ask yourself, "Which consciousness lifestyle might I have right now? "

Although you won't be able to tell for sure, you might make a pretty good guess. If you like, you can always schedule a session with any Energy Spirituality™ expert and receive an expert opinion — plus help, if needed, for improving your consciousness lifestyle.

#1. Spiritual Enlightenment

Spiritual Enlightenment is THE consciousness lifestyle of self-actualization. Quite distinctively, when you compare this way of living to any other way, what stands out most? How you're far more strongly connected to God.

Besides that, you're using your full potential as a person. For example, in Enlightenment you enjoy maximum creativity, bringing a very human-and-useful degree of resourcefulness to life.

Summing up, Enlightenment could be called the spiritual glory of human life.

The Typical Range for Positioning Consciousness

Usually whenever awake, a person in this category experiences life with a component of Divine Vibrational Frequency... mixed together with experience at a Human Vibrational Frequency.

During Technique Time, a person experiences with a component of Divine Vibrational Frequency... mixed with experience at an Astral Vibrational Frequency. Or sometimes it's all experience at the Divine Vibrational Frequency.

As you know by now, during the Age of Awakening, one is either in Traditional Enlightenment or in Age of Awakening Enlightenment; living one version or the other. Both have additional attributes, depending on the particular version. Here I've described what both of them have in common.

Why It May Seem Like Enlightenment
Spiritual Enlightenment seems like Enlightenment... because it is. Ironically, this glorious consciousness lifestyle is totally lacking in astral flash. For that reason, many folks wouldn't be particularly impressed by meeting such a person.

Keep reading further and you'll learn about flashier consciousness lifestyles — many of which are extremely *far away from* Enlightenment, yet the resulting auric modeling might seem *more impressive* to those who lack discernment. Real-deal Enlightenment doesn't necessarily impress casual lookers.

#2. Human-Based Spirituality

Folks in **Human-Based Spirituality** are evolving fast, although probably not as fast as what you'll read about as Consciousness Lifestyle #3.

Meanwhile, what's the great thing about this particular consciousness lifestyle? Folks living in Human-Based Spirituality aren't living in Options #4-7 on this list. Instead, folks maintain strong interest in their human lives — rather than what? Rather than the not-great alternatives you'll be reading about soon enough!

The Typical Range for Positioning Consciousness
Usually, while awake, a person in this category will position consciousness at a Human Vibrational Frequency.

During Technique Time, consciousness can be positioned at an Astral Vibrational Frequency or even, sometimes, at the Divine Vibrational Frequency.

Why It May Seem Like Enlightenment
Because, by and large, these folks don't come across as "weird." Not too shabby, actually!

Otherwise, even though Human-Based Spirituality is pretty darned great, guess what?

Usually the corresponding auric modeling fails to impress other folks, not unless these folks have become skilled aura readers who've developed expertise at discerning consciousness lifestyles.

Unfortunately, some people in Human-Based Spirituality can be pretty stuck in their spiritual evolution, such as alcoholics or porn addicts or just plain haters.

Fortunately, though, millions with this consciousness lifestyle are progressing very beautifully toward the goal of Spiritual Enlightenment. While researching auras of those in Human-Based Spirituality, I find more variation within this consciousness lifestyle... than any other.

#3. The New Strong

Ever hear of this consciousness lifestyle? **The New Strong** is an upgrade from Human-Based Spirituality, and your very best choice for evolving spiritually at the fastest possible rate.

In case you're wondering, while pursuing our Program for Spiritual Enlightenment, automatically, you will be living The New Strong, a consciousness lifestyle that you can maintain for the rest of your life.

Imagine, there's nothing to stop you until-and-unless God gives the okay for you to cross the threshold into Enlightenment; failing that, it's still pretty great to be living The New Strong.

What's with that name, "The New Strong"? This signifies the notable inner strength that you can develop through this Program for Spiritual Enlightenment; personal strength being just one of the cumulative improvements you can expect.

- You might do fine on your own, without personal sessions, simply using what's in this book.

- If you start feeling stuck, please consider booking a personal session with an Energy Spirituality™ expert, or somebody else with that degree of energetic literacy and problem-solving know-how.
- Also, presumably you can gain this consciousness lifestyle through involvement in any other *effective* program for spiritual evolution in the Age of Awakening.

What's most vital for all of you who seek Enlightenment in the Age of Awakening? Gain a practical understanding of your Consciousness Positioning Superpower, and then proceed to use it productively.

With our Program for Spiritual Enlightenment, I'm coaching you to do just that. As a supplement, you're learning how to follow the Six Sweet Golden Rules for this program. Provided that you're doing reasonably well, aura-wise, this program will help you to live The New Strong.

The Typical Range for Positioning Consciousness

Usually, when living The New Strong, while awake you will position consciousness at a Human Vibrational Frequency.

In addition, it's typical to just plain *enjoy* human experience; often enjoying life considerably more than somebody who's living in Human-Based Spirituality.

During Technique Time, consciousness can be positioned at an Astral Vibrational Frequency or even, sometimes, at the Divine Vibrational Frequency.

Why It May Seem Like Enlightenment

What would other people notice about your living The New Strong? Most likely, you'd seem to be enjoying your life more than most, and somehow you have developed an underlying emotional stability; also, that you act naturally in different human-type situations.

("Naturally"? For comparison keep reading about Consciousness Lifestyles #4-7, ugh!)

#4. Spiritual Shutdown

Oh, the wondrous sense of superiority! You see, **Spiritual Shutdown** is the ultimate "Know It All" way of living.

> See the irony, Smart Spiritual Seeker? Those of us who are willing to learn: We admit we don't have all the answers. Consider this lack of superiority to be a necessary price we pay for evolving spiritually.

In reality, life's most knowledgeable people typically have less confidence than life's (proudly ignorant) know-it-alls. *Socially* you've probably encountered quite a few of them already, long before the Shift. Since 12-21-12, you can appreciate that usually (though not always) know-it-alls have the consciousness lifestyle of Spiritual Shutdown.

Although they often act smugly superior, hello! From a spiritual perspective that smugness typically indicates something altogether different: Being spiritually stuck.

In relationships, those in Spiritual Shutdown tend to be proudly insensitive; in religion, they veer toward the Fundamentalist side of that religion; atheism is also a possibility.

The Typical Range for Positioning Consciousness

Usually, when awake, consciousness for a person in this category will stay put at a Human Vibrational Frequency; if there's a brief bit of experience at an Astral Vibrational Frequency, the person reflexively uses consciousness to race back to a Human Vibrational Frequency, thereby no longer feeling "off" or "weird"; "like a snowflake," etc.

Why It May Seem Like Enlightenment

Folks in Spiritual Shutdown tend to believe they're ideal. What if you or I were to tell them about the concept of Spiritual Enlightenment? Probably they'd respond, "Sounds like me. Let me tell you all about it."

Incidentally, here's one human tipoff to this consciousness lifestyle. In my experience, folks in Spiritual Shutdown seldom do any effective form of Technique Time, such as those you have read about in Chapter 26.

#5. Spiritual Addiction

The beauty of **Spiritual Addiction** is how it feels like such an advantage in life. (In reality, that's untrue. Oh well.) Neither emotional growth nor spiritual evolution is possible; and why not?

Because folks in Spiritual Addiction keep positioning consciousness at an Astral Vibrational Frequency. This prevents these people from progressing spiritually. Even worse, it's common for them to keep spiraling ever-deeper into their astral wonderland.

Often they have brag-worthy "Positive Vibes," but this comes at a price, since these folks use only a fraction of their potential in life.

But isn't it obvious to people when they start slipping into this consciousness lifestyle?

Not really. Smart Spiritual Seeker, think back to one of the most important things you've learned about humanity's new Consciousness Positioning Superpower: How effortless it is.

No wonder then, how somebody in Spiritual Addiction seldom knows it; the addiction develops effortlessly; moreover, life seems far prettier than it does for those of us who routinely position our consciousness at Human Vibrational Frequencies.

Maybe you're wondering, what causes this consciousness lifestyle? By now, Smart Spiritual Seeker, you know the answer.

Taking recreational drugs, or drinking alcoholic beverages is incompatible with our Program for Spiritual Enlightenment. You also know why.

Even without a chemical assist, millions fall into Spiritual Addiction, drifting away from human reality because they're doing more than 20 Daily Minutes of Technique Time, Tops. For example, when blogging in 2020 I researched many of America's top yoga teachers and Tai Chi masters.

Nearly all of them were living in Spiritual Addiction. These beautiful people exemplify what I've previously called "casualties of the Shift into the Age of Awakening." Still, it's definitely possible to overcome this stuck consciousness lifestyle. Our Program for Spiritual Enlightenment can sometimes be all that's needed.

The Typical Range for Positioning Consciousness

Most often, during waking hours, someone in Spiritual Addiction will position consciousness at an Astral Vibrational Frequency. As this consciousness addiction progresses, one may feel actively uncomfortable with positioning consciousness at a Human Vibrational Frequency.

Interestingly, this consciousness *process* is often supplemented by a lot of Energy Talk (*content*). Also, it's not unusual to use language from Enlightenment teaching, only not using those words quite right.

Why It May Seem Like Enlightenment

As a result of Spiritual Addiction, many traditional attributes of Enlightenment can appear to be a feature of that person's behavior (and auric modeling):

- Mellow
- Even-tempered
- More Spiritual than Thou

Except what shows with skilled research into the auras of folks in Spiritual Addiction? Oboy, you'll encounter something far less beautiful than Spiritual Enlightenment.

> Bottom line: People living in Spiritual Addiction do not evolve spiritually... at least, not until they improve their consciousness lifestyle.

Reality Check

Even if you don't yet have expertise at researching consciousness lifestyles, have you ever known a friend who turned into a pothead?

Suppose we're talking about your friend Zeke. These days, whenever you visit, Zeke invites you to join him in getting high. Inevitably, he regales you with his "great insights into life."

Of course, these are a byproduct of his stoned state (*process*); to you, Zeke's "great insights" don't seem the least bit impressive (*content*).

Such a heartbreaking illusion! Zeke feels like he's growing so much spiritually.

Yet to you it's as plain as the (still-human) nose on his face: Zeke is stuck, not growing at all, despite making some pretty pathetic attempts to persuade you and others to get high with him.

How about those who get high "naturally," due to over-using their Consciousness Positioning Superpower? Lacking energetic literacy, it's so easy to unintentionally move into Spiritual Addiction.

Far too many idealists today have discovered that they can live with a "natural high," caused by noticing energies as much as possible. In other words, they're doing way more than 20 Daily Minutes of Technique Time.

In reality, this natural mellowness isn't the triumph these folks think. Despite feeling full of ineffable wisdom, in reality, their auras are a mess; and humanly, they're using just a fraction of their potential in life — at least, until they swap out that consciousness lifestyle for something better.

#6. Psychological Overwork

Maybe you didn't know there was a consciousness lifestyle called "**Psychological Overwork**."

Well, there sure is. Can you guess what is meant by that name? The problem involves spending too much time on analyzing one's life, one's relationships, one's anything.

Sound to you like Technique Time? Sure is. Accordingly, "playing therapist" for more than 20 minutes per day causes Psychological Overwork, that simple.

To be clear, a bit of self-inquiry doesn't distort anyone's aura, but now that everyone's got that new Consciousness Positioning Superpower, what happens? Focusing on our motivations, doing this for 3 minutes here, 30 minutes there? That's like the summertime game of focusing a light onto a magnifying glass.

No, that excessive amount of Technique Time won't start a physical fire, but we sure can mess up some of our chakra databanks for a while, with specific problems distinctly observable to anybody with skills for discerning such things.

And speaking of discernment, mental health professionals are not doomed to live in Psychological Overwork.

As my Energy Spirituality™ clients, many of them did begin with this consciousness lifestyle, but a bit of mentoring helped them to quickly move into Human-Based Spirituality, or The New Strong, or even Spiritual Enlightenment.

For therapists, the trick is to guide clients without joining them in subconscious spelunking. What does it take to do better? Usually, therapists need just one mentoring session; sometimes some extra coaching (with Consciousness Positioning Consults®, etc.) can make all the difference.

And Speaking of Psychotherapy, Here's a Related Joke

When you just read this introduction to Psychological Overwork, how did that make you feel?

Granted, this jokey idea is no more hilarious than all the other variations you've encountered by now, where your friend plays "therapist" and keeps asking you, "How does that make you feel?"

But maybe this sort of joke can provide a practical clue for seeking Enlightenment:

1. Just as some folks move into Spiritual Addiction through overdoing spiritual, religious, and/or energetic forms of Technique Time...
2. Others move into Psychological Overwork by over-using Technique Time to constantly analyze their lives and the lives of other people, using pop psychology.
3. Either way, that person's Consciousness Positioning Superpower is being misused.
4. And yes, some hardworking seekers manage to do both kinds of overwork, managing to develop a mixed consciousness lifestyle of Psychological Overwork PLUS Spiritual Addiction.

Everything you've read in this chapter about the disadvantages of Spiritual Addiction... will apply equally to this psychologically-oriented consciousness lifestyle.

And equally true, after folks move into Human-Based Spirituality or The New Strong, they can resume emotional growth, spiritual evolution, and a more successful life in general.

The Typical Range for Positioning Consciousness

Most often, during waking hours, someone living in Psychological Overwork will position consciousness at an Astral (i.e., Subconscious) Vibrational Frequency.

As Psychological Overwork progresses, that person may feel *actively uncomfortable* when consciousness is positioned at a Human Vibrational Frequency.

Often, this consciousness *process* is accompanied by a lot of conversational *content* in the form of Psychology Talk.

Why It May Seem Like Enlightenment

Probing for psychological insight can seem superior to any other way of life. For that reason, many folks in Psychological Overwork believe they're in Spiritual Enlightenment, only better.

Even worse, they may impress other people as if in Enlightenment; for instance, seemingly possessing superior knowledge of other people's subconscious motivations.

Quite acrobatic, these folks may seem, due to using their new Consciousness Positioning Superpower to leap back and forth, alternating between human anything and describing the underlying subconscious pattern.

To those who "worship" at the altar of Freud — sure, I've just used ironic quotes here, since Freud was famously an atheist — what could seem better than fabulous psychological insights?

Well, Enlightenment is better, I'd say; certainly, Spiritual Enlightenment is a completely different consciousness lifestyle. Arguably, pop psychology has become an even more influential topic in Collective Consciousness than religion.

Yet auras of folks in Psychological Overwork aren't superior; they're stuck-stuck-stuck.

#7. Extreme Spiritual Addiction

This consciousness lifestyle is a one-way street. To my knowledge, nobody comes back from **Extreme Spiritual Addiction,** at least, not for the rest of that person's lifetime.

Already that sounds pretty scary, right? It is. Only here's the most important thing to know about this consciousness lifestyle:

Never does it *just happen* to anyone. Rather, the problem is the result of a series of choices; choices that are completely avoidable.

What's involved in that kind of slippery slope? Making one compromising choice at a time, a person keeps on encouraging energy sensitivity and astral influences... until the process of aura-level corruption passes a point of no return.

The Typical Range for Positioning Consciousness

Consistently, in Extreme Spiritual Addiction, the person's waking hours are spent with consciousness locked into Astral Vibrational Frequencies.

Besides automatically positioning consciousness that way, as a default, there's an added complication: Discarnate entities have gained access to that person's aura.

Icky but true, for folks with this consciousness lifestyle, at any given time, discarnate beings are physically present in that human being's chakra databanks; basically, opportunistic entities take turns making their human puppet walk and talk.

Why It May Seem Like Enlightenment

Can you guess?

What's the main allure of folks in Extreme Spiritual Addiction? Astral flash, of course.

Picture a wannabe rock star, all decked out in garish colors and sequins. Why does that over-the-top kind of costume work so well in Vegas?

Because audiences in Vegas aren't seeking Spiritual Enlightenment, nor even a refined experience. Quite the opposite, right?

Fact is, multitudes *anywhere* prefer entertainment that's larger-than-life. Sleazy sex sells, and so does every other kind of garishness, including astral flash.

To some spiritual seekers — and others — astral flash can seem incredibly wonderful. At least, certain folks feel that way, and you need not be one of them.

How about YOUR Consciousness Lifestyle?

Maybe you're wondering, "What if I'm living in Consciousness Lifestyles #4, 5, or 6?"

Following this Program for Spiritual Enlightenment might give you all the knowledge you need to get back on track with your spiritual evolution. Otherwise, what if you still feel a bit stuck? Then you might consider a personal session with me for Enlightenment Teaching.

I've helped many Smart Spiritual Seekers to progress beyond less desirable consciousness lifestyles #4 and 5; some of them have eventually moved into Enlightenment.

What if I'm living with Consciousness Lifestyle #7?

Guess what: Based on my experience, if you really were living that way? It's unlikely that you'd have read more than a chapter or two of this book. Living in Extreme Spiritual Addiction provides its own kind of high, often with an easy kind of contempt for anybody not living the exact same way.

So fear not, Smart Spiritual Seekers. And now, here's a well-deserved treat for us all.

Let's Officially Solve the Church-Wenters Mystery

Already you know that folks in certain occupational groups are especially at risk for Extreme Spiritual Addiction: psychics, energy healers, actors and other performers, politicians seeking power, spiritual teachers. Well, guess what? Another high-risk group is definitely clergy.

Ever since the New Age Years, so many churchgoers have wanted to *feel something*. Well, what could guarantee excitement better than astral flash?

First came the megachurches; later came outlets like YouTube and TikTok. Did you ever wonder who lands those highly competitive influencer jobs?

Astral flash has brought success to many religious leaders like Carlton, whose messed-up aura we researched in Chapter 20. Of course, many of his churchgoers would find him irresistibly charismatic, spell-binding, superb. When it comes to auric modeling, entities at a HIGH Vibrational Frequency put on the flashiest show.

On the Other Hand

Certain other churchgoers have more discernment about auric modeling. Think for a moment:

> *What would you do if you were born and raised to attend a certain house of worship? But then, over the years, your subconscious mind began warning you with more and more urgency:*
>
> *"This pastor may be famous, but something here is very, very wrong."*

Human nature being what it is:

- Some folks would *consciously* find reasons to leave the church.
- While others might not yet be strong enough to consciously admit the truth to themselves; instead they'd be guided *subconsciously* — until "for some reason" they'd keep forgetting to go to church.

And Now a Special Nod to You Faithful Churchgoers

Many factors may have contributed to your ongoing religious practice. For example:

1. Clergy at your particular house of worship might have an excellent consciousness lifestyle, such as Human-Based

Spirituality. Therefore, their auric modeling would continue to inspire, and you'd encounter none of the ick factor which has caused others to become Church-Wenters.

2. Another possibility is that you might be well on your way to Spiritual Enlightenment. Even if you haven't yet crossed the threshold into Enlightenment, you could have plenty of inner access to God; doing that in your own way and, therefore, spontaneously, yes! You might see only the good in your beloved religious service.

That second possibility would bring a blessing to you and — through your own auric modeling — subconsciously inspire the clergy and fellow churchgoers where you worship.

Wherever You Worship

I think you're fortunate indeed if you can belong to organized religion and be nourished by it. Through your example, worshipers like you can help to pull Age of Faith institutions into the Age of Awakening.

My only additional recommendation to you is that you follow this Program for Spiritual Enlightenment. Even if you already have a beautiful faith, Enlightenment would only improve it.

This I know from having helped people like you to move into Spiritual Enlightenment. Before, they already loved God; since then, their love and service have only turned more glorious.

Protecting Yourself as a Member of Organized Religion

Specifically, I mean protecting yourself from clergy with corrupted consciousness lifestyles. It's my hope that the clarity you've gained in this chapter can help you to discern more clearly what's currently true for you, regarding your religious community.

Please pay attention to what really works for you *now*, compared to what you've loved in the past.

If applicable, what you've learned here may help you to stop making excuses for certain fellow worshipers and clergy; those whose consciousness lifestyles involve Spiritual Addiction, Psychological Overwork, or Extreme Spiritual Addiction.

Recognizing this possibility doesn't make you judgmental. Nor, of course, are you responsible for other people's choices. Since you believe in God, perhaps you can trust God to help everything turn out right, eventually. (I do.)

In Conclusion

Of course, Smart Spiritual Seeker, long before developing energetic literacy, you can benefit in practical ways from what you've learned here about consciousness lifestyles.

After all, this Program for Spiritual Enlightenment was designed by a teacher who is also a consciousness engineer, cocreating with the Divine. Long story short, I believe you will benefit by following our Six Sweet Golden Rules.

Practically speaking, what you've read in this chapter can help you to avoid common problems that disallow progress toward Enlightenment. Granted, the research you've read about here isn't mainstream yet — not by a long shot — but why sit around and wait? Become a *leader* of the Age of Awakening. Get in on the ground floor!

Thanks for taking this time to educate yourself through this chapter, and all the chapters that preceded it. Now you can more fully appreciate what *isn't* in this Program for Spiritual Enlightenment, as well as what *is*.

All in all, you're ready to move forward, learning just a bit more, encountering more advanced — and spiritually yummy — details.

Let the big fun begin.

CHAPTER 29

How this Program for Enlightenment Helps You

I do believe we're all connected. I do believe in positive energy. I do believe in the power of prayer. I do believe in putting good out into the world.

Harvey Fierstein, Actor

....

If you'd like to help to change this world for the better...
Alternatively, if you'd simply like to personally progress toward Spiritual Enlightenment...
Either way, what's important to know?
Stop believing in feel-good ideas about energy. Daydreaming like that won't make a lick of difference. Wake up, people!

Rose Rosetree

....

Chapter by chapter, you've been learning how to pursue Enlightenment as somebody living now, in the Age of Awakening; you're seeking Enlightenment in an era when many traditional rules for attaining Spiritual Enlightenment have changed.

Enlivening your self-authority, you've smashed illusions regarding leftovers from the Age of Faith.

And so far, in Part III, you've learned about five of the Six Sweet Golden Rules in our Program for Spiritual Enlightenment. What's left?

Saved the Best Golden Rule for Last

It's so very Age of Awakening!

Golden Rule 6. Integrate Spiritual Expansion into Your Human Life

Smart Spiritual Seeker, in order to follow this rule, you'll do a two-step process: Spiritual Expansion followed by Spiritual Integration. Precisely that combo will help you to progress most rapidly toward your goal. But first things first....

What Is Spiritual EXPANSION?

Spiritual Expansion is a more precise term for something you're already familiar with, *spiritual awakening*. What makes them different from each other?

Spiritual awakening comes from an Age of Faith model for seeking Enlightenment: Traditionally, spiritual teachers emphasized waking up from "ignorance."

Ideally, this awakening allowed the spiritual seeker to gradually emerge from a maya-like, illusion-drenched, sleepy **State of Consciousness.** Perhaps entering into a **Satori** or **Samadhi** kind of experience, totally emerging from a sleepy-like state of consciousness into the fully awake, illusion-free, way to be human: Spiritual Enlightenment.

My view is different: Understanding Spiritual Expansion is essential for an up-to-date, effective way of seeking Enlightenment.

Absolutely, Spiritual Expansion helps us move toward **Self-Realization, Self-Actualization, "Solving the Mystery of the Self,"** or other names you may prefer to use for Spiritual Enlightenment. Including "Enlightenment"!

For sure, Smart Spiritual Seeker, in this chapter you'll learn more about the expansion of awareness. Equally important, you'll learn about something unknown to the ancients.

When you think of Buddha, as traditionally depicted in statues, he's laughing a lot, right? Well, I suspect he'd get quite a giggle out of what you're about to read next. Despite his magnificent wisdom, I doubt that Buddha had a clue about this kind of thing.

Nor did Jesus, Krishna, Kwan Yin, Isis, Athena, or other spiritual teachers — whether avatars, gods, goddesses, or ascended masters.

But you? Because you're living in the Age of Awakening, I'm quite sure that you'll easily understand the truth of what follows.

Smart Spiritual Seeker, You're a Person, an Individual

Seeking Enlightenment in the Age of Awakening is no longer the story of a nondescript sort of surrendered everyman, obediently surrendered, nourished by faith; eventually becoming enough of a nothing to receive The Big Prize.

Have you noticed yet? Smart Spiritual Seeker, you are a person, an individual, not merely some random "whoever." Actually, that's a mild understatement. Let's go for this version instead:

> **You are important-and-distinctive, evolving as a soul, engaged in living this unique human incarnation. No matter how many times you incarnate further, never again will you be this particular individual, with the distinctive qualities you have right now, alive at this time on Earth.**

Living as that unique person you are — and without even breaking a sweat — you already have a degree of sophistication unknown to humans from yesteryear.

And yes, that includes countless lifetimes spent by spiritual seekers whose highest spiritual aspiration was to become the nameless, faceless servant of God.

When traditional Enlightenment teachings first emerged, thousands of years ago, was there even such a thing as a person? I think not: not in humanistic ways that we, living now, would consider *being a person*.

Far More Sophisticated than People in Olden Days

That's you! Suppose that like me, back in the day, you spent countless hours reading the Vedas, a core scripture of Hinduism. My former guru, Maharishi Mahesh Yogi, insisted that his advanced initiators do that; he also told us the Vedas were 10,000 years old.

Pretty far back into the Age of Faith, right? Although Hinduism isn't the world's oldest religion, it may well be the oldest tradition for seeking Spiritual Enlightenment.

Not to criticize exactly, but hey, did you know this?

> **Something pretty important was missing from all of humanity's oldest scriptures.**

Colors

That's right, certain colors were missing; most of the colors that people living now — including you and me — take for granted.

Amazing but true, in the mid-1800's, scholars began to notice the strangest thing about colors in ancient writings, including the Old Testament, the Koran, Homer's Iliad and Odyssey, and more.

Color descriptions were mostly black or white, sometimes metallic; very rarely you'd read about yellow or red.

By now, linguistic scholars have explored this idea more extensively, determining that languages worldwide always started with just two words for color, *black* and *white* (or, sometimes, dark versus light).

In what sequence, then, did people all over the world begin to use additional words for colors? Next came *yellow*, and then *green*. (Although in some languages this order was reversed.)

Long story short, which was the last essential color to appear in every human language? *Blue.*

What, Ancient Spiritual Teachers Couldn't See BLUE?

Makes sense if you read more of the research that I'll summarize here. Smart Spiritual Seeker, one of my hobbies is studying the history of ideas, through books like *The Timetables of History*.

Over the centuries, important new ideas have been born and, eventually, gone mainstream. You see, humanity is evolving intellectually, cognitively, perceptually; we're not only evolving in the biological sort of way that fascinated Charles Darwin.

During my college days, I studied Homer's Iliad and read descriptions like the *wine-dark sea* and *gray-eyed Athena*. Only more recently did I think, "Huh? Never the *blue* sea? And not a single person in Homer's masterpieces ever had *blue* eyes? Not even *green* eyes, like Harry Potter?"

Over the millennia, and especially during the century before the Shift, human experience has evolved exponentially. In terms of emotional development, spiritual awakening, and everyday perception of life, humans have developed far more discernment.

At least as exciting as discovering the color blue, what else has emerged? Nothing less than the concept of *being a distinctive human individual!*

In this context, who deserves a shout-out? Humanistic psychologist Carl Rogers, who published *On Becoming a Person* in 1961: Although Dante Alighieri was a great poet, he never got anywhere close to writing about individual personhood, but Rogers sure did.

In Dante's *Divine Comedy*, published around 1319, the narrator traveled through Hell, then Purgatory, and finally he entered into Paradise. Along the way this great poet described many historical characters, such as the Roman poet Virgil. But are these larger-than-life characters ever really depicted as human individuals, like folks you'd meet at the local supermarket? I don't think so. Do you?

Deservedly, many ancient masters, poets, and seers are venerated to this day, but let's admit the truth. Despite their awesome wisdom, the ancient masters couldn't even see the color blue. Nor did they likely care much about people as individuals, their "personalities" or "preferences" or "interests." Let alone their "personal growth."

Look, it was enough to establish that somebody was male or female, able-bodied or not, obedient or rebellious; maybe more important was how, within society, one held a certain status, such as one's birth order.

Smart Spiritual Seeker, in your personal experience, has birth order been discussed by your parents as though this were highly significant? By contrast, you might remember traditional fairy tales, like those you read in childhood. Weren't the heroes usually the oldest son?

Is that just a coincidence? Maybe not. In China today — yes, *today's* China — parents with three sons will give them names like Joe or Charlie or Sven (only the Chinese versions.) Except, in everyday life, what will members of that family call each kid?

- Eldest Son
- Middle Son
- Or Youngest Son

Caring about individuality is hardly traditional, you see, so why be surprised that even the revered leaders of today's Enlightenment Establishment... never got that memo.

Thousands of Years Ago, Did Individuality Matter?

Not when it came to seeking Enlightenment: Individuality was hardly deemed significant. For instance, when it came to reading people's energies, back in the day, what *did* matter?

Aura skills emphasized a person's subtle flows of physical energy. Vedic seers would research the **Nadis**, so useful for ancient Enlightenment teaching; later, Chinese sages began to track the flow of energies through **Meridians**.

Both terms, of course, are used to this day. Clearly, this info must be useful to some. But hello! None of this takes into account that the spiritual seeker is a person, an individual.

Smart Spiritual Seeker, antique versions of energetic literacy don't take YOU into consideration; you, a person with a unique individuality, distinctive life experiences, and curiosity. Instead, old-timey energetic literacy concerns itself with how well you're working as an **Energy Machine.**

Honestly! Smart Spiritual Seeker, don't you consider yourself more than a human machine, somebody whose energies can flow either correctly or incorrectly?

Fortunately, in the Age of Awakening, buh-bye to Psychic Barrier, and hello to new insights into being a person. After the Shift it became possible to read chakra databanks — today's upgrade of the nadis.

And what a world of difference that makes, especially from the perspective of a self-actualizing individual like you. In a nutshell:

- Nadis have names about energy flow, like *Ida* and *Pingala*. Research them and what *won't* you find? Anything remotely individual. Zilch.
- Rather you'll learn about the human animal as an energy machine. Admittedly that could be useful for some purposes, but inadequate if you're seeking Enlightenment in the Age of Awakening.
- By contrast, today's chakra databanks have names like the *Root Chakra Databank for* **Presence in the Room** and the *Root Chakra Databank for* **Connection to Objective Reality.**

Remember these from our snapshots of consciousness in Part II? Every chakra databank informs you about one aspect of living humanly; living as a quirky individual, an incarnated soul; living the way you are now; living as a uniquely valuable YOLO human person.

That difference is abundantly clear to me and my Enlightenment students. Assisting them to evolve spiritually always involves helping them to develop as people: learning about themselves as people; setting personal goals as distinctive people. For this Enlightenment Teacher, each student contains a unique puzzle about self-actualization. Cocreating with Divine help, plus my student's active participation, we lovingly put that puzzle together.

Altogether it's the most delicious-and-sacred progression you can imagine, until finally I have the privilege of validating Enlightenment for that unique individual.

Today's Spiritual Enlightenment Glorifies Your Humanity

Yes, glorifies it. Rather than ignoring it or dismissing it as "ego involvement." Moreover, as a spiritual seeker today, there's no need for you to check your ego at the door to the temple. (Or even go to a temple in the first place, unless that's required by your religion.)

Seeking Enlightenment in the Age of Awakening, we shouldn't have to — and probably can't — ignore our *highly individual experience of being a person*. For this reason, following our Program for Spiritual Enlightenment will be a heck of a lot more interesting-and-personal than the olden ways.

Typically what was required of those seeking Enlightenment in the Age of Faith? Mostly, the striving included these variations on Spiritual Expansion.

1. Purify your body.
2. Awaken your energies.
3. Recognize illusions.
4. Detach from human reality (which supposedly is sooooo unspiritual).
5. And surrender, surrender, surrender.

For us, Living Now, Spiritual EXPANSION Matters

Seeking Enlightenment in the Age of Awakening demands that you fulfill your unique potential as an individual. No wonder, Spiritual Expansion matters greatly, and so does Spiritual Integration.

At this point in our chapter, you're finally ready for our official definition of **Spiritual Expansion:** This counts as *the first part of a two-step process* that helps you to evolve spiritually.

Technically, this expansion occurs whenever you position consciousness for several minutes or more at an Astral or Divine Vibrational Frequency.

Overall, this stretches your direct experience of life (*process*) at a vibrational frequency which is more abstract than anything available at a Human Vibrational Frequency. Well-designed Technique Time allows Spiritual Expansion to happen, and sometimes this also occurs spontaneously as well.

Now, Smart Spiritual Seeker, let's explore this topic still further. In that last paragraph did you notice how I just used the phrase "your direct experience"? If not, go back and take another look.

"Direct experience" is your tipoff to *process* rather than *content*. Moments of Spiritual Expansion matter because they're like exploring a new territory, one you haven't seen before.

Notably, this exploration is not merely waking up from a drowsy state of "ignorance." Traditionally this was accomplished through spiritual teachings (*content*) revealing important philosophical ideas about the meaning of ancient cognitions, scriptural writings, right living, and parables.

Drawing closer to Spiritual Enlightenment, you will attain a more expanded awareness — not as a theory but as direct experience.

Sounds good, right? But maybe you're wondering….

Isn't the Point to Keep on Expanding-Expanding-Expanding?

Your answer to that question depends on *when* you're seeking Enlightenment. Smart Spiritual Seeker, during the Age of Faith, moments of spiritual awakening were prized as all that really mattered. Authentic spiritual awakening was also extremely rare. Remember why?

The Psychic Barrier pretty much locked people in, consciousness-wise; nearly always, folks were paying attention at a Human Vibrational Frequency.

Consequently, spiritual seekers could safely meditate-and-pray all day long, seeking precious moments of spiritual awakening. The longer you spent on your spiritual practices, the better your chance at experiencing *something, anything* beyond Human Vibrational Frequencies.

By contrast, here we are in the Age of Awakening, with the Psychic Barrier gone forever, with that old limitation replaced by our new Consciousness Positioning Superpower.

Living now, we're brilliant at this: Doing any good version of Technique Time, we'll succeed at Spiritual Expansion (formerly known-and-prized as "spiritual awakening").

Even better, we'll succeed extra by selecting an EXCELLENT form of Technique Time, rather than guessing about what might be good.

Back in Chapter 26, why didn't I simply tell you which one form of Technique Time would be the very best? Instead, as you'll recall, I invited you to choose from a variety of options.

1. *Obeying* me wasn't the point.
2. *Having faith* in Rose's ability to decide which technique you-and-everybody-else needed? Hardly the point, either!

Seeking Enlightenment now, we can afford to get real — humanly real. Smart Spiritual Seeker, of course you may have definite preferences regarding Technique Time. Your fave might even change from one day to the next. Individuals like us are like that. Human individuals have preferences.

....

No longer must every spiritual seeker do the exact same Technique Time routine as every other monk in the monastery, faithfully "meditating your brains out"; constantly aiming for more-more-more.

....

Rather than obeying and surrendering, now you get to have some fun: **Smart** Spiritual Seeker's fun!

What's the Catch?

Hey, having fun is great. Choosing your favorite form of Technique Time for now is awesome. But what won't help you at all? Doing all you can to keep on expanding-expanding-expanding: Now that we're living in the Age of Awakening, what would be the consequence of doing that?

Remember, living now, consciousness lifestyles no longer come in only two flavors; either *"nothing special"* or else *achieving Enlightenment.*

Sure, Smart Spiritual Seeker, you could easily do more than 20 Daily Minutes of Technique Time. But what would be the result of all that unrestricted Spiritual Expansion?

Here's your short answer: You would move into the consciousness lifestyle of Spiritual Addiction, Psychological Overwork, or (depending on some complex factors) even Extreme Spiritual Addiction — that's what. Ouch!

To Protect Yourself, Start by Using Today's Language

Please, swap out the old-fashioned favorite "spiritual AWAKENING" and replace it with today's more up-to-date version, "Spiritual EXPANSION." Because these two terms are not merely two different ways of saying the same thing.

- Essentially, spiritual awakening was about having fun, akin to eating your favorite fancy dessert. (A scarce kind of treat for most of the Age of Faith; now scarce no longer.)
- By contrast, the term "Spiritual Expansion" helps to remind you: Don't snack on your favorite dessert all day long. (Expand only so much, at least if you know what's good for you.)

Smart Spiritual Seeker, is it dawning on you yet? Of course, Spiritual Expansion makes a far better ideal on our Program for Spiritual

Enlightenment. For one thing, you're more likely to stick to 20 Daily Minutes of Technique Time, rather than adding on 10 minutes here, 3 hours there, supplemented by a 14-day Magic Mushroom Retreat in Sedona.

In addition, swapping out Age of Faith lingo can protect you against craving the glamour of astral flash, which is like adding five scoops of ice cream onto your slice of cherry pie.

Wisely, avoid too much Spiritual Expansion. After you're done, pivot over to increasing your Spiritual Integration. That way, the sequence will work more like this:

1. *Eat* your food.
2. Then stop eating for several hours; which will allow you to *digest* the food.

Continuing with this analogy to nourishing yourself, have you ever noticed? You have an entire digestive system, not only a very active mouth with pleasure-seeking taste buds.

Like that, when seeking Enlightenment in the Age of Awakening, digest the spiritual goodies by living with your human individuality. *Alternate* Spiritual Expansion with Spiritual Integration: For today's spiritual seekers, that's the truly delicious, soul-nourishing combo.

How Can You Tell If This Alternation Is Working for You?

Smart Spiritual Seeker, expect to find results in human contexts, like developing better relationships and earning more money at work.

Unlike 10,000 years ago, you might well own a watch. All the easier, then, for keeping your Spiritual Expansion time to 20 daily minutes. You'll find practical details laid out in our final chapter, which will summarize how to do our entire Program for Spiritual Enlightenment.

What if I want to monitor that my consciousness isn't in Technique Time? You know, so I can avoid doing too much Spiritual Expansion.

Avoid monitoring yourself, for heaven's sake. This "monitoring" would count as extra Technique Time, since you'd detach from life in order to evaluate your consciousness.

Talk about counterproductive! Glad to say, our Program will work just fine if only you follow our simple, practical DOs and DON'Ts.

Speaking of which, one of our Program DON'Ts goes like this:

Don't take your consciousness "temperature" all day long. Instead, place your attention squarely where it belongs, at least where it belongs for today's Smart Spiritual Seekers. Take an interest in your human life. That way you're achieving Spiritual Integration.

Makes sense, right? Besides being practical, this choice will help your spiritual evolution. Take an interest in yourself and the other human beings you love; also helpful is caring about what happens in objective reality; who says what and does what.

Especially helpful for your Spiritual Integration is solving everyday human-type problems. Who would've thunk!

Golden Rule 6 Invites us to Integrate, Not Show Off

Astral flashy moments are often prized, as if they signify more than they really do. By contrast, authentic Spiritual Expansion isn't something to brag about — not that I'm accusing you personally, Smart Spiritual Seeker.

Just that it will serve you well to become crystal clear about the following: When you're doing an EXCELLENT kind of Technique Time, usually it will feel natural and normal, as if "nothing special is happening." Yet you're evolving the smart way.

How could this be? Why wouldn't we have to struggle to attain Spiritual Expansion?

Hey, you've got that Consciousness Positioning Superpower, remember? It's new, and it works. In that sense you're "special," but so is everybody else with that superpower. ***Using this*** *isn't the challenge for most of us, so much as to avoid* ***over-using this.***

In my experience of teaching real-life Enlightenment students, everyday Spiritual Expansion isn't flashy or weird, nor is it like taking any kind of recreational drug.

Also, know that your personal Technique Time doesn't need to be documented in books, tweeted about, or used to curate your life on Facebook.

Never feel pressure to make your spiritual life about showing off. Simply follow our Program for Spiritual Enlightenment. For you, Smart Spiritual Seeker, Golden Rule 6 may come as a relief. Benefit from the combo of Spiritual *Expansion* PLUS Spiritual *Integration*.

Consciousness is a flow. Following this program, you'll give your consciousness a direction; which is to say that you'll give it a chance.

Being human, during your waking hours, make human reality your default.

What if you realize you've been spacing out, feeling energies, analyzing etc.?

Simply come back to human reality; effortlessly reinsert your consciousness into objective reality; that is, Human Vibrational Frequencies. (As you've already learned to do.) Following those 10 seconds, get busy doing something human.

Your 20 Daily Minutes of Technique Time will provide just enough Spiritual Expansion daily, while the rest of your waking hours will provide Spiritual Integration.

Voila, that's the essence of our Program for Spiritual Enlightenment.

In Conclusion

During your waking hours, Spiritual Integration comes from doing your reasonable best to fulfill your personal goals in life, such as:

1. *Explore* some aspect of human life.
2. *Enjoy* yourself.
3. Develop meaningful *personal relationships.*
4. Include *service* to others in your day — just not at the expense of also *sticking up for yourself.*
5. Gently explore *your own personal relationship* with the Divine. (This will happen as a *process,* your direct experience: Avoid collecting more and more godly-type *content.*)

Maybe our program sounds simple to you. Well, why wouldn't it? Had you been given Spiderman's superpowers, would you find it terribly hard to cling to a wall?

Remember, you have been blessed with that Consciousness Positioning Superpower. True, you're not the only person on earth to have it. Nonetheless, *you've got it.*

For extra encouragement, turn to our next chapter.

CHAPTER 30.

Where You're Headed

*The long and winding road
That leads to your door...*

> **Paul McCartney, Songwriter and Beatles Star**

....

As a Smart Spiritual Seeker, aim to find a road that won't be unnecessarily winding or long.

> **Rose Rosetree**

....

By now you've learned a lot, Smart Spiritual Seeker. Although I have more to teach, you're well on your way. Thanks to your persistence, you've given yourself a thorough preparation for faster spiritual evolution. Our final chapter here will summarize all the practical DOs and DON'Ts, adding up to our complete Program for Spiritual Enlightenment.

Before then, yes, I think you deserve some encouragement. So let's consider where you're headed. Inquiring minds need to know *stories*.

Real stories, from Smart Spiritual Seekers like you: Each of the five volunteers contributing to this chapter has a story to share. All five have received Enlightenment Validation from this teacher, so you could simply generalize that "They're all in Enlightenment." Only that doesn't begin to do justice to their individual stories.

No two candles burn with an identical flame. Like that, each spiritual seeker's story is different. May you find inspiration in these five descriptions of seeking — and finding — Enlightenment in the Age of Awakening.

Success Story 1. Theodore Scott

What's a Feature, Versus a Bug?

I find it fascinating, the little visual shorthands and signifiers that pop culture uses to denote Enlightenment.

All-white yoga clothing, meditative pose, blissful grin, prayerful gesture... I mean, do we even need to pop the hood, here?

I still find it hard to talk about being in Enlightenment: Nine years later, I don't think I've ever really gotten past the feeling that I, personally, would be bragging to mention it.

To be very clear, nobody I know who has mentioned it ever struck me as being engaged in bragging. I mean, we need to be able to actually talk about it, right? Necessarily, that demands certain bare statements of fact, like "I am living in Spiritual Enlightenment."

This is just a personal problem of mine — one of many that Enlightenment did not automatically solve. In the words of the old saying, "It ain't bragging if it's so".

Unfortunately, the mainstream discourse on Enlightenment sucks, frankly. So, it's good if people with direct, lived experience can speak more on the topic. Even if we're not all completely at ease doing so.

All the pop culture nonsense about what Enlightenment is supposed to be like? These traditional ideas can make the lived experience of Enlightenment feel way, way more confusing than it needs to be.

- Why do I still get angry?
- Why do I still have bad habits?
- Why is life still frequently difficult?
- Isn't Enlightenment supposed to do... something... about all that?"

Yes, a Feature, Not a Bug

It took me a while to realise that I found these (and similar) unmet expectations to be a feature, not a bug. The persistence of human difficulties? This also represented the persistence of opportunities for growth.

If we assume that one of the major attractions of being human is growth... Then the notion of *ceasing* to grow, *because* I had grown to a certain point (reached Enlightenment), would seem to have an uncomfortable, restrictive irony.

Recently I have come to see God's gift to me of Enlightenment as an act of great mercy, coming as it did mere weeks before the Shift.

For reasons I won't go into, my life became dramatically more difficult shortly after the Shift. (I *will* say that this mess is thankfully now mostly sorted out. Thanks, Rose!)

I believe God saw this coming for me. I do not know if I would have made it this far, lacking that extra support of Divine connection (in addition to all the crucial support I received from my wife, my sister, my friends, and a certain teacher).

Theodore Scott from Canberra, Australia

....

Success Story 2. Steve

Living with Just Enough Bliss

Lucky us! For those of us living now, two different kinds of Spiritual Enlightenment are available.

Traditional Enlightenment is far better known than Age of Awakening Enlightenment, since humankind has existed for many thousands of years before the Shift on December 21, 2012.

During that Age of Faith, Traditional Enlightenment was humanity's only option.

From what I understand, that version of Enlightenment involves the near-extinction of a personal sense of self, plus a ton of Divine bliss.

Accordingly, the trials and tribulations of everyday life do not register except for witnessing them at a distance. Amazing right?!

- Your cat dies? Bliss.
- Your mom dies? Bliss.
- There's a revolution in your country, with murders in the street? Bliss.

Yet, perhaps, that level of bliss, and the ensuing detachment from life, can also be disorienting to others, even unhelpful.

Equally limiting, somebody with that much bliss might not have much skin in the game of life.

- Would YOU really care about achieving goals at work?
- Would it matter if YOUR wife is satisfied in your marriage?
- How about caring much if YOUR kids hated school?

Far as I'm concerned, there is such a thing as too much bliss.

My Soul Wanted Age of Awakening Enlightenment

What if you, who are reading this, also consider it important to care about people? Suffice it to say, you're living at the right time in human history, since an alternative version for using your full potential is available now. That would be Age of Awakening Enlightenment.

My teacher, Rose, has told me that our soul decides which kind of Enlightenment we will move into, if that time comes. Personally, I'm very glad that my soul prefers this kind, not Traditional Enlightenment.

All in all, I consider myself doubly fortunate. First, I'm grateful to be living that new kind of Spiritual Enlightenment, Age of Awakening Enlightenment.

Second, I feel fortunate to have found Rose, since among Enlightenment Teachers she is a visionary leader, a clear-sighted leader. Here are just some of the reasons why I think so.

1. Rose Rosetree has been a leader at energetic literacy.

For example, she was the first person to discover "chakra databanks." If you don't know much about them yet, you will.

For now, suffice it to say that just as math is the basis for most scientific discoveries, good skill at reading auras is the basis for assessing emotional growth and spiritual awakening.

Personally, I've learned good aura reading skills, and they sure help me to see through illusions. Combine that with Age of Awakening Enlightenment and you can have such an adventure every day.

2. Also, speaking of visionary, did you know? Twenty years ago, Rose launched the field of Empath Coaching. She developed the system of Empath Empowerment® and published the first how-to book for helping empaths to become more effective in life.

Search at Amazon.com and you'll see the latest figure on how many books for empaths they're selling now. Last time I checked, it was over 9,000.

Often imitated but never equaled — no kidding, I haven't seen anyone else's work that comes close to Rose's. Empath Empowerment changed my life, and it sure helped me to move toward Enlightenment.

3. I was already studying with Rose by 2012, when she moved into Enlightenment. Shortly after that *she* became an Enlightenment Teacher.

Again, more leadership. Using her skills of energetic literacy, and also skills for cocreating with the Divine, Rose became the first Enlightenment Teacher to publicly recognize this new kind of Enlightenment.

I can't imagine how much courage it takes to spread the word about Age of Awakening Enlightenment, but that's what she continues to do.

Seems like, Rose's distinctive method for helping people to evolve faster spiritually is also far ahead of her time — although I'm living proof, her method sure does produce results at THIS time in human history.

The Only Tough Part

What's the only tough part for me, living in Spiritual Enlightenment?

I'd have to say, it's how most other people are not doing as well those of us in Enlightenment. Like, not nearly as well as they could be doing.

As a general rule, my spontaneous way of living is one of good will, curiosity, and usually kindness (not always — still hate that traffic). But many people do not live like that. At all.

I wish they would. I believe they could. I can even recommend a certain great teacher who could probably help a lot!

In these weird early days of The Age of Awakening, it's a huge boost to learn skills that can help us to grow and evolve, skills that can lead to living in Age of Awakening Enlightenment.

Those of us with this "consciousness lifestyle" definitely have an advantage in life. If you're reading this, very possibly, I could be talking about you.

Although circumstances continue to challenge all people, those of us in Age of Awakening Enlightenment are more resourceful at solving problems — and we're always growing full speed ahead.

Steve from Bethesda, Maryland
....

Success Story 3. Akira

Not the Kind of Person Who Was Seeking Enlightenment

Receiving Enlightenment Validation from Rose was a surprise. I'm grateful this happened for many reasons.

More than ever, I appreciate the good relationships and the everyday joys of being alive. Besides that, I can tell what isn't so good. No more making excuses, the way I used to do! And no more blaming myself for other people's mistakes.

I am not coming from a religious background, so speaking about God feels awkward. After I crossed the threshold into Enlightenment, I learned how to cherish my relationship with God, and my trust in God grew stronger.

God is always deep within us. This quiet, dependable presence has made it much easier for me to find human kinds of truth, such as having more clarity about whatever is happening in my life.

I mean, seeing what's *really happening* in objective reality.

Enlightenment Is Like Having Better Spiritual Eyesight

I believe I can build a good life for myself. It helps that now I can see through many illusions and confusions.

At first, it was so hurtful to see the truth about people who were trying to use me, and so forth. You know what? It was even harder, at first, to tell when I was kind of lying to myself, like when I'd pretend that everything was fine.

Sometimes everything wasn't fine. At first, it felt scary to admit to myself, about this person or that job or whatever, "I deserve better."

Other times the truth has been more like: "I could change in this particular way. Would I really prefer to stay stuck?"

In my experience, inner truth doesn't come like a push or a shove from within. It's more like a quiet invitation.

Now I'm More Likely to Use My Free Will

I've had this consciousness lifestyle for a few years by now. What am I finding? Life is so much better than I ever thought it could be. Included is how I appreciate what is true for me.

Sometimes there isn't anything to do about the truth, other than to accept that, "This is how things are."

Other times, improvement at recognizing truth in my life is empowering. Once I see the truth, I have a choice about whether or not to do something about it.

That combo of truth and free will is allowing me to make better choices. For example, after moving into Enlightenment I found the courage to change my career.

Previously, I worked in a restaurant as a server. By now I've studied technology skills, and I'm in my first professional job. It feels good.

Look, I have a lot more to learn and grow, of course, but a big milestone has been reached. Enlightenment doesn't mean no more learning or growing, just the opposite.

Akira, Born and Raised in Russia, Now in New York

....

Success Story 4. Roger

A Bubblehead No More

Yes, I'm one of Rose's Energy Spirituality clients who was validated as having moved into Age of Awakening Enlightenment.

I strongly believe that if I hadn't discovered this teacher, taken some personal sessions, and studied some Energy Spirituality books, I probably would have gone in a direction that *wouldn't* have included living my full potential in life.

To put it mildly.

Before reaching Enlightenment, I'd compare my experience to living like a bubblehead. I had a very strong desire to grow emotionally and spiritually; however, it was as though I was living in my head, like in a bubble.

Looking back, I lacked clarity in life. Again, to put it mildly.

One of THE most important things that I recognize about having Rose Rosetree as my Enlightenment Teacher is her emphasis on being human. To see what I mean, just check out other teachers. You may find a very different emphasis.

How Exactly Does "Human" Play out in My Life?

Ever since I crossed the threshold into Enlightenment, all this and more has been happening:

1. I recognize my talents, and actively use and improve upon them.
2. When a problem arises, instead of being wishful and living in my head, I emphasize saying and doing things in objective reality. (By consistently doing this, I've become far more effective in life than I ever dreamed possible.)
3. I continuously learn and practice new human-type skills to improve my life, such as communication skills, financial skills, graduating from old habits of shyness.
4. I very much value what I can do as a grown-up, and independent, human being.
5. Equally I cherish every moment of those 20 Daily Minutes of Technique Time, essential for my spiritual growth within Enlightenment.
6. Although I can choose from plenty of ways to spend that Technique Time, I especially enjoy using my energetic literacy (and doing other techniques where I get to co-create with the Divine Being of my choosing).
7. Enlightenment helps me to stand up for myself. To live my truth no matter what.

In retrospect, before studying with Rose I lacked any real standards for choosing a spiritual teacher. Typically, when I didn't see any results based on their teachings, or things even got worse for me, what did I do?

Again and again, I blamed myself for those failures. It never occurred to me to question the effectiveness of that particular spiritual teaching.

Seeking Enlightenment, Choose Your Teacher Wisely

That's my advice, anyway. Enlightenment isn't a status symbol, like buying the latest iPhone. Enlightenment is a consciousness lifestyle, a way of life that is real. Definitely doesn't have to involve any belief system, not any more than being awake rather than sleeping involves belief.

When you're living in Age of Awakening Enlightenment, all day long your life is so much more enjoyable. And meaningful.

For example, I've developed a much stronger discernment about teachers of personal development. No longer do I assume that what's popular will necessarily be valuable for me.

And I sure don't assume that random "experts" on YouTube videos have the standing to teach about Enlightenment, just because they say so.

What does it feel like, living in Age of Awakening Enlightenment? To me it's like this: Discovering my personal talents and interests, then making really good use of them.

Does Spiritual Enlightenment mean that I'll automatically grow spiritually? Or I'll live happily ever after without any worries? Or that I'll live in a passive state of bliss?

Not at All

To me, Enlightenment means this: Depending on how I use my free will as a human being, and thanks to a strong Divine presence within me — now I'm considerably stronger than pre-Enlightenment.

As a result, I can keep on growing in the human ways that matter most to me.

In case you're wondering, Enlightenment doesn't fix everything. I still need to actively do my human part.

When problems arise, what's different now? Using my full potential as a person allows me to actively solve my problems. I keep coming back, not expecting every solution to work immediately.

Sometimes, though, I do find myself solving a problem quite elegantly.

To sum up, Enlightenment means a strong presence of God within me, a strong sense of self, and unprecedented resourcefulness as an individual. On a daily basis I'm learning new skills and breaking illusions. I'm continuing to progress on my chosen path.

Energy Spirituality isn't my path. That's something I choose for myself. Energy Spirituality is simply a resource, available as I need it.

Roger, Raised in Turkey, now from Montréal, Canada

....

Success Story 5. Tim

**My Eyes Were on Human Me.
Yet I Landed in Enlightenment.**

Like any Millennial, I take pride in shaping my own path in life. Rose's contributions supplement that. For instance, I still choose to be somewhat involved in the religion I was raised in. Politically I'm quite active.

You get the idea. This is my life, thank you very much. I'm the one in charge of shaping it. Quite simply, Enlightenment makes everything better.

Speaking for myself, what was it like to progress toward Enlightenment? My experience of studying with an Enlightenment teacher was human, not churchy; and it wasn't like talking to some kind of big authority about spiritual teachings.

(You could call Rose that, but it's not how she comes across, not at all.)

After a while I started doing 20 Daily Minutes of Technique Time, as she recommended: Doing my choice of techniques; and just 20 minutes, turned out to be a whole lot easier than working on myself all day long.

In addition, I chose to have some Energy Spirituality™ sessions over the years. These weren't necessarily about Enlightenment, more about removing garbage ("STUFF") from my aura. Gradually I learned to express myself better as who I can be in this life.

Practically speaking, these sessions helped me to solve human-type problems. Some of the growth areas for me have been these:

- Developing better skills for dating.
- Upgrading how to solve problems with difficult people in my workplace. Moving on from past relationships that seemed totally sticky.
- And did I mention, how I used to have problems with drinking? And weed?
- Also, at the time I couldn't stop picking up women in bars.
- All of which is history now, has been for years.

All This and More Has Changed for Me

Big changes in the direction of becoming the kind of man I've wanted to be! These changes happened gradually. Meanwhile, in the background, it turns out that I was preparing to move into Enlightenment.

During my Energy Spirituality sessions, Rose made everything seem easy and natural. Yet I'm enough of a spiritual seeker to have encountered others who teach about Self-Realization and Spiritual Enlightenment. What a refreshing contrast! I'd also call it an Age of Awakening contrast!!

> In my experience, traditional teachings around spirituality and religion involve abstractions, detachment, other-worldliness, and a whole lot of faith.
>
> It's as if the messy details of life are stupid distractions away from the point. But why wouldn't making a good life for myself BE the point?
>
> Hey, like I said, I'm a Millennial. At 35 I'm still learning how to live independently as an adult. Life around me is crazy complicated. Haven't you noticed the same thing?
>
> Working with Rose as my Enlightenment Teacher, I feel heard and seen. She treats me as though my life is important, interesting, even sacred.
>
> Traditional teachings seem to disrespect human struggles and desires. Not so when I've studied with this teacher. Positive results kept surprising me, and most surprising of all was the day when my teacher told me:
>
> "Tim, we've just been doing Enlightenment Validation. Yes, you're in Age of Awakening Enlightenment. Congratulations."
>
> ***Tim from Dallas, Texas***
> ....

CHAPTER 31.

Summing up Your Program For Spiritual Enlightenment

Why create the Universe if not to see what happens?

Theodore Scott, Acupuncturist, in Enlightenment

All of us humans are improvising how to live well in the Age of Awakening, ways that are new and simple and sacred.

Rose Rosetree, Enlightenment Teacher

Thank you for reading all the way through to the end of this book. You've learned so much, Smart Spiritual Seeker. I hope it's typical of you that when you decide to do a thing, whether to read this book OR to follow this program, you do it.

All that remains is to sum up exactly what's involved in our Program for Spiritual Enlightenment. One chapter at a time, you've learned the WHY'S behind the WHAT'S. As for those WHAT'S? They've been surprisingly simple, haven't they?

Everyday-Glorious Human Life

Give yourself credit. Your new Consciousness Positioning Superpower is everyday-glorious. Use it wisely; don't overuse it. As a result, human-type clarity will start spilling over into your relationships and career. During your waking hours, take an interest in life, *your human life*. Set goals, and do your reasonable best to fulfill them.

Make money and gain success; among other reasons, caring about these things is perfectly compatible with this Program for Spiritual Enlightenment.

Take an interest in people, *making the most of each relationship* — even while you recognize that all relationships won't necessarily be The Best.

As a Smart Spiritual Seeker, you can also do your reasonable best to help your physical body *stay healthy*. That means good sleep, enough exercise, meeting your sexual needs as best you can, eating food that agrees with you. Human bodies respond well to a fairly predictable routine.

Unless it's your official Technique Time for the day, don't play around with astral anything. As needed, reinsert yourself into human reality. Remember what that means? If you start slip-sliding into energy space-out — or psychological analysis — move one chosen part of your body for 10 seconds. (Next time, choose a different body part.)

If stuck in a boring conversation, ask a question, a question to which you'd like to know the other person's answer. Don't secretly detach from the conversation, positioning your consciousness at some astral happy place. What else will help you to seek Enlightenment in the Age of Awakening?

Do 20 Daily Minutes of Technique Time, Tops

Here you can shine, Smart Spiritual Seeker. Avoid letting a day go by without doing your Technique Time. Because this is when you're purposely using your new Consciousness Positioning Superpower.

Gain Spiritual Expansion by doing those 20 Daily Minutes of Technique Time. Then achieve Spiritual Integration by living like the person you are, pursuing happiness.

What if you'd like to fine-tune your Technique Time choices? First of all, you can learn a lot at my blog, *Deeper Perception Made Practical*. Even better, if you can swing it, would be booking a personal session with me for Enlightenment Teaching. (For details, see the rose-rosetree.com website.)

Bring to your appointment a list of Technique Time options that interest you. Once our personal session begins, let me know if you would like to explore this kind of mentoring, Enlightenment Coaching.

Summarizing Your Six Sweet Golden Rules

Here they are, all in one place:

- Golden Rule 1. Value Your Experience at Human Vibrational Frequencies.
- Golden Rule 2. Do 20 Daily Minutes of Technique Time, Tops.
- Golden Rule 3. Choose Your Technique Time WISELY.
- Golden Rule 4. Avoid Social Pressures that Could Lead You Astray.
- Golden Rule 5. Understand What Enlightenment IS and ISN'T.
- Golden Rule 6. Integrate Spiritual Expansion into Your Human Life.

That simple. The *process* is just that simple.

Enjoy Your Sacred Path, Smart Spiritual Seeker

Supporting your desire for Enlightenment, God will do God's job. But who's responsible for the human-type choices that make your life worth living? You, of course. Now that you're graduating from our Part III, you're in a position to see for yourself... What will the results of our program be for *you*?

Smart Spiritual Seeker, I think you'll find that this Program for Spiritual Enlightenment is highly effective. And if you have fun along the way... and sometimes you even help other people... so much the better.

Afterword

Assuming that you move into Enlightenment, *your soul will choose which kind.*

Yes, your soul will choose one of today's two different varieties of Enlightenment, since both are now available to humanity. The majority of my students have moved into the newer kind, *Age of Awakening Enlightenment*; while a few have moved into the kind you're more familiar with, what I call *Traditional Enlightenment*.

> **That new kind sounds really important. A new kind of Enlightenment? Can you tell us more?**
>
> *Sure, but not so much in this book. For now, trust me on this: Our Program for Spiritual Enlightenment can get you there. And by "there," I mean helping you to attain whichever form of Enlightenment is your soul's preference.*

Many a spiritual seeker today is familiar with standard teachings about Traditional Enlightenment, but how about the newer option? At this writing, the Enlightenment Establishment hasn't much recognized the existence of today's newer kind of Spiritual Enlightenment.

Expect that to change, once the public demands that spiritual teachers equip themselves with up-to-date knowledge of energetic literacy and consciousness lifestyles.

Meanwhile, are you curious to sample what it's like, living in Age of Awakening Enlightenment? You already have. All five success stories in Chapter 30 were written by folks in this new-and-more-popular version.

Perhaps in the future I'll publish a book about this but, really, hasn't this one taught you plenty about seeking Enlightenment in the Age of Awakening? This had to come first.

Until I can return with a rigorous model to help you comprehend the fine points about this new kind of Enlightenment, maybe you'll simply do as I did for the first couple of years that I spent in Age of Awakening Enlightenment, and just let your heart appreciate the wonder of it.

And while we're considering good things that could potentially happen — really-truly happen in your lifetime....

Let's Set a New Standard for Enlightenment Teaching

Smart Spiritual Seeker, you may recall what you saw on the back cover of this book:

Everything you've been told about Enlightenment — and how to achieve it — is beautiful. Except for being like a can of delicious soup, now long past its expiration date.

No way was I trying to insult my colleagues, others who have dedicated their lives to elevate humanity; to me, they're like my brothers and sisters. Specifically, whom do I mean by "colleagues"?

The list includes professionals like the following, who have built their lives around dedicated training and specialized service:

1. Priests, Ministers, Rabbis, Imams
2. Leaders of religious communities, both official leaders and also each group's real movers and shakers.
3. Psychologists, psychotherapists, psychiatrists, neuroscientists
4. Counselors, life coaches, pastoral counselors
5. Yoga teachers, Tai Chi instructors
6. Meditation teachers
7. Spiritual and religious influencers, vloggers, bloggers, authors

Members of the Enlightenment Establishment, more is still needed. All I'm suggesting is a little tweak to the "soup recipe," some updating of knowledge.

Knowledge Leading to More Effective Service

Just because, know it or not, like it or not, all of us living now are in the Age of Awakening: If only today's spiritual leaders knew what you know by now! Think about that for a moment.

So many experts in the professions just listed... might need only a tiny download of knowledge, and then they can take it from there.

Reading about this Program for Spiritual Enlightenment might show these experts all they need to start updating their skills; while some might choose to fine-tune further.

As is the case for you, Smart Spiritual Seeker, what *isn't* necessary? In order to *benefit personally* from our program, these experts don't need to develop good quality energetic literacy; it's enough for them to learn the practical parts, such as to stop overdoing Technique Time, to gain a working knowledge of our common Consciousness Positioning Superpower, and so forth.

Yet, in order to *guide other people*, such as gaining more clarity about who's taking an inner side trip, I would recommend developing the skills of Stage 3 Energetic Literacy.

But first things first. Please consider giving a copy of this book to leaders you know, leaders in personal growth and/or spiritual awakening, even clergy members. Remind them, if need be, that Energy Spirituality isn't a path. They're the ones teaching a path, not me. I'm not *competing* but, perhaps *completing*.

As an Enlightenment Teacher, my job is simply to help every good path work better. Traditional teachings haven't included all that we need to know now, living in the Age of Awakening. That's nobody's fault.

Smart Spiritual Seekers, making use of personal contacts, reaching others through the power of social media, you and I are in a position to make a positive difference. Wouldn't that be a worthwhile project, helping today's Enlightenment Establishment to do a bit of fine-tuning! And how long would all this have to take? Maybe 10 years?

Please, step up. In your own way, join with me to help this world's beautiful spiritual teachers, sources of psychological wisdom, and other influencers. In our lifetimes, millions — even billions — of people can move into Spiritual Enlightenment.

Moreover, you know what else is possible? Not only can people like us stop feeling homesick for Heaven. We can lift up this world, this Earth School, this so-human world with its magnificent beauties but also its shabbiness, injustice, pain, and confusion... *together we can make this world a lot more like Heaven.*

About the Author

Rose Rosetree lives in Sterling, Virginia with her husband Mitch Weber; their Millennial son Matt Weber lives in San Francisco and works with computers. (Shocking? Not so much.)

Rose is the founder of Energy Spirituality™. Also, as you know by now, she's an Enlightenment Teacher.

Her 1,000+ media interviews include the *Washington Post*, the *Los Angeles Times*, *USA Today*, *The Catholic Standard*, and "The View."

Most of Rosetree's books have been independently published, with 42 foreign rights sales to established publishing houses, including a national bestseller for Random House Germany.

Follow Rose's latest discoveries at her website and blog, www.rose-rosetree.com.

....

Please Review This Book

Unless you're living in a monastery or convent, it seems like everybody you meet wants your stars. These days maybe even renunciates are asked to give them too; reviews by everyone from the person who cuts your hair... to the checkout cashier where you buy toothpaste.

No wonder I'm asking you too. Weird in a way, an Enlightenment Teacher (for crying out loud) is asking you for ratings! Why would that be? Fact is, some readers won't even *consider* buying a book — especially one from an indie author — unless they see plenty of 5-star reviews.

Your review can help inform people like you about this leading-edge resource, *Seeking Enlightenment in the Age of Awakening*. Please, spend a few minutes spreading the word at book review sites, social media, blogs, and so forth.

By now you know how to like and tweet and follow and friend. You can make such a difference by letting others know about this particular book.

Granted, folks sometimes worry that it's a serious technical challenge, submitting a *book review* at Amazon.com or wherever. Not so. Your review can be just a sentence or two, mentioning something about this particular book. Plus those stars.

As an indie publisher, I would appreciate your help. So may people who read your words; and if they choose the same book you've just recommended, *your* words might help *them*, too.

Neither you nor I know how many people could benefit from this Program for Spiritual Enlightenment. Wouldn't it be something if folks you've never met would wind up moving into Enlightenment, and why? Because they saw stars contributed by YOU.

More Books by Rose Rosetree

*Purchase these Energy Spirituality™ Books
At your favorite bookstore.
Explore inside info at www.rose-rosetree.com/books-2/*

Energy Spirituality™ Energy Reading

Book One. *The NEW Power of Face Reading*
Improve Communication (and Self-Esteem) by learning the system of Face Reading Secrets®

Book Two. *Aura Reading Through All Your Senses*
Over 100 techniques bring energetic literacy to life.

Book Three. *Read People Deeper*
Make deeper perception *practical* with secrets of Body Language + Face Reading + Auras.

Energy Spirituality™ Energy Healing

Book One. *Use Your Power of Command*
For Spiritual Cleansing and Protection

Book Two. *Cut Cords of Attachment for Self-Healing*
Cord-Cutting Made Simple and Effective

Book Three. *The New Strong:*
Stop Fixing Yourself—And Actually Accelerate Your Personal Growth!

Empath Empowerment® Books

Book One. Empath Empowerment in 30 Days
Enjoy Your Life So Much More

Book Two. The Empowered Empath — Quick & Easy
Gain more practical skills as an empath

Book Three. The Empowered Empath (Expanded)
Owning, Embracing, and Managing Your Special Gifts

Book Four. The Master Empath
Turning on Your Empath Gifts At Will in Love, Business and Friendship (Includes Training in Skilled Empath Merge)

Enlightenment Teaching for the Age of Awakening

Bigger than All the Night Sky
The Start Of Spiritual Awakening. A Memoir

Book One. This One!

Book Two. Let Today Be a Holiday
365 Ways to Co-Create with God

Book Three. Magnetize Money with Energetic Literacy
10 Secrets for Success and Prosperity in the Third Millennium

---

By 2022 Rose has signed 42 different foreign rights contracts, including a national bestseller for Random House Germany. Altogether, authorized editions of books in the emerging field of Energy Spirituality™ have been published in Arabic, Bulgarian, Chinese, Czech, Estonian, German, Japanese, Kurdish, Lithuanian, Russian, Spanish, and Turkish.
